D0046131

Freedom
from
OIL

Mel —
Double 6's! Great to see you.
love to Jill — David

Nov. 07

Freedom
from
OIL

*How the Next President Can End the
United States' Oil Addiction*

David Sandalow

David Sandalow

New York   Chicago   San Fransisco   Lisbon   London   Madrid   Mexico City
Milan   New Delhi   San Juan   Seoul   Singapore   Sydney   Toronto

The **McGraw·Hill** Companies

Copyright © 2008 by David B. Sandalow. All rights reserved. Printed in the United States of America. Except as permitted under the United States Copyright Act of 1976, no part of this publication may be reproduced or distributed in any form or by any means, or stored in a data base or retrieval system, without prior written permission of the publisher.

1 2 3 4 5 6 7 8 9 0   DOC/DOC   0 9 8 7

ISBN-13: 978-0-07-148906-5
ISBN-10: 0-07-148906-1

This publication is designed to provide accurate and authoritative information in regard to the subject matter covered. It is sold with the understanding that the publisher is not engaged in rendering legal, accounting, or other professional service. If legal advice or other expert assistance is required, the services of a competent professional person should be sought.

—From a *Declaration of Principles Jointly Adopted by a Committee of the American Bar Association and a Committee of Publishers and Associations*

McGraw-Hill books are available at special discounts to use as premiums and sales promotions, or for use in corporate training programs. For more information, please write to the Director of Special Sales, Professional Publishing, McGraw-Hill, Two Penn Plaza, New York, NY 10121-2298. Or contact your local bookstore.

This book is printed on acid-free paper.

For Holly

Contents

Foreword

THE UNITED STATES MUST END ITS ADDICTION TO OIL. Yet there remains despair that we can actually do so. Such defeatism is unworthy and unwarranted. Thanks to technology and the new economics of energy, the time is ripe to launch an energy revolution. David Sandalow's *Freedom from Oil* helps show how.

As Sandalow points out, the need to end our oil dependence is clearer by the day. Oil is a magnet for conflict, a weapon for petro-states and a stimulant for terrorism. The volatility of world oil markets hurts American families and businesses. Petroleum is a leading source of heat-trapping gases that contribute to climate change.

During many years of service on the Senate Foreign Relations Committee, I have seen oil dependence threaten our national security countless times. Today, oil addiction is a six-pronged threat. First, oil supplies are vulnerable to natural disasters, wars and terrorist attacks that can disrupt the global economy. In the last several years, the international flow of oil has been disrupted by hurricanes, unrest in Nigeria and continued sabotage in Iraq. Al-Qaeda and other terrorist organizations have openly declared their intent to attack oil facilities to inflict pain on Western economies.

Second, as large industrializing nations such as China and India seek new energy supplies, oil and natural gas will become more expensive. As we approach the point where the world's oil-hungry economies are competing for insufficient supplies of energy, oil will become an even stronger magnet for conflict.

Third, adversarial regimes from Venezuela to Iran to Russia are using energy supplies as leverage against their neighbors. We are used to thinking in terms of conventional warfare between nations, but energy is becoming a weapon of choice for those who possess it. Nations experiencing a cutoff of energy supplies, or even the threat of a cutoff, may become desperate, increasing the chances of armed conflict, terrorism and economic collapse.

Fourth, the revenues flowing to authoritarian regimes often increase corruption, allowing these regimes to insulate themselves from international pressure and the democratic aspirations of their own peoples. We are transferring hundreds of billions of dollars each year to some of the least accountable regimes in the world.

Fifth, threat of climate change is advancing due to inefficient and unclean use of nonrenewable energy. This is bringing drought, famine, disease and mass migration, all of which lead to conflict and instability.

Sixth, much of the developing world is being hit hard by rising energy costs, which often cancel the benefits of our foreign assistance. Without a diversification of energy supplies that emphasizes environmentally friendly energy sources that are abundant in most developing countries, the national incomes of energy-poor nations will remain depressed, with negative consequences for stability, development, disease eradication and terrorism.

In my judgment, meaningful progress to relieve energy dependence will require almost a single-minded national focus on solving specific energy deficiencies. The key word in that sentence is "specific." A broad, unfocused campaign to achieve an ill-defined state of "energy independence" almost guarantees that no objective will receive the resources and attention necessary to overcome technological obstacles and societal inertia. Like a military campaign, we need to maintain pressure for change on a broad front, but we also need to achieve breakouts that yield rapid results and demonstrate what is possible.

We can do this. We should start by establishing a national goal of making competitively priced biofuels available to every motorist in America. Ethanol is already revitalizing towns across the American heartland. Such an accomplishment would transform our transportation sector.

In addition, we should radically increase the miles per gallon of America's auto fleet. The federal government has numerous tools to make this happen, from direct federal support for research to government fleet purchasing to market regulations and incentives.

We should also build a new generation of "plug-in" cars. As Sandalow points out, the United States' far-reaching infrastructure for generating electricity can be a powerful tool for reducing oil dependence.

In fact, we can combine all these steps. We can build flex-fuel, plug-in, highly efficient cars that can get hundreds of miles per gallon of oil. It's time to get on the road to doing that.

David Sandalow's *Freedom from Oil* should be required reading for all concerned citizens and elected officials. Sandalow explains the national security, environmental and economic problems with oil dependence. More important, he explains how to solve these problems. Sandalow makes clear that we have the tools we need, from ethanol and other biofuels to electrification of the auto fleet to technologies for improving fuel efficiency. Even more important, we have the determination and commitment of the American people.

Freedom from Oil also offers an important lesson in government, shedding light on how important decisions are made. Many readers may embrace some of the book's proposals, while questioning others. But good policy emerges from serious debate, informed by the facts. Today we need bold new approaches for forging bipartisan coalitions to solve the problem of oil dependence.

—RICHARD G. LUGAR
United States Senator

Introduction

IN SUMMER 2006, I had lunch with Newt Gingrich. Within weeks, I had dinner with Howard Dean.

Gingrich, a conservative firebrand and prominent Republican for more than two decades, took questions from dozens of guests, covering a wide range of topics. Dean, a liberal firebrand and chairman of the Democratic National Committee, did the same.

At these meals I asked Gingrich and Dean the same question: "What should the United States do about its dependence on oil?"

Both men gave basically the same answer.

Both Gingrich and Dean said oil dependence is a pressing national security problem that must be addressed as a matter of priority.

Both Gingrich and Dean said ethanol is an important part of the solution.

Both Gingrich and Dean said a Manhattan Project-type program is needed to develop technologies to help free us from oil dependence.

Both Gingrich and Dean said the fuel efficiency of our auto fleet must improve.

At the time, I had already started researching a question I'd wondered about for years: Why has the United States made such little progress in reducing its dependence on oil?

Politicians have been talking about this problem since the 1970s, after all. The oil shocks of the 1970s were deeply traumatic. (Prices nearly quadrupled in three months and drivers waited in long lines to get gas.)

Oil played an important role in the decision to go to war in the Persian Gulf in 1991. Oil plays a central role in global warming. Drivers complain almost every summer, when gasoline prices rise.

Yet today oil provides more than 96% of the fuel for our transportation fleet, scarcely different than three decades ago. Why? Could that be changed?

Hearing Newt Gingrich and Howard Dean utter almost the same words was an "aha!" moment for me. If Newt Gingrich and Howard Dean mostly agree, I wondered, might it be possible to get something done?

Washington, D.C., these days is consumed by a poisonous political culture. Deep disagreements divide liberals and conservatives on most issues. But this issue seemed different.

I started cataloguing the positions of other major political figures on oil dependence. I discovered an astonishing amount of agreement across the political spectrum. The consensus was not complete, by any means. Yet the similarities far outweighed the differences.

I discovered that politicians from President George W. Bush to Senator Richard Lugar (R-IN) to Senator Tom Harkin (D-IA) to Gov. Brian Schweitzer (D-MT) were highlighting the importance of the issue and calling it a pressing national priority. I discovered that an overwhelming majority of the American public believe oil dependence is a problem that must be solved.

So I dug deeper. I explored the ways we use oil, the reasons we do so and the problems oil creates. I researched substitutes for oil and ways to use oil more efficiently. I examined the policies we've adopted so far, why they've had such limited success and what it would take to do more.

This book is the product of those efforts.

For me, three insights about oil are central.

First, oil is everywhere. Everyone reading this book will use oil—directly or indirectly—in the next day. If you travel beyond your neighborhood, you will almost certainly use oil, because our transportation infrastructure is utterly dependent on it. (There are almost no vehicles on the road today that move without oil.) If you stay at home, you will use goods that were shipped with the use of oil, as well as goods that were made with it.

As Daniel Yergin wrote in *The Prize*, his Pulitzer Prize-winning book on the history of the oil industry: "Today we are so dependent on oil, and oil is so embedded in our daily doings, that we hardly stop to comprehend its pervasive significance."[1]

Second, drivers have no substitutes for oil. Most goods in our economy have substitutes. If the orange crop fails and juice prices rise, for example, you can switch to milk, soda or water. But when it comes to oil, there are no widely available substitutes. If events in some distant land cause gasoline prices to rise, you have two choices—pay more or drive less.

We grew up with this lack of substitutes, as did our parents and grandparents. We consider it normal. But it is deeply abnormal. (What other essential commodities have no substitutes?) It damages our national security, natural world and pocketbooks. It is the most fundamental problem we face when it comes to oil.

Third, our political dialogue about oil is stuck in the 1970s, focusing on just one part of a larger problem. During the 1970s—an age before the Internet, personal computers or cell phones—the phrase "independence from foreign oil" became emblazoned in our national psyche. We started paying attention to the percentage of oil imported each year as a central measure of the success of our energy policy. We continued doing that, even as oil imports climbed from 34% in 1973 to 60% in this decade.

Today, oil imports are indeed a problem, adding to the trade deficit. But they are hardly the *fundamental* problem when it comes to oil. Even if imports dropped dramatically, we would still face serious national security threats from the world's dependence on oil. (We haven't imported a drop of oil from Iran in more than 25 years, but that fact doesn't prevent Iran from playing its oil card in negotiations over its nuclear program.) We'd still face serious environmental threats from heat-trapping gases. (Emissions from imported and domestic oil are the same.) We'd still face wild price swings. (In the summer of 2000, British truckers went on strike over rising oil prices. At the time, the United Kingdom was energy independent, exporting oil into world markets. That fact didn't protect British truckers from rising world prices.)

The fundamental problem with oil is that we have no substitutes. If every American could choose between oil, ethanol, biodiesel and electricity from the grid when fueling their cars, Saudi Arabia's influence would decline sharply. Emissions of heat-trapping gases would plummet. Drivers' exposure to swings in world oil markets would fall.

To become independent of foreign oil, we must become independent of oil. That doesn't mean no oil in our vehicles. It means giving drivers a choice between oil and other fuels.

This conclusion is not radical. Experts across the political spectrum have been saying it, in different ways, for many years. But it has not permeated our political dialogue on the topic of oil.

Which leads to a fourth insight: Ending oil dependence will require presidential leadership.

The changes required to end oil dependence are far-reaching. Lead times are long. Many current proposals are far too small. For the scope of change needed to solve this problem, Presidential leadership is essential.

Perhaps I came easily to this conclusion, influenced by my own experience. For several years during the mid-1990s, I had the privilege of working as a member of the White House staff. Such jobs are exhausting but exhilarating, providing the chance to support the President and Vice President of the United States as they grapple with the most challenging issues of our time.

During my years at the White House, I worked on two "policy councils"—the National Security Council and the Council on Environmental Quality. For a staff member on one of these councils, a core part of the job is seeking input from federal agencies as the President and Vice President develop new policies. These agencies are filled with impressive and knowledgeable experts on a wide range of topics. Not surprisingly, these experts don't always agree. Members of the White House staff are charged with distilling information from the agencies, identifying and resolving differences, and (on the really big issues) shaping options for the President for decision.

When the President of the United States decides to tackle the problem of oil dependence as a matter of top priority, it will be a very big decision. Input from many sources will be needed. Far-reaching and consequential decisions will be required.

That insight led to this book.

★ ★ ★ ★

This book tells a story. It tells the story of how the President of the United States could help end our dependence on oil.

This book also provides a policy analysis. Based on research and interviews, it critically examines the problem of oil dependence and proposes a plan to solve this problem in a generation.

To do both these things, I have created a series of "memos to the President" from around the federal government. They are not real—I wrote every one. The sources cited in these memos are quite real, however. If you're interested in further reading on this topic, these sources may be a good place to start.

I've also written short profiles of nine extraordinary individuals, each of whom I've had the privilege to speak with during the past year. The profiles are in the form of newspaper or magazine articles. These "articles" aren't from actual newspapers or magazines—I wrote every one for this book. The people profiled are very real, however. We can all learn from them.

The book ends with a speech by the President, proposing a path forward. If you have time for only one chapter, I hope you'll read that one.

★ ★ ★ ★

Finally, a caveat. I do not put forward the proposals in this book as the only answer to the problem of oil dependence. There are many good ideas. Events change quickly. Different measures may be appropriate several years from now. Yet the proposals put forward here could change the lives of our children and grandchildren. They are an attempt to grapple with one of the most challenging questions of our time. I hope you'll consider them.

PART I

The Problem

MEMORANDUM FROM THE PRESIDENT

TO: SECRETARY OF STATE
SECRETARY OF THE TREASURY
SECRETARY OF DEFENSE
SECRETARY OF THE INTERIOR
SECRETARY OF AGRICULTURE
SECRETARY OF COMMERCE
SECRETARY OF LABOR
SECRETARY OF HOUSING AND URBAN
DEVELOPMENT
SECRETARY OF TRANSPORTATION
SECRETARY OF ENERGY
SECRETARY OF HOMELAND SECURITY
ADMINISTRATOR, ENVIRONMENTAL
PROTECTION AGENCY
UNITED STATES TRADE REPRESENTATIVE
ASSISTANT TO THE PRESIDENT, NATIONAL
SECURITY AFFAIRS
DIRECTOR, OFFICE OF MANAGEMENT
AND BUDGET
CHAIR, COUNCIL OF ECONOMIC
ADVISERS
CHAIR, COUNCIL ON ENVIRONMENTAL
QUALITY
CHAIR, NATIONAL ECONOMIC COUNCIL
DIRECTOR, OFFICE OF SCIENCE AND
TECHNOLOGY POLICY

SUBJECT: Oil Dependence Speech

I plan to deliver an address from the Oval Office one month from today.
The topic will be oil dependence. This memorandum seeks
recommendations for that speech.

BACKGROUND

Oil dependence threatens all Americans. Our national security is
threatened by the need to protect oil flows from unstable regions. Our

natural world is threatened by heat-trapping gases from the burning of oil. Our prosperity is threatened by volatile world oil prices.

Fortunately, technologies to help end oil dependence are at hand. Plug-in hybrid engines can connect cars to the electric grid. Ethanol and other biofuels can diversify the fuel supply while renewing rural America. Many well-known technologies can dramatically improve the fuel efficiency of new cars.

In one month, I hope to present the nation with a plan for ending our dependence on oil. To do that, I need your help. Below is a list of topics central to shaping this plan, with a lead author next to each. Please deliver a memo (10 pages maximum) on each topic for which you are identified as lead author by the date shown. These memos should provide both background information and policy recommendations.

Your departments are filled with experts familiar with many facets of this complex topic. Please draw on their expertise in preparing these memos.

As part of my speech, I plan to highlight several individuals who have demonstrated extraordinary leadership on topics related to oil dependence. Please provide recommendations along with sample press clippings concerning these individuals.

In making your recommendations, please be guided by the words: "Make no small plans, for they have no power to stir the soul."

TASKINGS
Due one week from today:
1. National Security Consequences of Oil Dependence—National Security Adviser
2. Environmental Consequences of Oil Dependence—Chair, Council on Environmental Quality
3. Economic Consequences of Oil Dependence—National Economic Council

Due two weeks from today:

4. Plug-In Cars—Secretary of Transportation
5. Biofuels—Secretary of Agriculture
6. Fuel Efficiency—Secretary of Transportation
7. Coal—Secretary of Energy
8. Hydrogen—Secretary of Energy
9. Smart Growth—Secretary of Transportation and Secretary of Housing and Urban Development
10. Strategic Petroleum Reserve—Secretary of Energy
11. Diplomatic Strategy—Secretary of State

Due three weeks from today:

12. Options Memo—Chief of Staff

MEMORANDUM FOR THE PRESIDENT

FROM: COUNSELOR TO THE PRESIDENT

SUBJECT: <u>Oil Dependence Speech</u>

I know you are considering a speech to the nation on the topic of oil dependence. Before you commit yourself to this publicly, I want to offer several strong notes of caution. I do this as a friend of more than three decades—someone who shares your values, who believes in you, and who above all wants to see you succeed as President.

You are undoubtedly correct that oil dependence is at the root of many of the problems facing our nation. Along with many others, I cheered you when you said this during the campaign.

However, the odds against you achieving anything significant on this issue are high. Others before you have tried and failed. Every President since Richard Nixon has decried our nation's dependence on foreign oil, yet that dependence has climbed steadily for more than three decades.

Last year oil provided more than 96% of the fuel for our cars and trucks. The dominance of oil in our transportation sector is almost complete.

There's a reason for this. Oil is a high-energy content, easily transportable liquid. Today there are literally trillions of dollars invested in the global oil infrastructure.

Your powers as President are considerable, but they are not infinite. Changing anything as deeply entrenched as our nation's dependence on oil will take perseverance, commitment and time.

Calling for an end to oil dependence is a terrific rallying cry. Most Americans support this at the level of rhetoric. You can win political points by echoing these sentiments. But actually taking the steps needed to solve this problem would not be easy. There will be many hurdles in your way.

You'll make enemies. You'll go down some wrong paths. Perhaps most troubling, complete success cannot come during the eight years in which (I hope) you will serve as President.

If you make oil dependence your top priority, you have the potential to change history. I think you sense that. You also have the potential to fail spectacularly, compromising other goals I know you have for your Presidency.[1]

Before you proceed irrevocably down this path, I hope you'll weigh the pros and cons carefully. If I can help as you do so, please let me know.

MEMORANDUM TO THE PRESIDENT

FROM: SECRETARY OF ENERGY

SUBJECT: Ten Facts about Oil

I read yesterday's memo on oil dependence from the Counselor. I agree with the memo's premise, in part. Ending oil dependence will take sustained commitment. Half measures will not be enough. Yet I do not share the pervasive sense of pessimism about your prospects.

This issue unites Americans. More than 90% of voters believe oil dependence is a serious problem. Politicians from both parties won wild applause by pledging action on this topic in the last campaign.

Furthermore, game-changing technologies are at hand. Plug-in hybrid engines can connect cars to the electric grid, transforming our transportation infrastructure. The transition to ethanol is already renewing rural America. A crash program to end oil dependence can revitalize the American auto industry as well.

Some basic facts about oil may be helpful. Ten are set forth here.

FACT 1: Oil provides more than 96% of the fuel for our transportation fleet.

Modern vehicles depend almost completely on oil. This fact is so basic— so utterly taken for granted—it's worth pausing for a moment to consider.

If you're thirsty and don't feel like a soda, you can drink water or orange juice. If you'd like to relax and don't feel like a movie, you can watch television or read a book. But if you want to travel more than a few miles and don't want to use oil, you're almost certainly out of luck. Perhaps you can buy "E85" (85% ethanol fuel, sold at fewer than 1% of U.S. gas stations) or biodiesel (even less available). Perhaps you can bike or ride an electric train. In most situations, though, you'll almost certainly need oil.

This lack of substitutes is central to several of the most serious problems caused by oil.

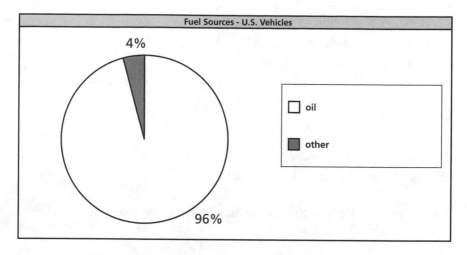

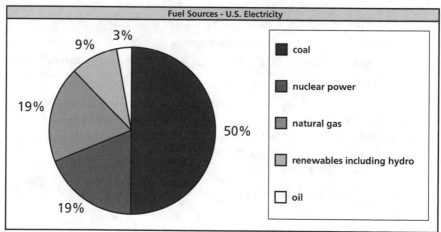

FACT 2: Oil provides less than 3% of electricity in the United States.

There are two energy markets in this country. In the first market, for transportation fuels, oil is overwhelmingly dominant. In the second, for electricity generation, oil is a very small factor. Half our electricity comes from coal; 19% comes from nuclear power; 19% comes from natural gas; 9% comes from renewable sources (hydro, sun and wind); and 3% comes from oil. Of the more than 20 million barrels of oil per day consumed in the United States, only 500,000 are used for electricity.[1]

One implication: technologies used to generate electricity—such as nuclear, wind and solar power—can't do much to help wean the United

States from oil without major changes to our vehicle fleet. Debates often rage about the choice between these technologies. Is nuclear power safe? Can renewables compete? Those debates have many important consequences. They have almost no implications for ending oil dependence, however, and won't until our cars can connect to the electric grid.

Nuclear power, solar power and wind power can't help wean the United States from oil without major changes to our vehicle fleet.

FACT 3: The United States consumes roughly a quarter of the world's oil.

The United States is the world's largest oil consumer, by far. We use more than 24% of the global total, followed by China at 9%; Japan at 6%; and Germany, Russia and India at just above 3% each. One of the fastest growth rates is in China, where tens of millions of people are buying cars for the first time.[2]

In the United States, the average person consumes approximately 2.8 gallons of gasoline per day. In Japan, the figure is 1.8 gallons; in Germany, 1.4 gallons; and in China, 0.2 gallons.[3]

The United States is to oil consumption what Saudi Arabia is to oil production— the biggest by far.

FACT 4: The Persian Gulf has the most oil in the world—and the cheapest.

More than half the world's proven oil reserves are in the Persian Gulf. Saudi Arabia alone has 20% of the global total and maintains the world's only spare production capacity, making its cooperation critical in managing world oil markets. The countries with the largest proven reserves, in order, are Saudi Arabia, Canada, Iran, Iraq, Kuwait, UAE, Venezuela, Russia, Libya and Nigeria. The United States has roughly 2% of the world's proven reserves.[4]

Furthermore, the cost of producing oil in the Persian Gulf is lower than anywhere in the world. Most Persian Gulf reserves sit just below the surface in vast pools easily accessed with drilling technology. In Saudi Arabia, production costs are often as low as $2 per barrel. In the United States, in contrast, production costs are generally $15 to $20 per barrel. In Canada, production costs above $30 per barrel are common.[5]

The United States has absolutely no comparative advantage in the production of oil. Why have we allowed ourselves to become so dependent on it?

FACT 5: Oil is a fungible product, traded globally.

The price of oil is set on a global market. Traders in New York, London and Singapore play an important role in establishing prices. Oil is cheap to ship across vast distances, facilitating international trade. Roughly 75% of oil produced each year is traded internationally.[6]

U.S. oil imports have grown from 34% in 1973 to more than 60% today. Our major trading partners are also dependent on imports: Europe gets 17% of its oil from the Persian Gulf and Japan gets 78%.[7] But the percentage of oil a country imports does not determine the price it pays. With very minor variations, the price of a specific variety of crude oil is the same all over the world.

A disruption in oil supplies anywhere can affect oil prices everywhere.

FACT 6: Oil is the United States' largest source of heat-trapping gases.

Forty-four percent of the United States' energy-related carbon dioxide emissions come from oil —more than from coal or natural gas.[8] The average car in the United States puts more than 1.5 tons of carbon into the air every year. Total emissions from oil use are climbing sharply, both in the United States and around the world.

Oil is carbon from living matter that has decomposed and been compressed below the earth's surface over millions of year. When oil burns, that carbon combines with oxygen to form carbon dioxide, a heat-trapping gas, which stays in the atmosphere for at least a century. By burning oil, we are taking carbon stored underground for millions of years and putting it into the atmosphere in a heat-trapping form.

Each year, we take millions of tons of carbon in underground oil reserves and convert them into a heat-trapping gas—carbon dioxide.

FACT 7: Roughly 69% of our oil is used in the transportation sector.

The United States uses roughly 20.8 million barrels per day of oil. More than 9 million barrels per day are used for gasoline alone. More than 3 million barrels per day are used by diesel trucks, buses and trains. Almost 1.7 million are used in airplanes. Oil is also used for home heating, in industrial boilers and as a chemical feedstock.[9]

During the past 30 years, oil use in industry, electricity generation and the building sector has dropped sharply in the United States. Use of oil in the transportation sector has climbed. U.S. refineries in general are designed to maximize production of gasoline.[10]

Demand for motor fuels determines demand for crude oil.

FACT 8: New car sales account for less than 7% of the total U.S. auto fleet every year.

More than 240 million cars and trucks are on the road in the United States today. (This is a huge capital stock, worth trillions of dollars.) Approximately 16 million new cars and truck are sold each year. Replacing our current vehicle fleet takes roughly 15 years.[11]

One implication: New oil-saving technologies will take years to permeate the vehicle fleet and have big impacts on demand. Our oil dependence developed over the course of a century and will not disappear overnight.

Ending oil dependence will take sustained commitment over many years.

FACT 9: The average household spends several thousand dollars per year on gasoline.

One 2005 study found the average household with two drivers spent more than $4100 per year on gasoline. Costs are especially high in rural areas. The poorest fifth of households, with incomes below $15,000, typically spend more than 10% of their incomes on gasoline. Household gasoline costs have varied widely in recent years, due to large oil price swings. When gasoline prices rise, Americans have two options—pay more or drive less.[12]

More than 92% of U.S. households own or possess a motor vehicle. Roughly 25% own three or more. The average car or light truck consumes 570 gallons of gasoline per year.[13]

Oil dependence exposes Americans to the volatility of world oil markets.

FACT 10: Huge majorities of Americans believe oil dependence is a serious problem.

Few topics unite Americans as much as oil dependence. National security hawks, environmentalists, farmers and consumers all agree that oil dependence is a serious problem. In one recent poll, 95% of respondents called dependence on Mideast oil a "serious" problem and 71% called it "very serious."[14]

Many voters are even willing to take unpopular steps to address this problem. In one recent poll, more than 85% of respondents said they opposed a gas tax increase, but more than 55% said they would *support* an increase that helped reduce dependence on foreign oil. Another poll found large majorities of the public looking to the government for solutions to this problem.[15]

Overwhelming majorities of Americans believe oil dependence is a serious problem. They will reward a political leader who takes serious steps to address it.

<u>CONCLUSION</u>
I hope these 10 facts provide helpful background.

I know you sought the Presidency to make a difference. Our nation's oil dependence is a festering problem that has lingered for more than a generation. You can help the United States solve it. This is worth every ounce of effort you can muster.

MEMORANDUM FOR THE PRESIDENT

FROM: NATIONAL SECURITY ADVISER

SUBJECT: Oil Dependence

You asked for a memorandum summarizing the national security threats posed by the U.S. dependence on oil. There are at least four.

First, oil dependence strengthens Al Qaeda and other Islamic terrorists.

The United States is in a long war. Islamic fundamentalists struck our shores and are determined to do so again. Like the Cold War, this struggle has many causes and will last for generations. Unlike the Cold War, oil dependence plays a central role in the struggle.

For more than 50 years, the need to protect oil flows has shaped U.S. policy and relationships in the Persian Gulf. During the Cold War, we supported the Shah of Iran and other unpopular leaders in part to keep oil flowing from the region. In 1980, with the Soviets in Afghanistan, President Carter declared that attempts by outside forces to gain control of the Persian Gulf would be considered "an assault on the vital interests of the United States" and be "repelled by any means necessary, including military force."[1]

In 1991, with Saddam Hussein in Kuwait, President George H. W. Bush told Congress that war was necessary because "[v]ital economic interests are at risk...Iraq itself controls some 10% of the world's proven oil reserves. Iraq plus Kuwait controls twice that."[2] Later, National Security Adviser Brent Scowcroft explained that "...what gave enormous urgency to [Saddam's invasion of Kuwait] was the issue of oil."[3] After removing Saddam from Kuwait in 1991, U.S. troops remained in Saudi Arabia where their presence bred great resentment.

These steps to secure oil flows have come at a cost. By making us central players in a region torn by ancient rivalries, oil dependence has exposed us to resentment, vulnerability and attack. Osama bin Laden's first fatwa, in 1996, was titled "Declaration of War against the Americans Occupying the Land of the Two Holy Places."

Today, deep resentment of the U.S. role in the Persian Gulf remains a powerful recruitment tool for jihadists. That resentment grows not just from the war in Iraq, but from the U.S. relationship with the House of Saud, the presence of U.S. forces throughout the region and a long legacy of perceived betrayals. Yet the United States faces severe constraints in responding to this resentment. With half the world's proven oil reserves, the world's cheapest oil and the world's only spare production capacity, the Persian Gulf will remain an indispensable region for the global economy so long as modern vehicles run only on oil. To protect oil flows, the U.S. policymakers will feel compelled to maintain relationships and exert power in the region in ways likely to fuel the jihadist movement.

Our other objectives in the region, such as protecting the territorial integrity of Israel, do not require the extensive presence in the Persian Gulf needed to secure reliable production and transit of oil.

Compounding these problems, the huge money flows into the Persian Gulf from oil purchases help finance terrorist networks. Al Qaeda raises funds from an extensive global network, with Islamic charities and NGOs playing an important role.[4] Saudi money provides critical support for madrassas with virulent anti-American views.

Fighting this flow of funds requires cooperation from many nations, yet leading oil exporters know we are poorly positioned to insist on it. Diplomatic efforts to gain Saudi assistance in choking off such funding, or investigating terrorist attacks, are hampered by the high priority we attach to preserving Saudi cooperation in managing world oil markets. As a result, millions of dollars of oil revenues each year work their way through an informal system of Islamic charities into terrorist coffers.[5]

Second, oil dependence strengthens oil-exporting nations that oppose U.S. interests.

Several leading oil exporters pursue policies that threaten the United States. The most serious threat comes from Iran, whose nuclear ambitions could further destabilize the Persian Gulf and put terrifying new weapons into the hands of terrorists. Yet efforts to respond to this threat with multilateral sanctions have foundered on fears that Iran would retaliate by withholding oil from world markets. Experts predict this would drive prices above $100 per barrel—a risk many governments are unwilling to accept.

Indeed Iran does not even need to withhold oil from world markets to play its "oil card." The mere fear it might do so can cause oil prices to climb, as traders build a "risk premium" into the cost of every barrel.[6] This puts pressure on governments around the world to minimize "saber-rattling" against Iran, in order to help control oil prices. The result—an emboldened Iran, more confident in its ability to pursue policies that threaten U.S. national security.

In short, three decades after the first oil shocks, and a quarter-century after the humiliating capture of U.S. diplomats in Tehran, we remain hostage to the world's continuing dependence on oil.[7]

Other oil-exporting nations pose problems as well. President Hugo Chavez of Venezuela, a leading exporter, fans anti-American sentiments throughout Latin American and castigates the United States on the floor of the U.N. General Assembly. Oil revenues not only help Chavez maintain his grip on power, they allow him to finance policies that put U.S. assets at risk in countries such as Bolivia and Argentina.[8] Russia has already demonstrated its willingness to withhold natural gas exports in a dispute and would certainly consider withholding oil exports as well.

The world's leading oil exporters (in order) are Saudi Arabia, Russia, Norway, Iran, United Arab Emirates, Nigeria, Kuwait, and Venezuela.[9] All export more than 2 million barrels per day. Today, Iran poses the most serious security threat among this group. But any significant oil exporter can play its "oil card" to threaten the United States and other nations. This is a strategic vulnerability we ignore at our peril.

Third, oil dependence endangers our men and women in uniform.

In Operation Iraqi Freedom, many U.S. military fatalities took place as part of fuel convoys. A high percentage of road-bound convoys were dedicated to fuel movement.

Dependence on oil jeopardizes the safety of our troops. Fuel convoys are often highly vulnerable to ambush, as the Iraq experience demonstrates. Diesel generators display a heat signature easily detected by some enemies. In many battlefield environments, the need to ship oil to the fight exposes our soldiers to considerable danger.

Oil dependence also threatens mission success. Attacks on rear logistics assets can quickly shut down a combat system if oil supply lines are compromised. High casualty rates of the kinds associated with fuel convoys can erode public support for many missions.

In July 2006, General Richard Zilmer, commander of coalition forces in western Iraq, made a "Priority 1" request for renewable energy systems at outlying bases. Maj. Gen. Zilmer noted the need for "frequent logistic resupply convoys," in particular for petroleum and the threat those convoys pose to U.S. military personnel. Zilmer wrote that without renewable energy systems: "… personnel loss rates are likely to continue at their current rate. Continued casualty accumulation exhibits potential to jeopardize mission success."[10]

In many Army deployments, oil makes up a staggering 70% of the tonnage transported to the front lines.[11] The cost of this fuel is high, with every $10 per barrel increase adding roughly $1.3 billion to Pentagon operating costs.[12] (The Defense Department is the nation's largest oil consumer, using roughly 0.3 million barrels per day.) Improvements in the fuel efficiency of combat platforms can be powerful force multipliers, reducing logistical and cost burdens as well as casualties.

Fourth, oil dependence undermines democracy and good governance around the world.

Oil wealth corrodes democratic institutions. This dynamic is not inevitable, but it is widespread. A growing body of scholarly work explores this topic, concluding that oil wealth is strongly associated with corruption and authoritarian rule.[13]

A few examples underscore this trend. Bahrain, the Persian Gulf country with the smallest oil reserves, was also the first to hold free elections.[14] As oil prices climbed in recent years, both Vladmir Putin and Hugo Chavez moved away from democratic institutions and toward more authoritarian rule. In Nigeria, oil abundance contributes to widespread corruption.

Several explanations have been offered. Oil-rich leaders can diffuse democratic pressure with low taxes and generous payments. They can use wealth to command the loyalty of internal security forces, stifling any democratic pressures that emerge. Income generated by exporting oil appreciates a country's currency, pricing out other local goods on the international market and further deepening the country's reliance on the income from the natural resource. Meanwhile, exports of oil do not create the skills or social patterns that lead to a vibrant middle class and, in turn, to democracy.[15]

Our dependence on oil, and in particular our consumption each year of more than 25% of global production, plays a central role in perpetuating these trends. Without the United States as a major consumer, prices for oil would drop and democratic pressures would grow in many countries around the world.

from the desk of the
ASSISTANT TO THE PRESIDENT FOR
NATIONAL SECURITY AFFAIRS

In your oil dependence memo, you asked for press clippings about individuals whose leadership on energy issues could be highlighted. I thought you might be interested in the attached article concerning General Richard Zilmer (USMC).

★★★★★

General Fights for Renewable Energy

General Richard Zilmer, a combat veteran with a chest full of medals, once served as commander of coalition forces in western Iraq. It's there that Zilmer first began pushing the Pentagon for renewable energy systems to replace oil.

The reason was simple: too many of his troops were dying in fuel convoys.

In July 2006, Zilmer made a "Priority 1 request" for wind- and solar-power generators. He wrote that the need to supply coalition bases with petroleum created a "constant threat," causing "preventable...serious and grave casualties."

Convoys were needed to supply frontline troops with food,

fuel and ammunition. But he singled out petroleum shipments in particular—a "preponderance" of the convoys—for placing "Marines, soldiers and sailors in harm's way."

In the dry words of a Pentagon memo, he wrote that "continued casualty accumulation exhibits potential to jeopardize mission success."

Fuel supply has been a factor in combat for more than a century. Winston Churchill converted the British Navy from coal to oil before World War I, improving the speed of the fleet but raising concerns about the security of Britain's fuel supply. Allied forces in World War II delayed their march through

Europe due to shortages of oil.

But the problem faced by General Zilmer in the summer of 2006 was especially acute. He needed fuel for vehicles and diesel generators. Yet shipping that fuel to the front lines created extraordinary hazards.

Western Iraq was in the throes of a major insurgency, with Al Qaeda rising in popularity.

U.S. troops faced constant attack from improvised explosive devices, rocket-propelled grenades and small arms fire. "Current solutions—such as providing additional security to our logistics convoys and conducting convoy operations during the hours of darkness—are inadequate," wrote Zilmer.

Against this backdrop, General Zilmer reached out for a new kind of solution. Iraq's abundant sunshine made it a perfect location for solar power. Wind turbines had potential too.

Why should his troops die to bring diesel fuel to the front lines, when they could generate power from the sun and wind?

Furthermore, Zilmer noted, renewable energy would be cheaper than petroleum. He noted that the "real cost" getting

diesel fuel to front lines is often four times greater than the regular purchase price. More than half the fuel used in combat operations is consumed by support troops, not on the front lines.

In recent years, the U.S. military has spent as much as $8 billion per year on fuel. Any system that can help cut these costs is potentially of interest.

Solar power is being used at the Coronado Naval Air Base in San Diego, CA. Wind power is being used at Warren Air Force base in Wyoming. Even geothermal power is being used at several bases.

Today, the Pentagon is starting to respond to Zilmer's request. Solar-powered battlefield generators are under development. A high-powered task force is looking at ways to cut fuel use in combat situations.

The results could make a big difference to our troops in battle. "By reducing the need for…petroleum at our outlying bases," says Zilmer, "we can decrease the frequency of logistics convoys on the road, thereby reducing the danger to our Marines, sailors and soldiers."[1]

MEMORANDUM FOR THE PRESIDENT

FROM: CHAIR, COUNCIL ON ENVIRONMENTAL
                 QUALITY

SUBJECT: <u>Environmental Consequences of Oil Dependence</u>

Oil is a leading cause of global warming. Oil also contributes to urban
smog, marine pollution and other environmental problems.

In recent decades, pollution control technologies have helped reduce
many of oil's environmental impacts. Gasoline engines burn much cleaner
than years ago. New tankers have double hulls to protect against spills.

Still, the environmental footprint of the oil industry remains large. The
global warming impacts of oil combustion, in particular, are a serious and
growing problem. This memorandum summarizes the principal
environmental consequences of oil dependence.

1. <u>GLOBAL WARMING</u>

  a. *The Problem*
The buildup of heat-trapping gases in the atmosphere is fundamentally
altering the Earth's climate. Concentrations of heat-trapping gases are
already higher than at any time in human history. If current trends
continue, by the end of the century, concentrations of heat-trapping gases
will reach their highest levels in more than 50 million years.

The principal cause of this build-up is well-known. Since the beginning
of the Industrial Revolution, human beings have been removing fossil
fuels (coal, oil and natural gas) from beneath the Earth's surface and
burning them for energy. When this happens, the carbon in those fuels
bonds with oxygen in the atmosphere to form carbon dioxide (CO_2), a
heat-trapping gas. Once released, carbon dioxide can remain in the
atmosphere for more than 100 years.[1]

For more than 650,000 years before the present era, carbon dioxide
concentrations in the atmosphere remained below 300 parts per million

(ppm).[2] Concentrations climbed above that level in the last century and have increased steadily ever since. Today, carbon dioxide concentrations are 380 ppm and increasing at roughly 2 ppm each year.

This buildup is having an impact. The world's leading scientific authority on global warming, the Intergovernmental Panel on Climate Change (IPCC), states that "warming of the climate system is unequivocal." It found that:

- Of the 12 warmest years on record, 11 have occurred since 1995.

- Mountain glaciers and snow cover are receding all over the world.

- Average temperatures in the Northern Hemisphere from 1950 to 2000 were likely the highest in at least the last 1,300 years.[3]

The IPCC concluded that human activities are "very likely" the cause of most of the increase in global temperatures during the past 50 years. For the IPCC, "very likely" means a probability of 90% or greater.[4]

However, the most serious consequences lie ahead. The IPCC predicts that increases in the 21st century will very likely be greater than those in the 20th century, if current trends continue.[5] Potential impacts include sea level rise, the spread of infectious disease, more severe and frequent storms, more severe and frequent droughts, shifts in farm regions, and loss of forest cover. The IPCC concludes with "high confidence" that:

- Rainfall will shift from the tropics toward the poles, potentially in significant amount by mid-century.

- Droughts and heavy rainfall will increase.

- Hurricanes and typhoons will become more intense, with higher peak wind speeds and heavier precipitation.

- The health of millions of people will suffer, with increases in malnutrition, deaths from heat waves and more heart disease due to local air pollution problems exacerbated by global warming.

- "The resilience of many ecosystems is likely to be exceeded...by an unprecedented combination of climate change, associated disturbances (e.g., flooding, drought, wildfire, insects, ocean acidification) and other global change drivers (e.g., land use change, pollution, over-exploitation of resources)."[6]

The IPCC said: "The last time the polar regions were significantly warmer than present for an extended period (about 125,000 years ago), reductions in polar ice volume led to 4 to 6 metres of sea level rise."[7]

The scientific consensus regarding the threat from global warming is very strong. The IPCC reflects the work of thousands of scientists over a five-year period using only peer-reviewed material. Donald Kennedy, editor in chief of *Science* magazine, has said that "consensus as strong as the one that has developed around this topic is rare in science."[8]

In June 2005, the U.S. National Academy of Science joined 10 other national academies from around the world in declaring that "the scientific understanding of climate change is now sufficiently clear to justify nations taking prompt action. It is vital that all nations identify cost-effective steps that they can take now, to contribute to substantial and long-term reductions in net global greenhouse gas emissions."[9]

b. *Oil's Role*
Oil is a leading cause of global warming. Worldwide, 40% of fossil fuel carbon dioxide emissions come from oil, roughly the same as from coal.[10]

This problem could get much worse. Today there are roughly 800 million cars and trucks on the road worldwide. This is projected to grow to more than 2 billion by 2030.[11] If most or all those vehicles run on oil, the global warming impacts would be extremely serious.

Oil is the single largest source of heat-trapping gases in the United States. In the U.S., carbon dioxide emissions from vehicles increased from 1.2 billion tons in 1980 to 1.8 billion tons in 2003. At current rates of increase, emissions would easily reach 2.5 billion tons by 2020.[12]

A gallon of gasoline, when burned, produces almost 20 pounds of carbon dioxide. Just over 5 pounds of carbon dioxide, on average, are emitted in producing and refining the fuel, so the average gallon of gasoline creates roughly 25 pounds of carbon dioxide. That means the average car in the United States puts roughly 6 tons of carbon dioxide into the atmosphere each year.[13]

There are no pollution control devices that can separate carbon dioxide from a car's exhaust. (In this way, carbon dioxide is different than many other pollutants, such as particulates or carbon monoxide.) The only ways to cut carbon dioxide emissions from vehicles are to improve fuel efficiency, substitute cleaner fuels or drive less. Vehicle fuel efficiency has been roughly constant in the United States for the past 20 years.

2. URBAN AIR POLLUTION

Air quality is unhealthy in dozens of cities around the United States The worst problems are particulate matter (commonly known as soot), ground-level ozone (the main component of smog), and carbon monoxide.

Oil causes more than half this pollution. Vehicles produce 45% of nitrogen oxides (NOx) and 36% of volatile organic compounds (VOC), which combine to make ground-level ozone. They also produce 77% of the carbon monoxide.[14]

The health consequences of this pollution are serious. Particulates trigger asthma, coughs and other respiratory problems. Ozone causes shortness of breath, wheezing and coughing. Carbon monoxide reduces oxygen delivery to organs and tissues, with especial impacts on those with cardiovascular conditions.[15]

Since passage of the 1970 Clean Air Act, urban air quality has improved dramatically in the United States. Pollution from vehicles has dropped sharply. Technologies such as the catalytic converter have helped cut tailpipe emissions from new cars by more than 90% in a few decades.[16]

Still, unhealthy air quality is a fact of life in many cities around the United States. Four cities in California—Los Angeles, Fresno, Bakersfield and Visalia—have some of the worst records for both particulates and ground-

level ozone. Pittsburgh, Detroit, Atlanta and Cleveland all have problems
with particulate pollution. Houston, Sacramento, Knoxville, Dallas and
Washington, D.C. all have problems with ground-level ozone.[17]

The worst air pollution in the world is in Mexico City. Beijing, Manila
and other Asian cities have horrific air pollution problems as well. In these
huge megacities, vehicles burning oil are a substantial part of the problem.
In some urban areas around the world, vehicles produce 50% to 90% of air
quality problems.[18]

3. OIL SPILLS
In the past 15 years, more than eight tankers have accidentally spilled more
than a million gallons of oil into the world's oceans.[19]

The results can be devastating. In 2002, the tanker Prestige broke up off
the coast of Spain, sending heavy oil to Spanish beaches nearby. In 2001,
the Ecuadorian ship Jessica spilled diesel and bunker oil into the sea off
the Galapagos Islands, imperiling one of the world's great ecological
treasures. In 1999, the Maltese tanker Erika split in two off the coast of
France, blanketing beaches in Brittany with a sticky black slime.[20]

The largest oil spill in American waters, the Exxon Valdez in 1989, spilled
almost 11 million gallons into U.S. waters, causing widespread ecological
damage.[21]

In a 2003 report, the National Research Council (NRC) stated:

> Petroleum poses a range of environmental risks when released into the
> environment (whether as catastrophic spills or chronic discharges). In
> addition to physical impacts of large spills, the toxicity of many of the
> individual compounds contained in petroleum is significant, and even
> small releases can kill or damage organisms from the cellular- to the
> population-level.[22]

The NRC found that the damage caused by an oil spill is "a complex
function of the rate of release, the nature of the released petroleum...and
the local physical and biological ecosystem exposed."[23] Recovery can take
many years.

MEMORANDUM TO THE PRESIDENT

FROM: ADMINISTRATOR, ENVIRONMENTAL
                        PROTECTION AGENCY

SUBJECT: Global Warming/Oil Dependence

I read the excellent memorandum from the chair of CEQ on the
environmental impacts of oil consumption. I agree with everything in it.
In particular, I agree that global warming is an epic challenge and that oil
is a leading cause.

However, the memorandum fails to make an important point: When it
comes to fighting global warming, some ways of reducing oil dependence
are much better than others.

Some alternatives to oil create small amounts of heat-trapping gases.
Others create roughly the same amount as oil. Some alternatives can make
the global warming problem *worse*.

Here's a quick summary:

1. FUEL EFFICIENCY
When it comes to fighting global warming, technologies that improve fuel
efficiency are best, since all existing fuels produce at least some heat-
trapping gases. Making vehicles more fuel efficient is a straightforward and
powerful way to protect the climate system.

2. BIOFUELS
When it comes to fighting global warming, biofuels are better than oil.
That's because the carbon released when biofuels burn is simply being
returned to the atmosphere after briefly becoming part of a plant through
photosynthesis. This short cycle—growing plants and then burning them
as biofuels—has no overall impact on global warming. Burning oil, in
contrast, puts carbon into the atmosphere that's been stored underground
for millions of years.

However, the amount of benefit from a biofuel depends on what it is made from.

- Among biofuels, ethanol made from sugar is best from a global-warming standpoint, with ethanol from cellulose close behind. Making ethanol from these feedstocks requires relatively little fossil energy. According to a study by Argonne National Laboratory, E85 (85% ethanol fuel) made from cellulosic sources reduces heat-trapping gases by 86% as compared to gasoline.[1]

- Ethanol made from corn also helps with global warming, though much less. Growing corn typically involves substantial fossil fuel inputs for energy and fertilizer. According to Argonne, E85 made with corn-based ethanol reduces heat-trapping gases by 21% to 29% as compared to gasoline.[2]

3. ELECTRIC CARS
Replacing oil with electricity using plug-in vehicles is also an improvement over oil. The extent of the improvement depends on how the electricity is generated.

- If the electricity comes from wind, solar or nuclear power, driving a plug-in hybrid creates almost no heat-trapping gases.

- If the electricity comes from natural gas, driving a plug-in hybrid creates modest amounts of heat-trapping gases.

- If the electricity comes from a coal plant, driving a plug-in hybrid creates heat-trapping gases, but still less than a car driven on oil. This is such an important point, I want to emphasize it. *Even when the electricity to run a plug-in hybrid comes from a coal plant, emissions of heat-trapping gases are less than from a conventiona car running on oil. This is because electric motors are much more efficient than* internal combustion engines.

- The U.S. grid as a whole runs about 50% on coal, so expanding the fleet of plug-in hybrids would significantly reduce emissions of heat-trapping gases.[3] As the U.S. power grid becomes cleaner in the decades ahead, the global warming benefits of plug-in hybrids will grow.

4. <u>COAL</u>

The worst fuel from a global warming standpoint—considerably worse than oil—is liquefied coal.

- Using conventional technologies, liquefied coal produces nearly twice the amount of heat-trapping gases as oil on a life-cycle basis. About half these emissions are released at the production facility and half from tailpipes when the fuel is burned.

- With advanced technologies, it might be possible to eliminate emissions from the production facility by storing carbon underground. It might also be possible to use byproducts from these facilities to generate relatively clean electricity. One source claims that, using these technologies, life-cycle emissions from liquefied coal could be cut to roughly 80% of those from oil.[4] However, this has never been demonstrated.

These topics may be explored in more detail in other memoranda you have requested. However, I thought it might be helpful to highlight them here.

from the desk of the
ADMINISTRATOR, ENVIRONMENTAL
PROTECTION AGENCY

I hope you'll use your oil dependence speech to talk about global warming. It's the single greatest challenge we face today, bar none. Here's an interesting article.

★ ★ ★ ★ ★

Messenger from the North

"The seasons are shifting on us," says Sarah James. "The elders used to be able to predict the weather. Now it's impossible."

Sarah James lives in Artic Village, Alaska. When she was young, says the 63-year-old Gwich'n tribe member, snow came in September. It melted in May. Year after year it was the same.

No more. In the 1980's, the seasons started changing. Rains fell when there should have been snow. Melting began sooner. Nature's patterns were jumbled.

Speaking to a rapt audience in Washington, D.C., James is confident and well-spoken. A winner of the prestigious Goldman Environment Prize, she is on a month-long trip to be sure Americans hear a simple message.

"Global warming has already hit the Arctic hard," she says. "It threatens the future of our people."

THE ARCTIC is often compared to a canary in a coal mine, offering an early glimpse of the changes under way from global warming around the world. Computerized climate models predict that, as heat-trapping gases pour into the atmosphere, temperature increases will be greatest at the poles. And that's what's happening.

During the past few decades, temperatures in the Arctic have increased almost twice as fast as those in the rest of the world.

In 2004, hundreds of scientists completed the first comprehensive assessment of climate change in the Arctic, using data from the physical sciences, computer models and testimony of native people. In a report titled the Arctic Climate Impact Assessment, the scientists found evidence of rapid climate change throughout the region.

Perhaps most dramatic, they found that Arctic sea ice is melting, fast.

The earth's northern pole is a vast ocean surrounded by several continents. (In contrast, the southern pole is a vast continent surrounded by ocean.) For all of human history, the Arctic Ocean has been covered with a permanent layer of ice.

But in the past 30 years, summer sea ice in the Arctic has declined 15% to 20%. At the current pace, according to the Arctic Climate Impact Assessment, summer ice will be gone during this century. In summertime, the Artic Ocean will be an ice-free zone.

The consequences will be far-reaching. Arctic species that depend on the ice, such as the polar bear and seals, may not survive. Weather patterns worldwide may change. "Climate processes unique to the Arctic have significant effects on global and regional climate," according to the Arctic Climate Impact Assessment.

When the Arctic Ocean is covered with ice, for example, most of the heat energy it receives from sunlight is reflected back into space. When that ice melts, however, most of the heat energy it receives is absorbed into the ocean. The result: a warmer planet.

Today, just three years after release of the Arctic Climate Impact Assessment, the lead author of the report thinks its conclusions were too cautious. Based on recent data, Bob Corell, a distinguished oceanographer and engineer, now thinks the Arctic Ocean could be ice-free in summer as early as 2030. By mid-century, he says, the odds the Arctic Ocean will be ice-free in summer are high.

FOR SARAH JAMES and other native Alaskans, the consequences will be far-reaching

In Arctic Village, she says, the wolves now come into town. Wolves run well on frozen tundra, James says, but not on melting mush. When wolves can't catch prey in the wild, they come looking for food where people live.

The fish stocks her people live on are declining as well. In much of northern Alaska, the riverbeds are permafrost, which provides an impermeable barrier water can't soak through. As this permafrost melts, riverbeds become more permeable, soaking up more of the water flowing through streams. The result: lower stream flows and problems for many fish stocks.

The same is true in lakes in the region, which used to be filled with whitefish, James says. Her people used to be able to rely on these stocks, but no more.

In much of Alaska, vast areas of forest are suffering from devastating invasions by pests. The Canadian bark beetle, for example, used to be killed during the summer months by night time frosts, helping keep the population under control. Now those frosts are fewer and far between. The result: vast swaths of forest decimated by the pest.

For James and her Gwich'n tribe, the impacts on the caribou are most devastating. The Gwich'n rely on the caribou for food and clothing. But global warming is disrupting the caribou migration routes and habitat.

In 2000 and 2001, for example, the Porcupine River thawed early, before the caribou herd could cross it. Thousands of cows died trying to cross the rushing rivers. Pregnant cows weren't able to get to their summer pastures before giving birth.

As she talks, Sarah James keeps returning to a simple point: The climate now is so unstable. In Arctic Village, for as long as anyone could remember, the weather used to be predictable. No longer.

For Corell, this point is central on a global scale as well. Corell notes that human civilization emerged roughly 10,000 years ago during a period of unusual climate stability. Ever since, global average temperatures have stayed within a narrow range.

Now, for the first time since the dawn of civilization, says Corell, temperatures will likely move out of that range.

SARAH JAMES picks up a small drum and punctuates her presentation with a haunting native song. Her audience is entranced. Later, the conversation turns to politics. I ask her what message she would give the next President of the United States.

"I would say you have the opportunity to change the world in a good way," James says. "We need some change. The next President will have that power."[1]

MEMORANDUM TO THE PRESIDENT

FROM: CHAIR, NATIONAL ECONOMIC COUNCIL

SUBJECT: Economic Consequences of Oil Dependence

Oil dependence exposes all Americans to the volatility of world oil markets. Because there are no widely available substitutes for oil as a transportation fuel, drivers face limited options in responding to price swings. When oil prices rise, many business and family budgets feel the strain.

However, the macroeconomic impacts of oil dependence are less clear. The dramatic increase in oil prices from 2003 to 2006 was not accompanied by a recession, in contrast with oil price increases in prior decades. This was attributable, in part, to energy efficiency improvements in the United States during the past 30 years. Monetary policies made possible by the lack of underlying inflation also played a role.

This memorandum provides background and summarizes the principal economic impacts of oil dependence.

1. BACKGROUND
The United States spends more than $450 billion annually on oil.[1] This amounts to approximately 3% of GDP.[2] More than 69% of this oil is used to make fuel for motor vehicles, including cars, trucks, and planes.[3]

a. *Oil Prices*
The price of oil is set on a global market. Production cuts or demand increases in one location can ripple through the entire global economy. Traders at commodity exchanges in New York, London and Singapore play an important role in establishing prices, based on the quality of crude oil being traded and detailed information about supply and demand around the world. Oil is cheap to ship across vast distances, facilitating international trade. Roughly 75% of oil produced each year is traded internationally.[4]

The price of refined petroleum products, such as gasoline and diesel fuel, often varies by location. One reason is differing taxes. Other factors include refinery and pipeline capacity, which can cause short-term variations. In fall 2005, for example, gasoline prices in the eastern United States skyrocketed when many refineries lost power due to Hurricane Katrina. Gasoline imports from Europe helped reduce prices to American consumers.[5]

Oil prices are very volatile. Prices quadrupled (from roughly $3 to $12 per barrel) during the first oil shock in 1973–1974 and then more than doubled (from roughly $14 to $35 per barrel) in 1979–1981. Oil prices fell steadily in the early 1980s, fluctuated between $12 and $25 per barrel from 1985 to 2003 and climbed from below $30 per barrel in 2003 to reach $77 per barrel briefly in 2006.[6]

Indeed, oil prices can fluctuate dramatically even over the course of several months. Between December 2006 and January 2007, oil prices fell from roughly $62 to $50 per barrel (a drop of almost 20%). In February 2007, prices climbed back up to roughly $62 per barrel. They then fell back to $57 per barrel, only to increase to $66 per barrel (a jump of almost 16%) in the last 10 days of March 2007.[7]

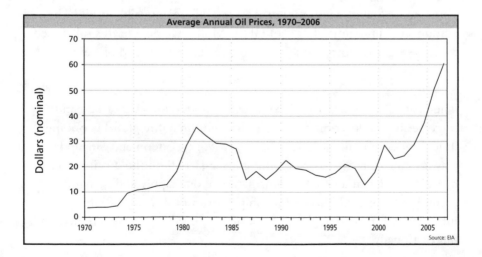

Average Annual Oil Prices, 1970–2006

Source: EIA

b. *Lack of Substitutes*

Oil's role in the U.S. economy is shaped by the fact that there are no widely available substitutes. The U.S. transportation infrastructure is almost completely dependent on oil. Although ethanol and other biofuels play a growing role, they make up less than 4% of the liquid fuel supply. Furthermore, the distribution network for biofuels is at present very limited. When oil prices rise, few businesses or individuals are able to find substitutes.

As a result, the "elasticity of demand" for oil is very low. Demand elasticity measures how purchases respond to rising prices. Essential goods with few substitutes, such as oil, are very "inelastic," meaning that demand drops very little even as prices rise. Based on data in the United States during the past several decades, economists estimate the short-run "elasticity of demand" for oil at less than 0.1, lower than tobacco and coffee and comparable to salt.[8] Over the long run, oil's demand elasticity is higher, as drivers have the chance to adjust, for example by purchasing more fuel-efficient cars.[9]

c. *Oil Supply*

Oil production requires enormous capital investment and long lead times. Unless production capacity is sitting idle, many years can elapse between decisions to produce additional oil and oil becoming available. As a result, oil supply responds slowly to price increases. Oil's "elasticity of supply," the measure of how supply responds to prices, is very low.[10]

Historically, Saudi Arabia has maintained considerable excess production capacity, in part to help stabilize world prices. Saudi Arabia has also sought to prevent oil prices from rising high enough to encourage alternatives, in order to maintain long-term demand for its product.[11] In recent years, however, Saudi reserve capacity has dropped as world oil demand climbed.[12] The result has been steep price increases and considerable oil price volatility.

Production costs for oil are much lower in the Persian Gulf than in the United States. The average cost to produce a barrel of oil in the Gulf is in the range of $2 to $5. In the United States, in contrast, production costs are generally $15 to $20 per barrel.[13]

About 90% of global oil reserves are owned by national oil companies. Concerns have been expressed about whether some of these state-run enterprises invest sufficiently in additional production.[14]

Since the 1970s, the Organization of Petroleum Exporting Countries (OPEC) has played an important role in shaping global oil markets. OPEC nations currently control 43% of global production. Members are Algeria, Angola, Indonesia, Iran, Iraq, Kuwait, Libya, Nigeria, Qatar, Saudi Arabia, the UAE and Venezuela.[15]

 d. _U.S. Statistics_
The United States is the world's leading oil consumer, using roughly 24% of the global total. We are the world's third largest oil producer, with roughly 8% of global production.

U.S. oil consumption has risen every year since 1985, with one exception (1990).[16] However, the U.S. economy uses oil more efficiently than several decades ago. Indeed the ratio of oil use to GDP is roughly half its 1970 level. In part, this is because of the improvements in vehicle fuel efficiency during the 1970s and 1980s. In part, it is because of the steep drop in oil use by electric utilities since then. The shift toward service and high-tech jobs, which tend to use less petroleum, has also played an important role.[17]

U.S. oil production peaked at 9.6 million barrels per day in 1970. It has been mostly declining (with a few modest annual increases) ever since.[18] Production in 2005 was 5.2 million barrels per day. Almost half this oil comes from Gulf of Mexico or Texas. Roughly 17% comes from Alaska and roughly 13% comes from California.[19]

This combination of rising consumption and falling production means that U.S. oil imports have been rising steadily for many years. Imports were 34% of total consumption in 1973 and are almost 60% today.[20] In 2006, payments to foreign oil producers totaled roughly $280 billion.[21] The largest single exporter to the United States is Canada, generally followed by Mexico, Saudi Arabia, Venezuela and Nigeria. The Persian Gulf region as a whole provides roughly 11% of U.S. oil each year.[22]

U.S. oil consumption per capita is still much higher than in most other industrialized countries. In the United States and Canada, oil consumption is roughly 2.8 gallons per person per day. The average for all other countries in the industrialized world is roughly 1.4 gallons per person per day, and for the world as a whole, just over 0.5 gallons per day.[23]

The United States has roughly 2% of the world's proven oil reserves.[24]

2. MACROECONOMIC IMPACTS

Between 2003 and 2006, oil prices rose from under to $30 per barrel to briefly reach more than $77 per barrel. During this period, the performance of the U.S. economy remained strong, with real GDP growth averaging more than 3% per year. Unlike previous episodes in which oil prices skyrocketed, the U.S. economy did not go into a recession.[25]

One reason: the improvements in energy efficiency of the U.S. economy discussed above. The additional amounts spent for oil were a smaller percent of GDP than during previous periods of rising oil prices.[26]

The relationship between oil prices and economic output has been studied extensively. Initial scholarship suggested a direct relationship between oil prices and economic growth.[27] This seemed to fit well with the experience of the 1970s, in which oil price spikes were followed by severe recessions.

In a series of papers, however, economist James Hamilton argued that the relationship was more complicated.[28] Hamilton's statistical analyses suggested that oil price increases tend to slow economic growth, whereas oil price decreases do little to boost it. Hamilton also found that oil price increases after long periods of stable prices have a bigger impact on the economy than increases that are part of short-term swings.[29]

In 1997, Ben Bernanke and colleagues presented an even more radical hypothesis: that "oil shocks, per se, were not a major cause" of the downturns in the 1970s.[30] Bernanke, now chair of the Federal Reserve Board, concluded that the response of monetary authorities to oil price increases had a larger impact on the economy than the price increases themselves. Bernanke's analysis indicates that a sound monetary policy could help significantly to reduce the negative impacts of oil price increases on the economy.

The results of the past several years are encouraging. We have come a long way since the 1970s in being able to manage the impact of substantial oil price increases on the economy. Improvements in energy efficiency and monetary policy appear to have played important roles. More sophisticated financial instruments, allowing businesses to hedge against oil price increases, may also have played a role.[31]

Such increases are not without significant costs, however. Every $10 increase in the price of oil, for example, adds roughly $50 billion annually in foreign payments.[32]

Furthermore, the ability of the U.S. economy to absorb price increase even greater than those experienced from 2003 to 2006 remains uncertain. According to one analysis, for example, an increase in oil prices to $120 per barrel would throw the world economy into recession, with U.S. GDP declining by 2.3% and global GDP falling even more.[33]

Unfortunately, there are several plausible scenarios in which price spikes of this magnitude might occur. These include a nuclear attack upon Saudi oil fields, a jihadist coup in Saudi Arabia and coordinated terrorist attacks on a small number of choke points in the global oil distribution network. In such scenarios, U.S. oil dependence would have severely negative impacts on the economy as a whole.

3. IMPACT ON FAMILY BUDGETS
Even if the macroeconomic impacts of oil price swings are manageable, the impact on many family budgets is not.

Between February, 2002 and September, 2005, average gasoline prices increased from $1.15 to roughly $3.00 per gallon.[34] For a car driven 12,000 miles per year getting 20 miles per gallon, that's $1,080 of extra cost. For a car driven 25,000 miles per year getting 15 miles per gallon, that's an annual difference of $3,000.

Median family income in the United States is roughly $46,000.[35] Furthermore, the average personal savings rate in the U.S. is negative, meaning that on average consumers not only spend all money earned, but use savings or borrow to supplement their incomes.[36] The capacity of many families to absorb gasoline price increases is poor.

Because there are no widely available substitutes for oil, most drivers are forced to simply absorb additional costs when oil prices rise. Some can shift daily patterns to drive less, but for many this is difficult or impossible.

Furthermore, deeply ingrained cultural patterns exacerbate the very real financial costs on many families. Gasoline prices are posted prominently at commercial street corners throughout the United States, constantly reminding drivers of additional costs. (Price increases for milk or orange juice, for example, don't receive nearly the same attention.) Media reports often highlight fluctuations in oil prices.

A severe disruption in oil supplies would bring catastrophic consequences for many families. One study found that with oil at $120 per barrel, household energy bills (including oil and heating gas) would roughly double.[37]

4. CONCLUSION

The U.S. economy maintained steady growth in recent years, even as oil prices climbed substantially. Energy efficiency improvements and sound monetary policies appear to have played important roles. However, these oil price increases were a considerable burden on some families and businesses. The United States remains vulnerable to severe economic disruption as a result of sudden and substantial oil price increases.

from the desk of the
SECRETARY OF COMMERCE

Fed Ex founder and chairman Frederick W. Smith is a highly visible leader on the topic of oil dependence. I thought you might be interested in the attached article.

★★★★★

Fred Smith on the Move

When I see Fred Smith, he's on his way to the White House. Not as a candidate, but as a messenger. He's joined by an admiral, two generals and an investment banker.

Their message is simple: it's time to get the United States off oil.

Thirty-five years ago, Fred Smith founded Federal Express. In doing that, he created not just a company, but an industry. Before Fred Smith, reliable overnight delivery service didn't exist. Today, people everywhere depend on it.

Thanks to Fred Smith and his team, FedEx is one of the nation's most successful companies. In a recent Wall Street Journal survey, FedEx ranked first in reputation, management quality and investor potential. In 2004, Smith was named CEO of the Year by readers of Chief Executive magazine.

With a net worth north of $2.2 billion, Smith could retire and go fishing. But instead he's walking the power corridors of Washington, D.C., and touring the country with a simple message.

"Oil dependence is heading this country toward a major economic disaster," Smith says. "Aside from the spread of weapons of mass destruction, it's the most critical national security threat we face today."

Smith knows something about oil dependence. Every day, FedEx trucks and airplanes consume a staggering amount of gasoline and diesel fuel. The company's annual fuel costs typically exceed $3 billion. When the price of oil climbs, so do FedEx expenses.

Several years ago, FedEx was approached by Environmental Defense, a national advocacy group, about working together on fuel-saving technologies for delivery trucks. Smith jumped at the chance.

FedEx and Environmental Defense teamed up to shape a set of fuel-saving goals and then find a manufacturer who could meet them. Eventually Smith chose Eaton Corporation, an Ohio-based manufacturer, to build the first hybrid electric delivery trucks.

Eaton's hybrid engine technology—similar to that found in the Toyota Prius—is perfectly suited for FedEx. It combines a classic internal combustion engine that runs on diesel with an electric motor that draws power from a battery. The battery is recharged in part with energy captured from the frequent use of the truck's brakes.

Today, FedEx has over 90 hybrid delivery trucks on the road. It's aiming for 30,000 by 2016.

FedEx also operates the largest solar power installation in California (at Oakland International Airport).

But Smith's interests extend beyond the company. He also spends time spearheading the Energy Security Leadership Council, a bipartisan group of business and military leaders committed to highlighting the problem of oil dependence. Over the course of a year, the group fashioned a set of proposals to help the United States kick its oil habit.

Smith's work on the group wins high praise. General P. X. Kelley, retired Commandant of the Marines and co-chair of the Council, says simply "Without Fred, I don't think we'd be where we are today."

Smith has emerged as a natural leader of the group and perhaps its most visible spokesman. He speaks with conviction about the dangers oil dependence poses to all Americans. Which is one reason he's on the way to the White House when I see him, ready to preach about the dangers of oil addiction.

The other reason, of course, is that oil dependence is a problem for his company. Smith is a savvy businessman and sees the chance to help his nation and his business at the same time.

What's good for FedEx is good for the country? Today at least, it's looking that way.[1]

Key points on oil dependence so far—

National security problems
- strengthens Al Qaeda
- strengthens oil exporters—eg. Iran, Venezuela
- jeopardizes troop safety (interesting! not widely known)
- undermines democracy

Environmental problems
- global warming
- local air pollution (smog)
- oil spills

Economic
- no recession in 2003-2006 despite rising oil prices
- price volatility
- big supply disruption could tank the economy

Still 96% of the fuel for our cars and trucks!
Why haven't we made more progress?!

MEMORANDUM FOR THE PRESIDENT

FROM: SECRETARY OF ENERGY

SUBJECT: <u>Trapped in the 1970s</u>

You asked why we've made such little progress in reducing oil dependence. After all, politicians have been talking about this problem for more than 30 years.

There are several reasons.

First, we have failed to comprehend the size of the problem. Oil is everywhere. In the United States, we spend a billion dollars on oil every day. Small measures will not be enough.

Second, we have failed to comprehend the time required. Oil dependence will not be solved in weeks, months or just a few years. Almost all of the more than 240 million cars on our roads today depend on oil. Less than 7% of the auto fleet is replaced each year. We can make important progress in the short term, but weaning ourselves from oil will take a full generation.

Third, we have failed to comprehend the nature of the problem. Trapped in a 1970s mindset, we have focused repeatedly on oil imports. Such imports are a problem, but they are not the fundamental problem when it comes to oil. The fundamental problem is that we have no substitutes. Only when we set a goal of providing all drivers with a choice of fuels will we have a chance of ending dependence on oil.

I'll elaborate on that third point in this memo.

1. <u>THE 1970s AND ITS LEGACY</u>
From the dawn of the automobile age until the early 1970s, the United States controlled the world price of oil. During World War II, the United States produced almost 90% of the oil used by the Allies. As late as 1970,

government agencies limited output by U.S. producers to prevent prices from falling too low. No country matched the U.S. impact on global markets.[1]

In the early 1970s, that changed. World oil demand was growing. U.S. oil production peaked, starting a downward trend that continues to the present day, and the excess capacity of U.S. producers disappeared. (In the words of Alan Greenspan, "rising world demand finally exceeded the excess crude oil capacity of the U.S."[2]) At the same time, production capacity abroad grew sharply. Between 1965 and 1974, Saudi production increased from about 2 million to more than 8 million barrels per day.[3]

Power shifted to foreign producers, who quickly used it. In October 1973, Saudi Arabia responded to U.S. support for Israel with a decision to cut oil production by 10% and ban shipments to the United States and the Netherlands. In the next three months, oil prices increased by almost a factor of four.

In the United States, gasoline prices skyrocketed. Many drivers, used to decades of low and stable prices, were shocked. As long gas lines appeared in many parts of the country, Americans struggled to adjust to a new and unsettling vulnerability. The impact on the national psyche was far-reaching and profound.

Prices stabilized at a new high level. Then, in 1979, it happened again. World oil prices more than doubled, as exports from Iran ceased amid widespread chaos and a radical Islamic revolution. In the United States, gas lines reappeared and the nation plunged into recession.

In the years since the oil shocks of the 1970s, many experts have pointed to a combination of causes. Spare production capacity dropped sharply in the early part of the decade, reaching a mere 500,000 barrels per day worldwide in 1973. (In tight markets, production cutbacks have large impacts on prices.) Price controls and complex regulatory schemes for allocating oil helped create long gas lines in the United States. The response of monetary authorities to rising oil prices contributed to some problems.[4]

But in popular discourse, there was only one cause for the trauma that befell the United States in those years: the nation's new "dependence on foreign oil."[5]

This was understandable. Saudi and Iranian production cutbacks were the most visible cause of the problems. If the United States could only return to the halcyon days when it produced its own oil, people thought, such troubles could be avoided. "Dependence on foreign oil" became emblazoned in the national psyche, where it remains today.

Of course there was a more fundamental reason the United States was vulnerable: our cars depended completely on oil. If drivers had been able to shift to fuels other than gasoline, the impact of Saudi and Iranian cutbacks would have been greatly reduced. Yet by the 1970s, vehicles had been depending almost completely on oil for more than 70 years. The most obvious culprit for our problems was not that dependence, but the newer need for foreign oil.

Much has changed since the 1970s—an age before the Internet, personal computers or cell phones. The United States is much more integrated into the global economy than three decades ago. Nations in Asia and elsewhere have undergone dramatic growth. Global warming has emerged as an epic environmental threat.

Oil markets have changed dramatically, too. Long-term contracts are much less important than in decades past. A vibrant international spot market and futures trading now dominates. Today, almost 240 million barrels of oil per day are traded on the London International Petroleum Exchange, three times as much as global consumption.[6]

Meanwhile, U.S. oil imports have climbed steadily. In 1973, imports supplied 34% of total U.S. consumption. By 1990, they had risen to roughly 40%. Today, imports supply roughly 60% of the oil we use each year.[7]

Yet one enduring legacy of the 1970s has been the constant focus in political dialogue on "foreign oil." Today, more than 30 years after the first oil shocks, is that the core of the problem?

2. THE IMPORTANCE OF IMPORTS

Unfortunately, cutting oil imports would not solve many of the national security, environmental and economic problems typically associated with oil. Many Americans would no doubt be surprised to learn this. But it's true.

Don't get me wrong—cutting oil imports is desirable. Oil expenditures contribute more than $270 billion to the trade deficit each year.[8] Spending money at home is better for economic growth and job creation than sending it abroad.[9]

But oil is a fungible product, traded globally, with a price set on a global market. As a result, many of the problems often associated with oil simply cannot be solved by replacing foreign oil with domestic oil. The problem is more fundamental.

a. *National Security*

Surprisingly, many national security vulnerabilities created by oil would remain even if the percentage of oil we import dropped significantly.

Consider: The United States hasn't imported a drop of oil from Iran in more than 25 years. Yet that fact doesn't prevent Iran from playing its oil card in international negotiations over its nuclear ambitions. In fact, even the possibility that Iran might play its oil card is enough to weaken the resolve of political leaders around the world when it comes to confronting Iran on the nuclear issue.

Iran's influence as an oil exporter is based on its importance to world markets. The fact Iran doesn't ship oil directly to the United States doesn't protect us or diminish Iran's influence.

Consider: Canada is our leading source of oil imports. Mexico varies between number two and number three.[10] Do imports of oil from Canada and Mexico threaten our national security?

Consider: Europe gets 17% of its oil from the Persian Gulf. Japan gets 78%.[11] In an interdependent global economy, our prosperity depends upon the prosperity of allies and trading partners. Imagine that U.S. oil imports dropped sharply, but Europe and Japan remained dependent on Mideast oil. In that scenario, the United States would still retain a vital interest the flow of oil from the Persian Gulf to world markets. Our continued economic growth would depend on it.

The issue is not the United States' dependence on imported oil. The issue is the world's dependence on oil.

Consider: Some funds sent to state-owned oil companies in the Persian Gulf are channeled to radical jihadists, threatening our national security. Funds sent to Venezuelan President Hugo Chavez empower a leader who wishes us ill. But U.S. oil imports could fall and funds from around the world would keep flowing to the Persian Gulf and Venezuela, if global oil demand remained high.

Money, like oil, is fungible. To minimize the problems posed by financial flows to oil-exporting nations, we need to reduce global demand for oil.

None of these facts means that oil imports are irrelevant. But together, they point to a clear conclusion: Focusing on oil imports isn't enough. To solve the national security problems created by oil, we need more fundamental change.

b. *Economic*

In summer of 2000, British truck drivers went on strike over rising oil prices. At the time, the U.K. was fully energy independent, a net oil exporter. However, that fact didn't protect British truckers from rising world oil prices.[12]

Reducing oil imports, even to zero, would not protect U.S. drivers from rising world oil prices. The price of oil is set on a global market. Crude oil prices within a country do not depend on how much oil that country imports or exports. Unless a country is willing to impose import quotas and export barriers, isolating itself from the world market, the percentage of oil it imports has little impact on prices paid by consumers.

It turns out, however, that there is one somewhat unusual situation in which the percentage of imports influences prices. Ironically, in this situation, imports help reduce prices at the pump.
In September 2005, gasoline prices in the eastern United States jumped to record levels. The problem wasn't rising world oil prices (although they were high). The problem was a massive but temporary disruption of U.S. refinery capacity in the wake of Hurricane Katrina. During September and October 2005, imports of refined gasoline jumped sharply, helping reduce prices at the pump in the eastern United States. Refinery capacity was soon restored. "Foreign oil" helped manage the crisis.

The economic impact of oil imports is complex. On the one hand, expenditures for foreign oil are the single largest part of the trade deficit. Funds sent abroad could contribute more to economic growth if kept at home. On the other hand, the percentage of imports has almost no impact on the vulnerability of consumers to the volatility of world oil markets. Integration with world markets can even protect U.S. consumers in the event of unusual disruptions.

c. _Environment_
Domestic oil offers no environmental advantage over imported oil.

First, the global warming impacts of domestic and imported oil are the same. The carbon content of petroleum varies somewhat from field to field, but petroleum produced in the United States is roughly comparable to petroleum from other countries in this regard. Furthermore, the carbon content of refined petroleum products, such as gasoline, varies only slightly depending on the source. To determine overall carbon dioxide emissions from the burning of fossil fuels, for example, the U.S. government uses a single "emissions coefficient" for all gasoline, not one that varies based on the gasoline's origin.[13]

The analysis is similar for other air pollutants produced by petroleum, such as sulfur dioxide. The sulfur content of petroleum varies from field to field. Domestic petroleum is typically low in sulfur (or "sweet," in the industry vernacular), but there are many sources of low-sulfur petroleum from other countries as well. In any event, most sulfur and other impurities are removed at refineries, so petroleum with a higher sulfur content (known as "sour") does not necessarily lead to higher sulfur dioxide emissions from the refined product.

Two of the leading oil exporters to the United States, Canada and Venezuela, produce "heavy oil," which requires large amounts of energy to extract, ship and refine. Lifecycle carbon dioxide emissions from heavy oil are especially high. Replacing Canadian and Venezuelan oil imports with some domestically produced oil would, therefore, have positive global warming impacts. However, replacing Canadian or Venezuelan imports with imports from Mexico, the North Sea, or Saudi Arabia would have the same benefits.

Oil drilling in sensitive ecological regions can cause environmental damage. There is growing concern among environmentalists, for example, regarding oil drilling in parts of the Amazon. Using oil from less pristine domestic regions, such as the western Gulf of Mexico, would be preferable from an ecological standpoint. However using oil from pristine areas within the United States, such as the Arctic National Wildlife Refuge, would raise concerns similar to drilling in the Amazon. There is no automatic reason to prefer domestic oil over imported oil from an ecological standpoint.

3. THE FUNDAMENTAL PROBLEM: LACK OF SUBSTITUTES
The core problem we face today when it comes to oil is lack of substitutes.

Mobility is essential to modern life. Long ago, many people lived much of their lives without traveling more than a few miles from their homes. In modern societies, that is unimaginable.

Yet our transportation system is almost completely dependent on oil. If you want to travel anywhere, you need oil. If you want to ship goods from place to place, you need oil.

That dependence confers extraordinary power on those who happen to be endowed with cheap oil in large quantity. It puts an unfair burden on drivers whenever oil prices rise. It put enormous stress on natural systems, when carbon stored in underground oil deposits for millions of years is pumped into the atmosphere as heat-trapping carbon dioxide.

Almost a century ago, Winston Churchill made the famous statement that "safety and certainty in oil lie in variety and variety alone."[14] In Churchill's time, it was possible to imagine that multiple suppliers of this one product might be enough. But times have changed.

Today the global economy is far more integrated than in Churchill's time. The cheapest and most plentiful oil, by far, is concentrated in a single unstable region. Environmental challenges barely imagined a century ago now threaten people everywhere.

Today, we need more than geographic diversity in the supply of a single fuel. We need diversity of fuels themselves. We need a transportation infrastructure that allows drivers—for the first time since the dawn of the automobile age—to choose what fuels they use to drive their cars.

This transformation is achievable; indeed it is already beginning. Today several technologies offer the promise of disrupting oil's deeply entrenched hold on the transportation fuels market. One alternative, ethanol, is beginning to have a significant impact in the market. Another, electricity from the grid, could have dramatic implications on oil dependence, soon. Meanwhile conventional hybrid engines are helping cars go 20% to 40% further on a tank of gasoline, with significant implications for long-term oil demand.[15]

You have requested papers on different technologies to help free us from oil. I recommend you apply these criteria in evaluating which have the most potential:

- technical feasibility

- low pollution

- low cost

- substantial reserve capacity (to help protect against supply disruptions).

It's time to move beyond the 1970s in our dialogue on oil. It's time to give drivers a choice between oil and other fuels.

PART II

Solutions

MEMORANDUM FOR THE PRESIDENT

FROM: SECRETARY OF TRANSPORTATION

SUBJECT: <u>Plug-In Hybrids</u>

To reduce oil dependence, nothing would do more good more quickly than making cars that could connect to the electric grid.

The United States has a vast infrastructure for generating electric power. However, that infrastructure is essentially useless in cutting oil dependence, because modern cars can't connect to it. If we built cars that ran on electricity and plugged into the grid, the potential for displacing oil would be enormous.

Plug-in hybrid electric vehicles (PHEVs) are a game-changing technology. They can break our oil addiction, cut driving costs and reduce pollution. To help end U.S. oil dependence, there is no higher priority than putting millions of plug-in hybrids on the road soon.

<u>A QUICK HISTORY OF ELECTRIC CARS</u>
The first cars ran on electricity. In 1900, electric cars outsold all other kinds. However, early electric cars could travel no more than a few miles on a single charge. Cars with internal combustion engines, fueled by petroleum, could go much farther. During the early decades of the 20th century, petroleum-fueled cars took over the market.[1]

For almost 90 years, electric vehicles were limited to niche applications. Golf carts and fork lifts used electric motors, but on-the-road vehicles almost never did. Then, in the early 1990s, the U.S. Congress and State of California passed clean air rules designed to spur innovation by major automakers. Several responded with new models of electric cars.

Unfortunately the electric cars of the 1990s produced more controversy than clean air. General Motors EV-1 was the most controversial. Leased mainly in California, with a range of 80-140 miles, the EV-1 won hundreds of wildly enthusiastic owners. But GM considered overall buyer interest inadequate and discontinued production. Major auto manufacturers lobbied successfully to change the California rules requiring them to build "zero emission" cars.[2]

In the late 1990s, Toyota and Honda began marketing the first "hybrid electrics."[3] A hybrid electric vehicle combines an internal combustion engine and electric motor. The engine runs on oil and the electric motor draws power from a battery. The battery is recharged with extra power from the engine (for example, when the car is going downhill) and energy captured from the brakes (in a process known as "regenerative braking"). When the battery is depleted, the vehicle runs on its gas tank. This solves the problem of short driving range that plagued other electric vehicles, while providing better fuel efficiency, torque and other measures of engine performance than a car with an internal combustion engine only.

Beginning in 2003, buyer interest in hybrid electric vehicles began to explode. By 2004, buyers were forced to wait months as dealers struggled to keep up with growing demand.[4] Worldwide, more than 1,000,000 hybrid electric vehicles have now been sold.[5]

2. THE NEXT STEP—PLUG-IN HYBRIDS
The next big step in automotive technology is the plug-in hybrid electric vehicle (PHEV). Like conventional hybrids, PHEVs combine an electric motor and internal combustion engine. But, as the name suggests, there is an important additional feature. Plug-in hybrids can be recharged from the electric grid. They can—quite literally—be plugged into a wall socket.[6]

The idea is simple, but the consequences are far-reaching:

- With plug-in hybrids, many drivers would need no petroleum for their daily commute. Cars could be recharged at night and many drivers could travel back and forth to work or around town using the car's electric motor only.[7]

- Driving costs would drop dramatically. At national average electricity prices, PHEVs would cost the equivalent of roughly 75 cents per gallon to drive when operating on their electric motors. (When charging, a plug-in hybrid car draws roughly the same amount of electricity as a home space heater.)[8]

- As with many electric cars, torque and acceleration would be excellent.

Said one enthusiast who converted his Toyota Prius to a plug-in: "Everyone wants to drive electric cars, they just don't know it yet."[9]

The biggest barrier to mass production is battery technology. Adding a plug-in feature to a conventional hybrid engine requires adjustments that increase the cost and size of the batteries, while shortening their expected life. Extra costs now run roughly from $8,000 to $11,000 per car.[10] These costs are expected to drop sharply, however, with mass production and advances in battery technology.[11] Many innovators—supported by substantial venture capital—are at work on new high-performance batteries.[12]

In late 2006, General Motors announced plans to produce a plug-in hybrid, known as the Chevy Volt, and displayed a prototype at the Detroit Auto Show. Toyota and other manufacturers have also indicated they are looking seriously at PHEVs. The time frame for bringing these cars to market is unclear.

Michigan Gov. Jennifer Granholm and a plug-in electric car.
Source: General Motors Corp. Used with Permission, GM Media Archives.

Plug-in hybrids are coming. Private investments and the predictable pace of innovation will help bring them to market, slowly, during the next decade. Federal policies could dramatically accelerate this pace. The balance of this memo summarizes the benefits of PHEVs and suggests polices to put millions on the road soon.

3. IMPACT ON OIL DEPENDENCE

Plug-in hybrids would cut oil use significantly. They would dramatically reduce U.S. vulnerability to disruptions in oil supplies.

With plug-in hybrids, many drivers would use little or no petroleum each day. National surveys have found that 60% of Americans travel 30 miles or less each day.[13] One recent study, using global positioning system (GPS) technology to track vehicles in St. Louis, found that 50% of vehicles monitored drove 30 miles or less each day.[14] With PHEVs, most or all of these miles could be driven using electricity instead of oil.

The oil savings would be substantial. With driving patterns observed in the St. Louis survey, a PHEV able to go 20 miles on an electric charge (a "PHEV20") would get approximately 70 miles per gallon on average. A PHEV able to go 40 miles on a charge (a "PHEV40") would get approximately 134 miles per gallon.[15] This is much better performance than a typical car (21 mpg average) or conventional hybrids.

One study found that, if all cars were PHEV20s, gasoline consumption would fall roughly 40%. Another study, using different survey data, put the figure at 50%. A third put the figure at 56%. For PHEV40s, studies project gasoline savings of more than 60%.[16]

Yet the contribution of plug-ins to ending oil dependence is much greater than the gallons saved. PHEVs would also allow our vehicle fleet to access an important reserve fuel source, dramatically reducing U.S. vulnerability to disruptions in oil supply.

Most utilities have substantial unused electric generating capacity at night, when loads are low. In addition, all electric utilities maintain reserve generating capacity—known as "peaking power"—for days of unusually high demand. (Typically, utilities use this peaking power only a few hundred hours per year.)[17] This excess and reserve capacity could provide an important backup fuel source for our vehicles, if cars could connect to the electric grid.[18]

Consider the impact of a significant oil supply disruption on two drivers: one with a conventional car and the other with a plug-in hybrid. Both drivers would face wildly inflated oil prices and, in the most extreme case, problems obtaining gasoline. The owner of the conventional car would be required to pay inflated gasoline prices or stop driving. The owner of the plug-in hybrid could shift more driving to the car's electric motor. This might cause some inconvenience, such as more frequent recharging or shorter trips. But driving costs would climb modestly, if at all. Even in the event of a catastrophic disruption in oil supplies, the second driver would be mobile.[19]

The presence of large numbers of PHEVs in the vehicle fleet would transform the relationship between the United States and leading oil exporters. We would retain an interest in reliable oil supply and stable prices, but our crushing dependence would be dramatically diminished.

This U.S. reserve capacity for generating electricity is an important asset, maintained at considerable cost. We should use it to help end our oil dependence. With plug-in vehicles, we can do just that.

4. ENVIRONMENTAL IMPACTS
Plug-in hybrids have two important environmental benefits. First, they dramatically improve urban air quality. Second, they significantly reduce emissions of heat-trapping gases.

PHEVs may have some small adverse environmental consequences as well. In some regions, plug-ins may cause more particulate emissions, mostly away from population centers. Disposal of used batteries may require additional landfill space, although most will likely be recycled.

a. Urban Air Quality
Plug-in hybrids emit nothing from their tailpipes when driving in all-electric mode. As a result, plug-ins would dramatically improve air quality in many cities. The exact amount of improvement would depend on

driving patterns, vehicle design, and other factors, but would almost certainly be substantial. One study predicts a 98% reduction in emissions of carbon monoxide, a leading smog precursor, for each PHEV.[20]

The benefits could be enormous. Vehicles are the largest source of air pollution in the United States, producing more than three fourths of the carbon monoxide and a half of the nitrogen oxides in the nation.[21] Better air quality would mean fewer children with asthma, greater worker productivity, and improved quality of life. In some cities, air quality could reach levels not experienced for more than 50 years.

b. *Global Warming*
Petroleum is a leading source of heat-trapping gases. By cutting oil use, plug-in hybrids can play an important role in fighting global warming.

Of course, the power to recharge a plug-in hybrid must come from somewhere. In much of the United States, that somewhere will be a coal-fired power plant. Yet coal produces more heat-trapping gases per unit of energy than oil. Does that mean that plug-in hybrids could make the global warming problem worse?

The simple answer: no. Plug-in hybrids reduce emissions of heat-trapping gases, even if the power to recharge batteries comes from a coal-fired power plant. The reason: A traditional internal combustion engine is astonishingly inefficient. With hundreds of moving parts constantly creating friction, an internal combustion engine wastes much of its energy in the form of excess heat. (That's the main reason for your car's cooling system.) The "thermal efficiency" of an internal combustion engine—its ability to convert fuel to useful work—is roughly 20%. The thermal efficiency of even an old-fashioned pulverized coal plant is roughly 33% to 34%. Newer coal units have efficiencies of more than 40%.[22]

Consider this calculation:
1. Burning a gallon of gasoline releases roughly 20 pounds of carbon dioxide into the atmosphere.[23]
2. A gallon of gasoline moves the average U.S. vehicle roughly 21 miles.[24]

3. That means *the average car releases just under 1 pound of carbon dioxide for each mile traveled.*
4. Generating a kilowatt-hour of energy at the average U.S. coal plant releases roughly 2.1 pounds of carbon dioxide into the atmosphere.[25]
5. A kilowatt-hour moves a first generation PHEV roughly 3 miles.[26]
6. That means a *first-generation PHEV recharged with energy from a coal-fired power plant will release roughly 0.7 pounds of carbon dioxide per mile* when driving on its electric motor.[27]

In other words, from a global warming standpoint, driving a PHEV charged with energy from a coal plant is *better* than driving an average vehicle filled with oil. Driving a PHEV charged with energy from a standard wall socket—which draws only part of its power from coal—is *much better* from a global warming standpoint

Roughly half of the electricity in the United States comes from coal. Other electric power sources emit far fewer heat-trapping gases than coal plants emit. Recent studies have found that, with today's grid and driving patterns, plug-in hybrids would reduce total emissions of heat-trapping gases from vehicles in the United States by 27% to 37%.[28]

Furthermore, it's possible to drive a plug-in hybrid without producing any heat-trapping gases at all. If a plug-in is recharged from a wind turbine or solar panel, for example, the miles driven on that charge have essentially no impact on global warming. In some regions of the country, wind resources are especially good at night, when many drivers will be recharging cars. PHEVs are an especially good way to capture wind energy.

The global warming benefits of plug-in hybrids will depend on many factors, including sources of electric power (coal, nuclear, natural gas, hydro, wind or solar) and driving patterns (miles driven on electricity versus miles driven on gasoline). With today's electric grid, the benefits are substantial. As the grid gets cleaner in the decades ahead, those benefits would grow.

c. *Particulates*

Increased coal generation due to PHEVs would lead to increases in other types of pollution. Many but not all of these increases would be offset by declining oil combustion or controlled through additional investment in pollution control devices at coal plants. However, emissions of particulates (better known as soot) would likely increase in some regions of the country with widespread use of PHEVs. The additional particulates would mostly be emitted away from urban population centers.[29]

d. *Battery Disposal*

Large-scale deployment of plug-in vehicles could add millions of additional batteries to the solid waste stream. However, this could be managed with minimal environmental problems at reasonable cost.

First, the batteries most likely to be used in plug-in hybrids are environmentally benign. Lithium ion batteries, for example, are nonhazardous and considered safe for disposal in municipal waste systems.[30] Nickel metal hydride batteries, used in the Toyota Prius and other conventional hybrids, are nonhazardous as well. Batteries with highly toxic elements such as lead, cadmium and mercury are very unlikely to be used to power plug-in hybrids.

Second, battery recycling programs are well-established and will likely be extended to batteries from plug-in hybrids. Today roughly 80% to 95% of car batteries are recycled.[31] The Rechargeable Battery Recycling Corporation runs a nationwide program dedicated to recycling used rechargeable batteries. Modifying and scaling up the programs already in place to handle the additional batteries from plug-in hybrids should not present significant problems. Indeed, many used PHEV batteries could be used by utilities or others for stationary energy storage.

Finally, the first plug-in hybrid batteries will not be ready for disposal for almost a decade. This will provide ample time to shape and implement programs for safe battery disposal.

5. IMPACT ON ELECTRIC POWER SYSTEMS

U.S. power plants are more than adequate to handle increased electricity demand from plug-in vehicles. Even with plug-ins making up half the vehicle fleet—several decades away under the most aggressive scenarios—electricity demand would increase only 4% to 7% from current levels. Much of this additional demand would be at night, when electricity loads are low and huge amounts of generating capacity sits unused. One recent study suggest that more than 200 million plug-ins could be driven daily in the United States without the need for new electric generating capacity.[32]

Plug-ins vehicles would provide utilities with a range of benefits. First, plug-ins would provide utilities with additional revenue. Second, plug-ins would reduce variations in electric load between night and day. (Such "load leveling" improves utilities' operating efficiency and reduces unit costs.)[33] Third, plug-ins could even become a *source* of power, helping utilities meet peak loads.

This final benefit—sometimes called "vehicle-to-grid," or V2G—could be especially compelling. Drivers could recharge car batteries at night and then sell electricity not used for driving back to the grid during the day. This would help many regions meet electric needs during summer months, when air-conditioning creates extraordinary daytime electricity demand. As "time-of-day metering" becomes more common, individuals could use this technique to help cut electric bills. Plug-in vehicles could also provide backup power to households during outages caused by downed wires or storms.[34]

Finally, plug-ins vehicles are an especially good way to use wind power. In most areas wind is greater at night, when electricity demand is low. With plug-ins, wind power could be used to recharge car batteries at night, essentially replacing the oil currently used to move vehicles with wind.

6. BARRIERS

Why aren't plug-in hybrids on the road today? Mainly, because the batteries required are expensive and might not last for the life of a car.

A plug-in hybrid needs a high-performance battery. PHEV batteries must deliver sufficient power for acceleration and high speeds. They must store enough energy for the car to travel many miles. They must withstand several thousand "deep discharge cycles." (The more often a battery is depleted, the shorter its life.) Performance requirements are especially great if the vehicle is designed to run entirely on its electric motor for a certain distance after each charge.[35]

At the same time, batteries must be small enough to fit within the car's frame, light enough to transport, and cheap enough to be competitive.

Not surprisingly, these battery design problems present a challenge. Lead-acid batteries, used for most car electrical systems, are far too heavy. Nickel-metal hydride batteries, used with great success in conventional hybrids, are too heavy for many plug-ins as well.

Much attention has focused on lithium ion batteries, the kind widely used in computer laptops. Lithium is the lightest metal (and third lightest element). Lithium ion batteries can deliver more power and energy per pound than any other battery on the market today.[36] More than $1 billion is being spent on research and development of these batteries each year.

However, lithium ion batteries are expensive. They generate lots of heat and have been known to catch fire, leading to widely publicized recalls of laptop batteries. Fortunately the fire risk, or "thermal run-away" problem, is easily solved by adding certain compounds to a lithium ion battery.[37] Standards requiring the addition of these compounds to any lithium ion car batteries would be in the public interest.

In designing batteries for plug-in hybrids, engineers consider many questions. Among the most important are:

- How much power can the battery deliver?

- How much energy can it store?

- How much does it weigh?

- How big is it?

- How quickly can it recharge?

- How many times can it be recharged?

- Does it lose charge with time?

- Can it operate in hot and cold temperatures?

- Does it present fire risks?

- How much does it cost?

At present, batteries that meet performance specifications for plug-in hybrids can be manufactured at a price premium of approximately $8,000 to $11,000 per vehicle. These costs would decline with mass production. In addition, energy capacity of batteries is improving at 5% to 8% per year, according to some estimates.[38]

At the same time, revolutionary advances in battery technologies may be near.

Nanotechnology may revolutionize batteries in the next few years. Nano processes can be used to make electrodes with much larger surface areas, for example, dramatically improving battery performance. At least one nanotech company claims its product can store 3 to 4 times the energy and last 20 times longer than an existing battery, while recharging in less than 2 minutes. Several companies are working to bring nanotech batteries to market.[39]

I believe that advances in battery technology will follow quickly from large orders for plug-in hybrids. Batteries that meet the needs of PHEV drivers are close. With leadership from the federal government, we can bring them to market soon.

7. <u>POLICY RECOMMENDATIONS</u>
During the next decade, plug-in hybrid vehicles will begin to enter the marketplace. However, the pace of commercialization will be slow. To dramatically speed the pace at which PHEVs enter the market, I recommend the five steps: federal purchases, consumer tax credits, a grand bargain with Detroit, a federal battery guarantee program and advanced battery research.

  a. *Federal Purchases*
Each year, the federal government buys more than 65,000 new cars.[40] These purchases should be used to transform the automobile industry.

I recommend that the federal government issue an open order for 30,000 plug-in hybrid vehicles, offering to pay an $8,000 premium for each one. The General Services Administration, which administers federal vehicle purchases, should commit to repeat this order every year after the first vehicles are delivered, with the premiums declining over time. All vehicles would need to meet basic performance requirements. I recommend stating a formal policy that 50% of noncombat vehicles purchased by the federal government be PHEVs, once they become commercially available.

These steps would quickly jump start the market for PHEVs by generating substantial new investment in battery technology, helping finance conversion of existing production lines, and creating economies of scale.[41] Total cost for the program would be $1.2 billion, spread out over roughly a decade.

State, utility, and private sector fleets are already making such commitments. Plug-In Partners, a campaign by several hundred state and local governments, utilities and nonprofits, has already generated more than 11,000 "soft orders" for PHEVs.[42]

b. *Consumer Tax Credits*
I recommend $8,000 tax credits for purchasers of the first million PHEVs. This would bring PHEV costs roughly in line with those of other cars. A smaller tax credit, say $4,000, could be offered for purchasers of the second million. This bold stroke would dramatically accelerate commercialization of PHEVs.

Credits should be fully refundable, so Americans with little or no tax liability could benefit.[43] Credits should reduce liability under the Alternative Minimum Tax, so the tens of millions of Americans affected by the AMT can benefit as well. Cars should meet strong fuel efficiency standards when driving on their internal combustion engines to be eligible.

The total of the cost of this program would be $12 billion, spread out over several years.

c. *Grand Bargain with Detroit*

The financial position of major U.S. automakers has never been worse, with some analysts speculating about impending bankruptcies. One reason is the cost of retiree health care. For the legacy automakers (GM, Ford and Chrysler), these costs average $680 per vehicle, hurting competitiveness and straining corporate balance sheets.[44] For financially weak companies, converting manufacturing facilities to produce plug-in hybrids or other fuel-efficient cars may be especially difficult.

I recommend you propose a federal trust fund to help automakers invest in plug-in hybrids and other fuel-saving technologies.[45] Several structures are possible. The fund could reimburse qualifying expenses involved in retooling production lines, or it could make payments based upon the fuel efficiency of new vehicles sold. Costs could be capped at any level, with funds allocated based upon superior performance in terms of oil savings or related factors.

d. *Federal Battery Guarantee Corporation*

Car makers identify battery life as a major barrier to mass production of PHEVs. Customers expect extended warranties on all major auto components, yet current batteries cannot reliably perform for extended periods. Providing extended battery warranties (such as for 10 years/100,000 miles) could be expensive.

There is a strong national interest in overcoming this barrier. One solution is a Federal Battery Guarantee Corporation, to help jump start the market for PHEVs by spreading the risk of battery obsolescence. The FBGC would reimburse car makers 100% of any costs incurred under extended battery warranties for the first 20,000 PHEVs sold. It would cover 80% of costs under extended battery warranties for the second 20,000 sold; 60% of costs for the third 20,000; 40% of costs for the fourth 20,000; and 20% of costs for the fifth 20,000. It could adjust this schedule, within limits, to help achieve the objective of bringing PHEVs to market.

Such a program would have three benefits. First, it would directly address a core concern of auto manufacturers reluctant to bring PHEVs to market. Second, it would reward early movers, giving the greatest benefits to those who bring PHEVs to market first. Third, it would stimulate improvements in battery technology, making the program itself less important over time.

Costs of the program are difficult to estimate, since the likelihood of battery obsolescence during the extended warranty period is speculative. With the schedule suggested above and average battery replacement costs of $8,000, the theoretical maximum would be roughly $500 million over 10 years, with most costs incurred toward the end of this period. Actual costs could be much lower.

e. *Advanced Battery Research*
The federal government should increase spending on battery research. Such research can make an important contribution to the performance of plug-in hybrids over time. Private sector research and development will remain focused on technologies with prospects for near- or medium-term commercial payoff. Federal research should focus on technologies where payoff will be over the long term.

The U.S. Advanced Battery Consortium, a partnership of the major U.S auto and the U.S. government, dates to 1991. The consortium has played a role in some battery advances in the past decade, but needs a more focused mission and additional funding.[46]

Over the years, federal energy research has helped produce important breakthroughs, such as electronic ballast for fluorescent lamps, low-e glass for windows and advanced turbine systems.[47] Growing federal support for battery research can help to accomplish the breakthroughs that will transform our children's lives.

8. CONCLUSION
Plug-in hybrid electric vehicles are a game-changing technology. They can break our oil addiction, cut driving costs and reduce pollution.

Some might object to the proposals above on the grounds that government should stay out of the marketplace. In fact, the federal government has been a central player in transportation and energy markets for many years. Federal funds built the interstate highway system and continue to provide much more support for road building than mass transit. Governments at all levels are central players in electricity markets. For more than a century, governments have been using eminent domain authority to help build a pipeline network for moving oil at low cost. Perhaps most centrally, the U.S. military helps protect oil flows around the world, transforming markets for that product.

Plug-in hybrids would help address important national security, environmental and economic problems. Bringing them to market quickly should be a top national priority.

Key points on plug-in hybrids—
- most promising technology for replacing oil
- biggest barriers: battery cost and battery life
- help fight global warming, even when electricity comes from coal (interesting!)
- don't need new power plants— lots of excess capacity at night

from the desk of the
SECRETARY OF TRANSPORTATION

Chelsea Sexton is an electric car advocate. Here's an interesting profile of her.

★★★★★

From Showroom to the Big Screen

Chelsea Sexton never expected to be a movie star. Jobs at car dealerships don't usually lead to that.

But Sexton, a tall energetic redhead, fell in love with her product. The company she worked for, General Motors, decided to discontinue it. The struggle that followed led to the award-winning documentary movie *Who Killed the Electric Car?*

Chelsea Sexton grew up in El Segundo, California, near the Los Angeles Airport. In 1993, at the age of 17, she joined General Motors as a marketing rep for Saturn.

Sexton was later assigned to market the EV-1, an electric car designed to meet California's clean air requirements.

At the time, California law required each car company to sell a small number of "zero emissions" vehicles. "Zero emissions" meant no air pollutants. Nada.

Chelsea's bosses at General Motors were trying to meet this requirement with a sleek two-seater that went from 0 to 60 mph in 8 seconds without using a drop of gas.

The EV-1 had the look and feel of a sports car. But the familiar "vroom vroom" was missing. The sound that drivers everywhere associate with fast cars and acceleration comes from compressed air and gasoline being forced through an internal combustion engine. The EV-1 ran entirely on an electric motor.

On the highway, the only

noise was from the tires. At lower speeds, the EV-1 was silent.

Many customers were thrilled. One said the car "was fun to drive, accelerated off the line like nothing else out there." Another said it "fit our needs perfectly."

Television and movie stars including Danny DeVito and Mel Gibson became enthusiastic drivers.

Chelsea Sexton says finding enthusiastic customers was easy.

But General Motors management says the picture was more complicated. Sales costs were being subsidized. Many customers were turned off by the car's maximum range—between 80 and 140 miles. Others lost interest after learning that the car needed several hours for recharging.

Although thousands of people expressed interest in buying the EV-1, only a tiny fraction, according to GM, were ultimately willing to do so.

Chelsea Sexton begs to differ. She says GM never really tried to sell the EV-1.

"Let's face it," says Sexton. "GM sent a car to market with one teaser ad and a bunch of print ads that barely showed the car and didn't tell you where to get it."

In fact, she notes, the cars weren't even being offered for sale. GM offered the EV-1s for lease only.

To Sexton and others, this reflected a lack of commitment. GM management says it was copying a Japanese marketing practice, in which prototype cars are offered for lease-only before being sold to a wider market.

Meanwhile GM was lobbying California regulators, trying to change the rule that required sales of zero emissions vehicles. One GM engineer—expressing a view held widely throughout the company—said the EV-1 was "a creature of government, not the market."

Controversy was high. Sales were low. Over the course of several years, General Motors leased only about 800 of the vehicles.

By 2001, GM had had enough. It stopped leasing new EV-1s. It refused to renew old leases, insisting that all cars be returned to the company.

Many customers wanted to keep their EV-1s. One driver described returning it as "one of the more heartbreaking moments of my life."

But GM insisted. By 2004, the company had collected all EV-1s ever made.

THEN it started crushing them.

EV-1s weren't sent to regular junkyards. A few were donated to universities and museums. The rest were sent to the Arizona desert for crushing.

The images of sleek new cars being compressed like pancakes are among the most memorable in Chelsea Sexton's film, *Who Killed the Electric Car?*

Why crush the cars? In fact, why not allow hundreds of enthusiastic owners to keep their EV-1s?

Liability concerns, says General Motors. "[P]arts suppliers quit, making future repair and safety of the vehicles difficult to nearly impossible," explains a GM spokesman. "We did what we felt was right in discontinuing a vehicle that we could no longer guarantee could be operated safely over the long term."

Chelsea Sexton and other advocates are skeptical. They believe the EV-1 threatened GM's business model and collided with a corporate culture that glorifies the internal combustion engine.

"The Detroit companies have composed their business models entirely around the engine," Sexton says. Besides, she says, "GM had an internal struggle about how to market the EV-1 as clean without suggesting that other products like the Suburban are dirty."

TODAY Chelsea Sexton has moved beyond the EV-1. She has a new passion: the plug-in hybrid.

Hybrid engines are already wildly popular. Models like the Toyota Prius combine a gasoline engine with an electric motor, delivering as much as 50 miles to the gallon. The electricity comes from a battery recharged each time the car stops, using a technique known as "regenerative braking."

A "plug-in hybrid" takes this technology one step further. The battery in these cars can be recharged by plugging it into a standard wall socket. This simple step promises to revolutionize the car industry and lots more.

Most drivers drive 40 miles or less to and from work. If they drove cars that could get 40 miles on an electric charge, many could do their daily commute without gasoline.

As Sexton says: "The best way to get people to use less oil is to give them the option to use none."

Sexton is executive director of Plug-In America, a coalition formed to fight for plug-in hybrids, and the founder of Lightning Rod, a nonprofit that also works to make clean cars and renewable energy a reality. She and a growing number of others believe these cars could reduce our nation's dependence on petroleum while improving the global environment.

And maybe, just maybe, Chelsea Sexton has a new ally. In late 2006, General Motors became the first major automaker to announce plans to build a plug-in hybrid.[1]

from the desk of the
CHAIR
NATIONAL ECONOMIC COUNCIL

Here's an interesting article for your oil dependence speech.

★★★★★

Electric Entrepreneur

As Martin Eberhard talks, someone at the next table is listening.

"Starting a car company is lots of work," Eberhard says. "But I know how to start companies. I've done that successfully a couple of times now."

Martin Eberhard is CEO and founder of Tesla Motors, the first new American car company in decades. Tesla's mission: to sell fast and fuel-efficient electric sports cars.

That's just the start. Eberhard wants to change the way we think about electric cars. And in doing so, help end our dependence on oil.

"As an electrical engineer, I know it's possible to make an electric car that rocks," Eberhard says. He's fed up with the electric "punishment cars" of the past—cars with "terrible range and embarrassing styling."

Great acceleration. Instant torque. Extraordinary energy efficiency. These are among the many advantages of electric motors, says Eberhard. Why not build a car that uses them?

Tesla Motors is doing just that. The Tesla Roadster is sleek two-seat all-electric convertible that goes from zero to 60 miles per hour in four seconds. Better performance than a Porsche or Ferrari, says Eberhard. Without a drop of oil.

Tesla's website describes a "favorite trick": Ask a passenger to turn on the radio and then accelerate. Because of the instant acceleration, "our passenger simply can't sit forward enough to reach the dials," the Tesla site claims.

Eberhard explains that, with an electric motor, "there's no tradeoff between performance and efficiency. The bigger you make them, the more efficient they are."

Earlier electric cars suffered from short driving range. Eberhard thinks he's solved that problem. The Tesla Roadster goes 200 miles on a single charge.

Tesla's innovation—making car batteries from the same small "cells" used in laptops and cell phones. Others companies have tried to invent specialty batteries for automobiles, Eberhard says. Tesla's strategy is to "ride on the commodity coattails of the highly competitive consumer electronics market."

So far, the reviews are good. Customers love the look and feel of the Roadster. But there's one big reason you'll never see millions of Roadsters on the highways.

I ask, "What about the $98,000 price tag?"

THE CALIFORNIA SUN streams through the restaurant window as Martin Eberhard explains his strategy. The man at the next table keeps listening.

"High-end is the only sensible way to enter a market," Eberhard says. Think of plasma TVs. Manu-facturers launched the product with $6,000 models, Eberhard notes, well beyond the budget of most consumers. That helped brand the product as cool and cutting edge, while more work on the technology brought costs down.

"Any new technology has high costs at first," Eberhard says. "Our strategy is to enter at the high end of the market, where customers are willing to pay a premium. Then we'll move to higher production levels and lower prices with each model."

Eberhard believes this will radically change public perception of electric cars. People who love cars and driving will want them. Tesla's next model will be a large four-door family car, starting at $50,000. Future models will be cheaper.

"Why aren't the major car companies doing the same thing?" I ask.

"Big company brain damage," Eberhard says, only half in jest. "If GM wants to sell electric cars, it should build electric Corvettes that could go from zero to 60 miles per hour in 4 seconds," he says.

"If I were Bill Ford," Eberhard adds, "I'd set a goal of selling 10%

electric cars within four years," he says.

Could this be done? "Of course." he says. "What Ford's doing now isn't working," he says. "Some of their cars, such as the Fusion, are actually very high quality, but people don't know it. Ford needs a big change."

I run through a list of issues sometimes raised by electric car skeptics.

Can batteries recharge quickly enough? How long does your cell phone take to recharge?" Eberhard asks in return. "Most people don't know. That's because you recharge it overnight, which is what most people will do with electric cars." Not a problem.

Will we face shortages of lithium, the metal used in the Tesla Roadster's batteries? "There's lots of lithium," Eberhard says. Furthermore, lithium batteries have high recycling value.

Will batteries be too heavy? "Lithium is light," says Eberhard.

"The main issue is battery cost, not the weight or size of batteries."

Why is he building an all-electric car, as opposed to a plug-in hybrid? "Plug-in hybrids make sense as a bridge technology," Eberhard says. "But in the long-run, cars will be all-electric."

THE MAN at the next table leans over a bit more. Eberhard asks him to join us.

The eavesdropper apologizes, explains that he's an alternative fuel enthusiast and says he couldn't help listening. Eberhard seems delighted to talk. The conversation turns to biodiesel, ethanol, fuel efficiency and much more. Eberhard is passionate about breaking the United States' dependence on oil.

One week later, Eberhard is in Washington, D.C., testifying before the Senate Finance Committee. Electric cars "are our best hope," he says. This time senators, reporters and a packed hearing room are listening.[1]

MEMORANDUM FOR THE PRESIDENT

FROM: SECRETARY OF AGRICULTURE

SUBJECT: Replacing Oil with Biofuels

I applaud your plans to deliver a major speech on oil dependence. I recommend the speech include the following:

- A strong endorsement of the role ethanol and other biofuels can play in helping end U.S. oil addiction.

- Praise for the role ethanol is already playing in renewing rural communities across the nation.

- Strong support for rapid development of ethanol from switchgrass and other "cellulosic" sources.

- Policies to ensure gas stations give drivers the choice to buy biofuels.

- Policies to prevent the U.S. biofuels industry from being crippled by O.P.E.C.

The U.S. biofuels industry enjoys strong bipartisan backing. I believe you will receive widespread support for these proposals. However, the rapid growth in the ethanol industry during the past several years has begun to spark a backlash. Skeptical questions are often raised. How much of our current oil consumption can biofuels displace? How much land will be required? What impact will biofuels have on food production? Will there be adverse environmental impacts? This memorandum examines these and other questions and provides recommendations for your upcoming speech.

1. BACKGROUND
"Biofuels" are liquid fuels made from living matter. Examples include ethanol—short for "ethyl alcohol"—and biodiesel. Ethanol is made by fermenting sugar into alcohol. Biodiesel is made from vegetable oil or animal fat.

Biofuels have a long history. Henry Ford expected his Model T to run on ethanol and, in 1925, described ethyl alcohol as "the fuel of the future."[1] Rudolf Diesel designed his engine to run on peanut oil and, in 1912, said that "the use of vegetable oils for engine fuels may seem insignificant today, but such oils may become, in the course of time, as important as petroleum and the coal tar products of the present time."[2]

a. _Ethanol_
Ethanol is the most widely used biofuel in the United States. The industry is in the midst of an historic expansion, with significant growth rates projected for years to come.[3]

Almost all ethanol in the United States is made from corn. Ethanol can also be made from sugar cane (the main feedstock in Brazil) and cellulose (the fiber in stalks, stems and leaves). One good source of cellulose is switchgrass— a summer grass native to North America that grows up to 12 feet tall even in poor soils with very small amounts of fertilizer.[4] Other sources include corn stover (stalks and leaves that remain after corn is harvested), miscanthus (a grass native to Africa and Asia) and fast-growing trees.

Switchgrass—a source of ethanol.

Cellulosic ethanol has received enormous attention from investors and political leaders in recent years. In part, this is because making ethanol from cellulose requires much less fossil fuel than making ethanol from corn. In part, this is because vast areas of the United States that are not suitable for corn production could be used to grow cellulose. However, cellulosic ethanol remains more expensive than either corn-based ethanol or gasoline. The first commercial-scale cellulosic ethanol plants are now being developed.

Adding small amounts of ethanol to gasoline helps improve engine performance and reduce emissions of some pollutants. "E10"—a blend of 90% gasoline and 10% ethanol—is popular throughout the United States. Almost all cars on the road today can run on E10.

Ethanol can also be used as the principal fuel to power a vehicle. "E85"—a blend of 85% ethanol and 15% gasoline—is sold at a small but growing number of gas stations.[5] An engine that takes E85 as well as gasoline (known as "flex fuel") costs approximately $100 more to manufacture than the same engine made for gasoline only. More than 6 million flex fuel cars are now on the road in the United States, with many more being sold each year.[6] General Motors, Ford and Chrysler plan to use flex fuel technology in half their cars by 2012.[7]

A gallon of ethanol contains roughly two-thirds the energy of a gallon of gasoline. That means, in today's cars, ethanol delivers fewer miles per gallon than gasoline. The exact difference varies. (Some drivers report that E85 delivers mileage almost comparable to gasoline, while others report penalties of up 28%.) Saab and other car makers are working on turbocharged engines that could deliver the same mileage using ethanol and gasoline.[8]

Ethanol is transported within the United States by truck and rail. Ethanol cannot be shipped through pipelines used for oil and gas, because it absorbs water and other impurities that petroleum products leave behind.

The cost of producing ethanol in the United States today depends mainly on the cost of corn. When corn costs $3 per bushel, ethanol costs roughly $1.45 per gallon to make. Each $1 increase in the cost of corn increases production costs for corn-based ethanol by approximately 35 cents. At present, making ethanol from cellulosic sources is much more expensive, mainly due to the cost of converting cellulose to fermentable sugars.

Ethanol receives considerable support from federal and state governments throughout the United States. Current federal policies benefiting the ethanol industry include:

- A 51-cent per gallon excise tax credit paid to fuel blenders who use ethanol. (This credit is not paid to corn farmers, although much of the benefit of the credit may be passed on to them.[9]) The credit will expire in 2010.

- A mandate requiring 7.5 billion gallons of ethanol be added to the nation's fuel supply by 2012. This level of production will likely be reached during 2008.

- A mandate requiring 250 million gallons of ethanol made from cellulose or waste materials be added to the nation's fuel supply by 2013.

- Loan guarantees for the construction of cellulosic ethanol plants.

- Tariffs of 54 cents per gallon plus 2.5% of value on any imported ethanol.

- A goal of 35 billion gallons of "renewable and alternative" fuels announced by President George W. Bush in his 2007 State of the Union Address. (This can be met with fuels other than ethanol, including liquefied coal.)

At the same time, ethanol production reduces costs to the federal government under traditional farm assistance programs. Since the 1930s, the U.S. government has protected corn growers from low crop prices with a variety of programs. In 2006, increased corn demand saved the federal government roughly $6 billion in subsidy payments.[10] This was more than twice the cost of the excise tax credit for ethanol.

b. *Ethanol in Brazil*

In Brazil, ethanol has replaced roughly 40% of gasoline. All gasoline in Brazil contains roughly 20% ethanol and pure ethanol is available at most service stations. More than 80% of new cars are flex-fuel. Some Brazilian ethanol is shipped through dedicated pipelines.[11]

Brazil's warmer climate, lower wage rates and long history of strong government support makes ethanol cheaper to produce than in the United States. Production costs vary with the price of sugar and other factors. In 2004, costs were in the range of 80 to 85 cents per gallon.[12]

c. *Biodiesel*
Biodiesel supplies a small but rapidly growing amount of fuel in the United States.[13] Sales volumes in the United States were roughly 25 million gallons in 2004, 75 million gallons in 2005 and 250 million gallons in 2006. Total diesel fuel sales in the United States are more than 60 billion gallons per year.

Biodiesel fuel is made primarily from soybeans and canola. (In Indonesia and some other countries, palm oil is the primary feedstock for biodiesel.) Like ethanol, biodiesel can be blended with petroleum in small amounts or used as a pure fuel. All diesel engines can take pure biodiesel. Biodiesel blenders receive tax credits of $0.50 to $1 per gallon, depending on the type of biodiesel used.

d. *Other Biofuels*
Biobutanol, an experimental fuel, has recently generated interest and attention.[14] It is similar to ethanol and can be made from the same feedstocks, such as corn. Biobutanol could offer several advantages over ethanol. For example, biobutanol has an energy content almost as high as gasoline, tolerates contamination well enough to be shipped through oil and gas pipelines, and can be used in most cars without modifications.

2. POTENTIAL TO REPLACE OIL
In the past several years, many experts have examined the potential of biofuels to replace oil. Estimates vary widely. Cautious estimates assume that productivity in the biofuels industry will grow slowly and land constraints will limit expansion.[15] More aggressive estimates assume that cellulosic ethanol will soon become commercially competitive and expand rapidly thereafter.[16]

I believe the United States could produce roughly 60 billion gallons of ethanol per year by 2025—15 billion gallons from corn and 45 billion gallons from cellulosic sources. With widespread adoption of plug-in hybrids and reasonable fuel efficiency improvements, this could represent roughly half the liquid fuel used by cars and light trucks.[17]

This projection assumes modest improvements in the technology for producing ethanol from corn and dramatic breakthroughs in the technology for producing ethanol from cellulose. Both of these assumptions are warranted.

- The technologies for making ethanol from corn are widely used and well-established. Such mature technologies typically show modest but predictable improvements over time.[18]

- The technologies for making ethanol from cellulose are currently the focus of extraordinary attention from the investment community and leading research scientists. Billions of dollars in capital and some of the nation's best minds are working on these technologies. Under these circumstances, it is reasonable to project dramatic reductions in costs. (In Brazil, ethanol production costs have fallen 75% in 25 years.)[19]

Similarly, this projection assumes small increases in the acreage under cultivation for corn and substantial increases in the acreage under cultivation for cellulose. Acreage used to produce switchgrass and other sources of cellulose need not be taken from land currently used for food crops.

- The United States has roughly 440 million acres of cropland. Of this, roughly 20% is typically planted with corn. In recent years corn planting has increased steadily, largely due to increased demand for ethanol. Yet there are tens of millions of acres of cropland in the United States where climate conditions and water availability permit corn production, but corn is not currently being grown. 100 million acres of corn could be planted in the United States, without disrupting agricultural markets.

- More than 30 million acres are currently in the Conservation Reserve Program. Some of these could be used for cellulosic ethanol production, although this would need to be managed very carefully with conservation values taking priority.

- Huge amounts of cellulosic ethanol can be produced from agricultural residues—as much as 40 billion gallons according to some estimates.[20]

This projection assumes infrastructure improvements in the United States, some of which will require federal leadership. Most important, gas stations must offer drivers the choice to purchase E85 or other biofuels. New cars must be flex-fuel—capable of taking either conventional gasoline or E85. Dedicated pipelines could help bring down the cost of shipping ethanol and should be built in select locations as production volumes increase.

In short, biofuels can make an important contribution to ending oil dependence in the United States. They can help achieve several other important objectives as well.

3. RURAL ECONOMIC IMPACTS
Ethanol is leading a renewal of rural America. The industry is creating jobs and opportunity in rural communities across the nation.

In Benton, Minnesota, an ethanol plant helped revitalize a community that had been losing jobs and tax base for years. In Hereford, Texas, a new ethanol plant brought new jobs and opportunity. In Dyersville, Iowa, home to the baseball field from the 1988 movie *Field of Dreams* (with its famous line "if you build it, he will come"), plans are under way to boost the local corn-based economy with a new ethanol plant as well.[21]

According to one study, a typical 40-million gallon ethanol plant increases the local tax base by more than $110 million, generates more than $1.2 million in tax revenues and creates almost 700 direct and indirect jobs. According to another, the ethanol industry added 153,000 jobs to the U.S. economy in 2005. Every billion gallons of additional ethanol capacity creates about 20,000 new jobs, according to the combined results of several studies.[22]

The ethanol industry is the leading edge of a deeper transformation in American agriculture. Today an increasing number of U.S. farmers are investing in businesses such as ethanol plants, vertically integrating beyond crop production. This trend should be encouraged as part of your broader strategy for revitalizing rural America. To quote the National Corn Growers Association, "Producer investment in value-added agriculture, not reliance on government programs, is the only way in which the future of rural America is more secure."[23]

Approximately half the ethanol plants in the United States are farmer-owned cooperatives.[24] Such farmer-owned cooperatives are an important tool for returning proceeds from the biofuels industry to rural communities.

4. ENVIRONMENTAL IMPACTS
Biofuels can make an important contribution to the fight against global warming. They can help reduce soot and smog. At the same time, expanded biofuels production could threaten natural forests, wildlife and soil quality.

a. *Global Warming*
Biofuels can significantly reduce emissions of heat-trapping gases. Today, the largest single source of such gases is oil.[25] When oil is burned, carbon stored underground for millions of years is released into the atmosphere as a heat-trapping gas, carbon dioxide (CO_2). In contrast, when biofuels are burned, carbon that was in the atmosphere until recently, but then briefly sequestered in plants, is simply returned to the atmosphere. This cycle—in which carbon is sequestered in plants and then burned as fuel—does not on its own add heat-trapping gases to the atmosphere.

However, the complete picture is a bit more complicated. Growing and transporting biofuels requires energy. That energy typically comes from fossil fuels such as coal, oil or natural gas. In the United States today, power to run ethanol refineries often comes from coal. Fertilizer for corn is typically made with natural gas. Making and shipping pesticides typically requires fossil fuels. As a result, the production of corn-based ethanol in the United States today is somewhat positive from a global warming standpoint. According to a study at the Argonne National Laboratory, E85 made with corn-based ethanol reduces heat-trapping gases by 21% to 29% as compared to an energy-equivalent amount of gasoline.[26]

Ethanol from cellulose is much better. Most sources of cellulose produce a by-product that can be burned to provide power in refineries, reducing the need for fossil fuels. Most cellulose sources are grown without intensive fertilizer or pesticides. Although the cellulosic ethanol industry is still in its infancy, and little data is available, the global warming impacts of cellulosic ethanol will certainly be much less than from either corn-based ethanol or oil. According to the Argonne National Labs, E85 with cellulosic reduces heat-trapping gases by 86% as compared to gasoline in energy-equivalent amounts.[27]

Ethanol from sugar also provides considerable global warming benefits. Most refineries in Brazil are self-sufficient from an energy standpoint, burning portions of the sugar crop for power. Indeed many Brazilian refineries export electricity to the electric grid.

b. *Local Air Pollution*
Biofuels can help cut local air pollution. Higher blends of ethanol (such as E85) reduce soot and smog. They produce fewer toxic air pollutants than gasoline. Replacing aromatics, a widely used octane booster, with biofuels in much of the nation's fuel supply could offer dramatic public health benefits.[28]

Lower blends of ethanol (such as E10) can also reduce local air pollution, although the complete picture is complex. In some situations, low blends of ethanol can increase emissions of nitrogen oxides and volatile organic compounds, both precursors of smog. This is more likely to happen in vehicles built before the mid-1990s. In some cities and in some seasons, air quality authorities may limit the use of low blends of ethanol.[29]

c. *Forests and Wildlife*
Expansion of biofuels production can threaten natural forests and wildlife. In general, this is more of a problem abroad than in the United States. In Brazil, new soy plantations are being cut into the Amazon, in part because of biodiesel markets. Cattle displaced by sugar production in southern Brazil are moving north, putting pressure on the Amazon.[30] In Indonesia, demand for palm oil is destroying large tracts of primary tropical rainforest.

In the United States, expansion of corn production for ethanol will lead to greater pesticide use and reliance on irrigation. Production of switchgrass, miscanthus and other sources of cellulose, in contrast, may deliver important environmental benefits. These crops can help control soil erosion and sequester carbon. They generally do not require pesticides or irrigation. They typically provide better habitat for wildlife than row crops.[31]

Much corn stover (cobs, stalks and leaves) is currently used as fertilizer. Using too much stover to make cellulosic ethanol could deprive the soil of needed nitrogen.[32]

5. IMPACT ON FOOD PRICES

As demand for ethanol has increased, so have corn prices. Between July 2006 and April 2007, prices jumped from $2 per bushel (the approximate average over the past few decades) to roughly $4 per bushel.[33] Increasing ethanol demand and shrinking corn stockpiles were the main reasons.

a. *Domestic*

Corn plays a central role in the U.S. food supply. More than a quarter of the products on supermarket shelves contain corn.[34] Corn is fed to livestock including cattle, dairy cows, hogs and chicken. Rising corn prices put upward pressure on a wide range of food products.

However, corn prices make up only a small percentage of the cost of most grocery store products. Indeed corn prices make up less than 5% of the cost of corn flakes.[35] (Packaging, advertising and distribution costs are substantial.) Furthermore, an ethanol by-product known as "distiller's grains" is widely used as an animal feed. Expanding ethanol production provides an additional source of this product.

U.S.D.A. chief economist Keith Collins projects annual increases of 3% or less in the Consumer Price Index for food for the next decade, despite dramatically increased ethanol production. The National Corn Grower's Association (NCGA) notes that, even as corn prices rose to record levels in the first quarter of 2007, prices of dairy products, poultry and pork in the United States mostly held steady from the prior year (and in some cases dropped). Citing Bureau of Labor Statistics data, the NCGA argues that grocery stores prices increased by 1.0% between March 2006 and March 2007, less than the 25-year average annual food inflation rate of 2.9%.[36]

As corn prices increase, land previously used for other crops will be planted with corn instead. This will tend to increase prices of other crops, affecting agricultural production broadly.

Overall, expanding ethanol production will put upward pressure on U.S. food prices, although the extent is uncertain.

b. *World Poverty:*
Experts offer sharply contrasting views about the impact of the biofuels industry on world poverty.

On the one hand, a growing biofuels industry will increase food costs for many desperately poor people around the world. Nearly a quarter of the world's grain exports come from U.S. corn fields. As higher U.S. corn prices ripple through the global food system, the impacts could be far-reaching. Many of the world's poorest people spend more than half their income on food. Price increases could cause substantial hardship.[37]

In Mexico in late 2006, for example the price of tortilla flour doubled, sparking riots. Although speculation and hoarding played an important role, many observers also noted the role of the U.S. ethanol boom, which drove up U.S. corn prices, reportedly leading several Mexican industries to shift from U.S. corn to Mexican varieties. This in turn drove up the price of Mexican corn, the main ingredient in most tortillas.[38]

On the other hand, poor farmers who are able to produce a marketable surplus of grains will benefit from higher prices. Furthermore, a thriving biofuels industry could reduce the cost of oil imports for many poor countries. (These costs have skyrocketed in recent years, often overwhelming the benefits of debt relief.) Local biorefineries can promote rural development. This creates jobs and reduces urban migration, while saving scarce foreign exchange.[39]

In addition, a thriving biofuels industry could help break the impasse that has stalled global trade negotiations. Disputes over agricultural subsidies have been a principal impediment to progress in these talks. Increased demand for biofuels could reduce pressures for price support programs in industrialized countries, helping break this logjam, with long-term benefits for economic growth in the developing world.[40]

6. POLICY RECOMMENDATIONS

Your oil dependence speech provides an important opportunity to promote biofuels, making them a principal part of our fuel supply in the decades to come. I recommend policies in three broad areas: (a) building a biofuels infrastructure, (b) preventing market manipulation by OPEC and (c) bringing advanced biofuels to market.

a. *Building a Biofuels Infrastructure*

Every driver who wants to buy biofuels should be able to do so. Yet today only a small percentage of U.S. cars can use E85. Only a small percentage of U.S service stations sell E85 or other biofuels.

Since 2006, U.S. auto manufacturers have been adding flex fuel technology to many new models. General Motors, Ford and Chrysler each pledge that half their new cars will be flex fuel by the year 2012. Costs are modest— approximately $100 per vehicle. This progress is laudable, but insufficient. Flex-fuel technology should be a standard feature in all new cars.

I recommend you shine a spotlight on this issue, urging all Americans to ask dealers whether a new car is flex fuel before purchasing. I also recommend you propose legislation requiring that automakers quicken the pace at which this feature is added to new models. For example, legislation could require that half of new cars sold be flex fuel by 2012, with required levels increasing by 10% per year thereafter.

E85 pumps are also essential. Today only a small percentage of U.S. service stations are equipped to sell E85 or other high blends of ethanol. The principal barriers appear to be the cost of converting gas tanks (approximately $4,000 apiece and franchise agreements that prohibit station owners from pumping ethanol at islands with petroleum fuels.[41]

Both these barriers can be overcome. I recommend legislation requiring all major oil companies to convert pumps for E85 at 50% of their owned or branded stations. Today there are almost 169,000 retail service stations in the United States, with roughly half owned or branded by the oil majors.[42] That means that under such legislation, roughly a quarter of the nation's service stations would have E85 pumps. I believe this would provide critical mass, allowing many drivers to find E85 without difficulty.

I also recommend legislation prohibiting franchise agreements that limit pumps for biofuels at service stations. These are contrary to the national interest. Such provisions in existing franchise agreements should be declared invalid.

Finally, I recommend legislation to encourage construction of ethanol pipelines along major corridors, as volumes grow to levels needed to make this economic. Federal legislation should guarantee the right to build ethanol pipelines on all existing pipeline right-of-ways and ensure that any benefits provided to oil and gas pipelines under state and federal law are also provided to ethanol pipelines.

b. *Prevent Market Manipulation by OPEC*

At present, American farmers are vulnerable to manipulation of world oil prices by OPEC. A decision by OPEC to expand production, causing world oil prices to fall temporarily, could force many ethanol producers out of business.

This is not a hypothetical concern. In the 1980s, low oil prices choked off the development of alternative fuels in the United States and elsewhere. (A decade later, when oil prices began a steady climb, drivers had no alternative to gasoline.) Saudi-Aramco, in particular, has pursued a strategy of keeping oil prices below the level that would lead to long-term reductions in demand.[43]

The best way to protect against this manipulation would be to adjust the ethanol tax credit based on the price of oil. Today, the subsidy is higher than needed to promote investment in ethanol production. There is a risk the subsidy could become inadequate, however, if OPEC sought to set prices at levels that would dampen investment in alternatives.

One simple adjustment formula would be to set the credit at zero whenever oil is $75 per barrel or more, but increase it by 2 cents per gallon for each dollar the price of oil falls below that figure. The result would be:

World Price of Oil	Subsidy for Corn-Based Ethanol
$75	No subsidy
$70	10 cents per gallon
$65	20 cents per gallon
$60	30 cents per gallon
$55	40 cents per gallon
$50	50 cents per gallon
$45	60 cents per gallon
$40	70 cents per gallon

This is intended as an example; the exact adjustment formula could be determined in the months ahead. Adjustments could be made annually (or perhaps more often).

The current ethanol tax credit of 51 cents per gallon will expire in 2010. I believe a credit for ethanol production is fully justified, in light of the benefits of ethanol and subsidies enjoyed by petroleum fuels.[44] I recommend extending the ethanol tax credit for another 10 years, while varying its amount as described above.

c. _Bringing Advanced Biofuels to Market_

Corn-based ethanol is just the beginning. Advanced biofuels such as cellulosic ethanol and biobutanol are essential, both to produce the volumes needed to help wean the United States from oil and to secure the environmental benefits possible from biofuels.

Considerably more research and development is needed to build a vibrant cellulosic ethanol industry. The private sector has begun investing heavily in this area, but more basic research is needed. The federal government should dramatically increase its research budget in this area, funding projects through universities and research centers. Federal support should also be increased for work on biobutanol and biodiesel fuels.

The federal government could spur the creation of cellulosic ethanol refineries with loan guarantees and other federal support. There is an existing program, but it can and should be expanded.

I recommend that cellulosic ethanol and other advanced biofuels receive a 30-cent-per-gallon "kicker:" that is, an excise tax credit 30 cents per gallon greater than the level for corn-based ethanol. This would be available for the first 50 billion gallons of advanced biofuels produced in the U.S. As part of a broader renewable fuels standard, a specific standard for advanced biofuels should be developed.

Recommendations

1. Urge all Americans to ask for flex-fuel cars.

2. Propose legislation to require that half of new cars sold be flex fuel by 2012, with required levels increasing by 10% per year thereafter.

3. Propose legislation to require major oil companies to install E85 pumps at half their owned or branded stations.

4. Propose legislation prohibiting service station franchise agreements that limit ethanol pumps and declaring any such provisions in current agreements invalid.

5. Propose legislation to guarantee the right to build ethanol pipelines on all existing pipeline right-of-ways.

6. Increased research and development for advanced biofuels.

7. Loan guarantees for cellulosic ethanol plants.

8. Renewable fuels standard with special provisions for advanced biofuels.

9. Propose legislation to extend the excise tax credit for corn-based ethanol for 10 years. The credit would vary with the world price of oil.

10. Provide an additional 30-cent-per-gallon excise tax credit for the first 50 billion gallons of advanced biofuels produced in the U.S., in addition to that provided for corn-based ethanol.

MEMORANDUM FOR THE PRESIDENT

FROM: U.S. TRADE REPRESENTATIVE

SUBJECT: Ethanol Tariff

I read the memorandum from the Secretary of Agriculture on your oil speech with great interest. I agree with its recommendations. However, the memo fails to raise an important topic: the 54-cent tariff currently imposed on all ethanol imports. I believe you should phase out that tariff to help end the nation's dependence on oil.

When it comes to your goal of ending U.S. oil dependence, our current trade laws are utterly illogical. We impose no tariffs or quotas on oil, despite the concerns you and others have voiced about our oil dependence. Yet we impose several restrictions on imports of ethanol, the leading alternative to oil, including a 54-cent per gallon tariff.

A phase out of the ethanol tariff would not hurt U.S. farmers, if designed correctly. Although a phase out of the ethanol tariff would be controversial, I believe it is an important part of any package to end the nation's oil dependence. Following are some background points and a specific proposal.

1. BACKGROUND
The United States currently imposes two tariffs on ethanol. Most important, ethanol imports are assessed 54 cents per gallon. In addition, these imports are assessed 2.5% of value. At wholesale prices of $2.00 per gallon—a rough average for recent years—this second tariff equals 5 cents, meaning the cost of each gallon of imported ethanol is increased by approximately 59 cents before it can reach U.S. drivers.[1]

The purpose of these tariffs is to promote the domestic ethanol industry. The 54-cent-per-gallon tariff is specifically designed to make sure that foreign ethanol producers do not gain the benefit of the ethanol excise tax credit. As currently structured, that credit reduces the tax liability of fuel blenders for every gallon of ethanol they purchase, without regard to the source. The tariff is intended to offset the benefits foreign producers receive under this provision.

There are several complex exceptions to these rules. Under the Caribbean Basin Initiative (CBI) and Central American Free Trade Agreement (CAFTA), ethanol from 24 Caribbean and Central American countries can enter the United States duty-free, in amounts up to 7% of U.S. production. This can include ethanol made with sugarcane from Brazil, if a minimal amount of processing occurs in a Caribbean or Central American nation. Ethanol from these countries can be imported duty-free in amounts above the 7% cap if certain requirements concerning local sugarcane content are met. In recent years very little ethanol has been imported duty-free under these provisions.[2]

2. ANALYSIS

The ethanol tariff contributes to U.S. oil dependence. Brazilian ethanol typically costs around $2.00 per gallon to deliver to the eastern United States, putting it in a strong position to compete against gasoline, depending on the relative prices of sugar and oil.[3] A charge of 59 cents per gallon has a substantial impact on the ability of Brazilian ethanol to displace oil. Some opponents of the tariff have urged that the United States set a goal of importing 15 billion gallons of ethanol by 2025.[4]

U.S. farm groups are strong advocates of the ethanol tariff and would fiercely resist proposals to end it. In general, farm groups are concerned that Brazilian ethanol would displace or compete against domestic ethanol. They note that labor costs in Brazil are much cheaper than in the United States and that Brazil has a long history of subsidizing its ethanol industry. Fair trade groups would tend to oppose ending the tariff as well.

Politicians from coastal states (with the easiest access to imported product) have tended to be most critical of the ethanol tariff. Sometimes this has created strange bedfellows. Opponents of the ethanol tariff have included Governor Jeb Bush (R-FL) and Senator Diane Feinstein (D-CA).[5]

The environmental implications of the tariff are mixed. On the one hand, ethanol from sugar—the kind most likely to be imported—creates far fewer emissions of heat-trapping gases than ethanol from corn. On the other hand, expanded ethanol production in Brazil or elsewhere could lead to increased clearing of tropical rainforests. In particular, there is concern that higher demand for ethanol will lead to more land being used for sugar cane in southern Brazil, which will displace cattle historically raised there to the Amazon region. Environmental groups have not considered the ethanol tariff to be a high priority.

Other countries impose tariffs on ethanol as well. As of early 2007, the Canadian ethanol tariff was roughly 19 cents per gallon, the European Union, 87 cents per gallon, and Brazil, roughly 20% of value.[6]

3. RECOMMENDATION

I recommend you propose a simultaneous change to the ethanol tax credit and ethanol tariff.

First, the ethanol tax credit would be paid directly to domestic ethanol producers, not to fuel blenders as it is today. The credit would be fully refundable, meaning that producers without tax liability to offset would get a cash payment.

Second, once this change is fully implemented, the ethanol tariff would be repealed.

These changes would have little impact on the relative price of domestic ethanol and imported ethanol. Just like today, domestic ethanol would have an advantage of more than 50 cents per gallon over imported ethanol. However, imported ethanol could then compete directly against gasoline, without complex off-setting tax and trade provisions. This would help promote rural development, minimize trade distortions and reduce oil dependence.

FROM THE DESK OF THE PRESIDENT

Key points on biofuels—
- could replace a third of gasoline
- ethanol from corn just the beginning—next step is switchgrass and other "cellulosic" sources
- renewing rural America
- on global warning—ethanol from corn is good, ethanol from cellulose is better
- small impact on domestic food prices
- impacts on world poverty complicated—could be good or bad

from the desk of the
SECRETARY OF AGRICULTURE

Here's a short article for your oil dependence speech.

★ ★ ★ ★ ★

I Am Indy

Buddy Rice took the straightaway at 160 miles per hour, his car burning 100% ethanol.

The noise at the Richmond International Raceway was deafening. Cars roared around the track, with the green flag waving. In the stands, fans wore ear plugs, using hand signals to communicate.

The sound of the track was familiar. The smell wasn't. The smell of gasoline—familiar at many racetracks—was missing. In its place was a faint smell. Somewhat sweet. The smell of burning alcohol.

Rice, winner of the 2004 Indianapolis 500, wasn't the only one with ethanol in his tank.

This year, for the first time, the Indy Racing League is being run entirely on ethanol.

SEVERAL DAYS BEFORE the Richmond race, Buddy Rice took time out to talk about the renewable fuel.

"It's pretty cool we can do this," Rice said. "There's lots of interest."

The Indy Racing League has not used gasoline in many years, Rice explains. Until last year, Indy racers used methanol, a fuel made from many sources but most frequently from nonrenewable natural gas. In 2006, Indy racers used a 90% methanol/10% ethanol blend. This year it's 100% ethanol.

The drivers like it, Rice says.

Ethanol is a high octane fuel. Very high. Gasoline has octane ratings in the high 80s and low 90s. For methanol, the figure is roughly 107. Ethanol's octane rating is 113 or higher.

In the words of the Indy Racing League, ethanol's "high octane rating delivers strong engine performance by helping engines resist detonation so they can run higher compression ratios."

Another benefit, according to Rice: smaller fuel tanks, since ethanol gets better mileage than methanol. That means shorter pit stops. It also means smoother handling on the track.

Rice says the switch to ethanol happened because of hard work by his former teammate, Paul Dana.

"Paul Dana deserves all the credit," Rice says. Dana's determination drove forward a deal between ethanol producers, technology vendors and the Indy league. "A tough group to pull together," according to Rice. Tragically, Paul Dana died in a race car accident in 2006.

But several Indy drivers are making sure Dana's work contin-ues. Rice has appeared at ethanol plants to promote the fuel and says he'll do it again. Jeff Simmons, who drives a car for "Team Ethanol," has done the same.

"I hope the public gets the message," Rice says.

If they do, race car drivers like Buddy Rice, Jeff Simmons and Paul Dana will be one of the reasons. And it turns out these three aren't the first race car drivers to be enthusiastic about ethanol. A driver named Leon Duray finished the Indy 500 in a car filled with ethanol—in 1927.

BACK AT THE RICHMOND RACEWAY, the checkered flag is down. Rice is fifth—seven positions up from where he started, not easy on a short racetrack. "A good race with a solid top-five finish," Rice says. "It gives us good momentum going into next weekend."

Buddy Rice is off to the next race, with a tank filled with ethanol.[1]

from the desk of the
CHAIR,
NATIONAL ECONOMIC COUNCIL

The attached article may be of interest in connection with your oil dependence speech.

★★★★★

From High Tech to Ethanol

"Why," I asked Vinod Khosla, "are you convinced cellulosic ethanol can completely replace gasoline in 25 years? I've read the technical literature on this. Your projection is very optimistic."

"Simple," said Khosla without missing a beat. "I know at least a dozen people who have bet more than $50 million on this technology, including me. More money is coming in fast. That type of money attracts top talent."

"I hope my own bets pay off," Khosla continued. "But if they don't, someone's will. With all this money and brainpower, we're going to see big breakthroughs."

Only time will tell if Vinod Khosla is right about the newest kind of ethanol, made from switchgrass, forest waste and other "cellulosic" sources. But his bets have paid off before.

In the 1980s, Khosla helped found Sun Microsystems, building it into one of the most successful computer companies of the decade. When Khosla stepped down as CEO, Sun had $4 billion of revenues and 12,000 employees.

In the 1990s, Khosla became one of Silicon Valley's top venture capitalists, betting on companies like Excite, Cerent, Juniper and Netscape. At Cerent, an optical networking startup, Khosla paid $8 million for a $30% stake, cashing out for $2.4 billion three years later.

"At heart, I'm a techie nerd," says Khosla. "I spend my time with engineers, learning. If technology can solve a problem, I want to be involved."

Vinod Khosla was born into a middle class family in Poona, India, in 1955. At age 20, he graduated with a degree in electrical engineering from the Indian Institute of Technology. He enrolled at Carnegie Mellon, where he earned a Masters in Biomedical Engineering, and then Stanford Business School, where he got his MBA.

Today Khosla has a professional passion: alternative energy. "We have a climate crisis and energy crisis," says Khosla. "We have a terrorism crisis and a foreign policy crisis and all of them are linked to oil."

"I'm looking for pragmatic solutions that can unlock the stranglehold gasoline has and open the field for innovation driven by our scientists and entrepreneurs," explains Khosla.

That search has led him to cellulosic ethanol and other cellulosic biofuels. Cellulose, explains Khosla, is a major component of grasses, wood and many agricultural residues (such as corn stalks). It can be broken down into sugars, which can then be used for ethanol production.

Historically, this process has been expensive, but costs are declining. Since sources of cellulose are abundant throughout the United States (and world), the impacts could be far-reaching. Furthermore, producing cellulose requires much less fossil energy than growing corn.

Ethanol made from cellulose, says Vinod Khosla, is "not your father's ethanol."

Khosla has become a leading apostle for the fuel, criss-crossing the country to tell audiences "we can replace most of our gasoline needs in 25 years with biomass from our farmlands and municipal waste." He has testified before Congress and appeared at countless conferences. He has co-authored opinion pieces with Sen. Richard Lugar and former Senator Tom Daschle.

But above all else, Khosla is a venture capitalist. He has put his money behind at least 10 companies doing research in this area.

"I'm trying to blanket every possible technical pathway" says Khosla, speaking about his investment strategy in cellulosic ethanol. "I'll fund any scientist with a clear idea I think has a shot at success."

In 2006, Khosla entered the policy arena by helping launch Proposition 87, a California ballot initiative designed to establish a $4 billion fund for alternative energy paid for with a tax on California oil production. Khosla co-chaired the campaign on behalf of the initiative. Oil companies reportedly spent more than $100 million opposing the measure, which was defeated 55%-45% in November 2006.

With his high profile, Khosla has drawn critics and detractors. One anonymous blogger wrote "Dear Mr. Khosla—I hope this letter finds you well. I have no doubt it finds you wealthy." Robert Rapier, a chemical engineer who maintains a blog on energy issues, has written lengthy postings challenging Khosla's assumptions and projections.

Khosla takes such criticism in stride. He submitted a lengthy response to Rapier's critiques. He has debated skeptics of ethanol's potential. After listening to one such debate, one observer said that while the critic saw a glass half-empty, "Vinod looks at this as an entrepreneur...and says the glass is half-full. Vinod always has an answer: 'It depends on innovation.'"

Khosla doesn't quarrel with that description. In fact, he embraces it. "I love science because it's a huge multiplier of resources" says Khosla.

"An entrepreneur," says Khosla, "is someone who dares to dream the dreams and is foolish enough to try to make those dreams come true. The power of ideas fueled by entrepreneurial energy can solve a lot of problems, including the energy and climate crises."[1]

MEMORANDUM FOR THE PRESIDENT

FROM: SECRETARY OF TRANSPORTATION

SUBJECT: Fuel Efficiency

You asked how to improve the fuel efficiency of the U.S. vehicle fleet. After reviewing this question with my staff, I conclude that:

- Many technologies are available to improve the fuel efficiency of the fleet at low cost.

- Fuel efficiency standards should be strengthened and reformed.

This memorandum will not address alternatives fuels, such as electricity from the grid, ethanol and biodiesel. Instead, it will focus on how petroleum-powered vehicles can be made more efficient. I would like to emphasize, however, that alternative fuels can be used in combination with the technologies discussed below to radically transform the transportation system. We can build plug-in, flex-fuel, highly efficient cars that run on a tiny percentage of the petroleum used in current vehicles.

1. CURRENT FUEL EFFICIENCY TECHNOLOGIES
Many widely used and cost-effective technologies can dramatically improve the fuel efficiency of the vehicle fleet.

a. *Conventional Hybrid Engines*
The most powerful technology for reducing oil consumption now available is the conventional hybrid engine.

A conventional hybrid combines an internal combustion engine and an electric motor. The internal combustion engine runs on gasoline and the electric motor draws power from a battery. The battery is recharged with extra power from the engine (such as when the car is running downhill) or with energy captured from the brakes (in a process known as "regenerative braking"). Unlike plug-in hybrids, not yet in widespread use, conventional hybrids cannot be connected to the electric grid.

The fact that hybrid engines can now be considered "conventional" reflects their astonishing success in recent years. The first hybrid engines were introduced in the United States in the late 1990s amid skepticism that they would find a market. Since then, demand has been growing steadily. Wait lists of several months have been common for the Toyota Prius (the most popular hybrid on the market today). More than 1,000,000 hybrid electric vehicles have now been sold worldwide.[1]

Hybrid engines can dramatically improve fuel efficiency. A standard Toyota Camry gets 24 miles per gallon, while a comparable Toyota Camry Hybrid gets 34 mpg—a 42% improvement. A standard Ford Escape FWD gets 23 mpg, while a comparable Ford Escape Hybrid FWD gets 30 mpg—a 30% improvement.[2] One study found that the Lexus SUV Hybrid, a luxury car, outperforms the average luxury SUV on fuel efficiency in city driving by more than two-to-one.[3]

The fact that an engine is a hybrid does not necessarily mean it will achieve substantial fuel savings. Hybrid technology can also be used to improve acceleration.[4] Yet even hybrid engines optimized for acceleration generally have somewhat better fuel efficiency than standard internal combustion engines. Most hybrid engines on the road today are designed with fuel savings as an important objective.

Hybrids are becoming an important part of the U.S. vehicle fleet. Each year since 2002, manufacturers have offered new hybrid models. One expert estimates that by 2012 more than 40 models will use hybrid technology, with annual production of more than 650,000 vehicles.[5] According to analysts at Alliance Bernstein, a leading institutional investment manager:

> The world is on the cusp of a major transition to hybrid-power vehicles ...This is a game-changing technology that promises to increase energy efficiency substantially, make a broad range of fuels available for powering vehicles and meaningfully reduce demand for oil from the transportation sector.[6]

These analysts predict the number of hybrids on the road will grow rapidly, eventually reaching 80% of the vehicle fleet. James Press, President of Toyota North America—the leading vendor of hybrids in the U.S.— predicts every car will eventually be a hybrid.[7]

Even if the percentage of hybrids in the fleet never reaches such heights, the impact on oil consumption could be dramatic. With rapid growth in hybrid sales, oil consumption could fall in the United States in the years ahead even as population and the economy continue to grow.[8]

Hybrid engines cost more. In recent years, retail price premiums (over comparable cars with internal combustion engines) have varied from $3,000 to almost $9,000.[9] These retail premiums are generally greater than the extra cost to manufacturers, reflecting the high demand for and limited supply of the product. The extra cost of a hybrid engine is getting smaller as volumes increase and may reach roughly $2,000 by 2010.[10]

b. *Clean Diesel*
Diesel engines are 30% to 40% more fuel efficient than comparable gasoline engines.[11] Historically, diesel car sales in United States have been limited by dirty exhaust and a reputation for poor quality, but these problems are being overcome. Diesels could make up a growing part of the U.S. vehicle fleet in coming years, helping save fuel.

A "diesel" is a type of internal combustion engine in which the fuel is ignited mainly with compression and high temperatures. (In a gasoline engine, the fuel is ignited with spark plugs.) The technology is named after Rudolf Diesel, who invented it in 1892.

In Europe, diesels make up roughly half of new car sales. In the United States, less than 4% of all vehicles are diesels.[12] Because they perform especially well carrying heavy loads at low speed, diesel engines are used widely in large trucks and heavy equipment. Several efforts to build diesel cars for the U.S. market ended in failure during the 1980s, plagued in part by the vehicles' quality problems.

Until recently, diesel engines generated considerably more soot and smog than gasoline engines. The black smoke belching from a large truck's exhaust, familiar to many Americans, comes from a diesel engine. European cities have tolerated higher levels of soot and smog than U.S. cities for the last several decades, in part because of Europe's reliance on diesels.

However, changes in fuel quality and engine design are producing a new "clean diesel." Under EPA regulations, all diesel fuel must be "ultra-low sulfur" by 2010. New pollution control devices are helping control particulates and other pollutants. (Some of these devices can be added to diesel engines already on the road at reasonable cost.) The result will be a diesel engine that produces roughly the same amount of soot and smog as its gasoline counterpart.[13]

The impacts on the U.S. market could be substantial. With pollution concerns less of a factor, diesel's many benefits could help sales grow quickly. Diesels have better torque and greater durability than gasoline engines. (Many diesel engines last more than 200,000 miles).[14] Roughly 40% of U.S. service stations already offer diesel fuel—far more than currently offer high-percentage ethanol blends such as E85. And of course the fuel efficiency benefits of diesel could be especially attractive during a period of high oil prices.

Diesel engines cost roughly $2,000 more than their gasoline counterparts.[15] Pollution control devices needed to meet U.S. emissions standards can add additional cost. However, purchasers of new cars with clean diesel engines may be eligible for up to $3,400 in tax credits, depending on weight, fuel efficiency and emissions level of the vehicle. The credits expire in 2010.

The market research firm J.D. Power & Associates predicts diesel sales will reach almost 12% of the U.S. market by 2015.[16] In the United Kingdom, diesel sales increased from 15% of new car market in 2000 to more than 40% in early 2007.[17]

c. *Other Technologies*

Beyond hybrid and diesel engines, there are many existing technologies that can substantially reduce fuel consumption without sacrificing performance, safety or comfort. The National Research Council (NRC) released a comprehensive assessment of these technologies in 2002, concluding that "technologies exist that, if applied to passenger cars and light-duty trucks, would significantly reduce fuel consumption within 15 years. Auto manufacturers are already offering or introducing many of these technologies in other markets (Europe and Japan, for example)."[18]

According to the NRC, options include low-friction lubricants (estimated savings of 1%), variable valve timing (2%–3%), cylinder deactivation (3%–6%), five-speed automatic transmissions (2%–3%), continuously variable transmissions (4%–8%) and many more.[19] Based on data from the NRC, the Union of Concerned Scientists found that raising the average fuel economy of new passenger cars and light trucks from today's level of 24 miles per gallon to 37 miles per gallon within 10 to 15 years would be technically feasible and cost effective for the consumer with gasoline at $2.50 a gallon.[20]

2. FUEL EFFICIENCY STANDARDS

Federal fuel efficiency standards are controversial. Advocates argue vigorously that these standards save fuel, cut pollution and help correct several market failures. Opponents argue with equal vigor that the standards don't work, waste money and cost lives. Rhetoric has often been heated on both sides.

This memorandum summarizes the main arguments for and against fuel efficiency standards. After considering these arguments, it recommends you propose overhauling current standards with several far-reaching reforms. In light of these reforms, the old label—corporate average fuel efficiency standards ("CAFE"), which dates to the 1970s—will no longer be appropriate. I recommend a new label: fuel reduction and energy efficiency—"FREEdom"—standards.

a. *Background on CAFE*

Federal fuel efficiency standards for vehicles were first adopted in 1975. Under these standards, each vehicle manufacturer was required to achieve certain average levels of fuel efficiency. One standard was established for cars and another for "light trucks" (a category that included pickup trucks, minivans and sport utility vehicles). Standards were the same for each manufacturer, regardless of the size of vehicles sold. Authority to set standards was delegated to the Secretary of Transportation, who was directed to set them based on "maximum feasible fuel economy."

These CAFE standards rose steadily during most of the program's first decade, contributing to significant fuel efficiency improvements. In 1978, new vehicles averaged 16 miles per gallon. By 1987, this had climbed to 22 miles per gallon, an increase of 37.5%.[21]

The CAFE program's precise role in these improvements has been debated. Some experts note that from 1978 to 1981, as oil prices climbed sharply, vehicle manufacturers regularly exceeded CAFE standards. Rising oil prices appear to have shaped production decisions more than the CAFE program during this period.[22] Others note that from 1982 to 1988, the fuel efficiency of new vehicles continued to increase as oil prices fell. CAFE standards appear to have been the driving force behind fuel efficiency improvements during those years.[23]

CAFE standards have changed very little since the late 1980s. Standards for cars reached 27.5 miles per gallon (mpg) in 1990 and remain at that level today. CAFE standards for light trucks were 20.0 mpg in 1989, 20.7 mpg in 1996 and 21.6 mpg in 2006. [24]

The fuel efficiency of new U.S. vehicles has also changed little in 20 years. Advances in engine design have typically been used to improve acceleration, not achieve fuel savings. The fuel efficiency of new passenger vehicles (cars and light trucks combined) peaked at 22.1 miles per gallon in 1987 and has trended slowly downward ever since.[25]

Ironically, the CAFE program played an important role in the rise of the gas-guzzling sport utility vehicle.[26] Because CAFE standards for light trucks were less stringent than those for cars, auto makers had an incentive to design light trucks for use as standard passenger vehicles. In 1975, light trucks made up about 10% of the U.S. vehicle fleet. Today, they make up about 50%.[27] This shift from cars to light trucks is the main reason average fuel efficiency of the U.S. fleet as a whole has declined slightly in the past 20 years.

Under new rules effective in 2006, different fuel efficiency standards are being established for different sizes of light truck. This is an important reform of the original program. Under the old system, a manufacturer could avoid improving the fuel efficiency of large inefficient vehicles by adding smaller ones to its fleet. Manufacturers of smaller vehicles sometimes faced no requirement to improve fuel efficiency at all. Under the new system, light trucks of all sizes will be required to improve fuel efficiency. The new system provides important benefits in terms of fairness, cost-effectiveness and safety.[28]

However, similar changes were not made to the CAFE program for passenger cars, due to concerns that the underlying statute would not allow it. Fuel efficiency standards for cars are still set under the old "corporate average" system.

b. _Other Countries_

U.S. fuel efficiency standards are much weaker than those in other industrialized countries or China. In Japan, new vehicles are required to achieve the equivalent of roughly 46 miles per gallon. In the European Union, the figure is 37 miles per gallon. Australia and China both require roughly 29 miles per gallon. Only Canada—at 26 miles per gallon— approaches the U.S. figure of roughly 24 miles per gallon (averaged for cars and light trucks). These other countries all have schedules for strengthening standards faster than the United States as well.[29]

c. _Arguments in Favor of CAFE Standards_

CAFE standards have helped the United States save huge amounts of fuel.

According to an authoritative 2002 report by the National Research Council (NRC), fuel efficiency improvements since 1975 save the United States about 2.8 million barrels per day of oil. The NRC found that CAFE standards are a "major reason" for these savings, noting that other factors, such as oil prices, also play "important roles."[30] The NRC found the CAFE program had been "particularly effective in keeping fuel economy above the levels to which it might have fallen when real gasoline prices began their long decline in the 1980s."[31]

More recent estimates put fuel efficiency savings from CAFE standards at more than 3.2 million barrels per day. At $50 per barrel of oil, annual savings from fuel efficiency improvements exceed $55 billion.[32]

By mandating fuel efficiency, CAFE standards help reduce the U.S. vulnerability to oil price increases. In 1973, the U.S. consumed 1.46 barrels of oil for every $1,000 of GDP. By 2006, that had fallen to 0.66.[33] This change is one reason rising oil prices in this decade have had much less impact on the economy than rising oil price during the 1970s.

CAFE standards also help cut pollution. Saving 3.2 million barrels per day of oil reduces carbon dioxide emissions by 436 million metric tons per year—roughly 7.5% of the U.S. total.[34] It also reduces smog in many of our nation's cities.

CAFE standards help correct a fundamental market failure. Reduced oil consumption has many social benefits—such as less pollution and greater strength in the war against Islamic jihadism—but no individual car buyer can realize these benefits by purchasing a more fuel efficient car. These benefits can only be realized if car buyers as a whole purchase more fuel efficient vehicles. This is a classic situation in which government standard-setting can provide important benefits.

Furthermore, most consumers only consider fuel saving benefits for the first few years when buying an automobile. Yet most vehicles stay on the road for many years. Society as a whole has a strong interest in ensuring that the fuel consumption implications over the lifetime of the vehicle are reflected in the initial purchase. This too is a classic situation in which government standard-setting can provide important benefits.

Similarly, investments in developing fuel efficient technologies have important social benefits, yet manufactures are unable to capture these. As a result, from a social standpoint, manufacturers underinvest in fuel efficiency research. Government can help ensure that the incentives of vehicle manufacturers are better aligned with the interests of society as a whole.[35]

d. *Arguments against CAFE Standards*

CAFE standards are an imperfect tool for reducing oil consumption. First, they affect new vehicle sales only. Since new vehicles make up roughly 7% of the U.S. fleet each year, it takes many years for a change in CAFE standards to have an impact on the fleet as a whole.[36] For example, if CAFE standards are strengthened by 4% annually—often considered to be a significant increase—fleetwide fuel savings five years later would be less than 2%. CAFE standards can have an impact, but they take time.

Second, CAFE standards don't reduce total driving. Fuel consumption is determined both by the fuel efficiency of the fleet and the total distance traveled by all vehicles (often referred to as "vehicle miles traveled," or VMT). If fuel efficiency improves by 4%, but vehicle miles traveled increase by 4%, fuel consumption remains unchanged.

In fact, perversely, CAFE standards increase total driving. More fuel efficient cars are cheaper to drive and, therefore, driven further. The amount of this "rebound effect" has been the subject of several studies. Based on a review of this literature, the National Research Council found that 10% to 20% of the fuel savings from an increase in standards are lost due to increased driving.[37] In a subsequent analysis, however, David Gerard and Lester Lave argue that such estimates overstate the "rebound effect." According to their data, a 3-mile-per-gallon improvement in fuel efficiency would—assuming a gasoline price of $2.50 per gallon—cut average driving costs by roughly a penny per mile, or 1.5% to 3% of total variable driving costs.[38] They question whether cost differences of that magnitude in fact alter driver behavior.

The most serious charge lodged against CAFE standards, as originally designed, is that they increased traffic deaths. First, CAFE standards gave a manufacturer selling large, highly profitable vehicles a powerful incentive to "downsize" other vehicles in its fleet. This bifurcated fleet—made up of some very large and some much smaller vehicles—added risks for occupants of smaller vehicles in two-car accidents.[39] Second, to the extent that CAFE standards caused the "rebound effect" discussed above, they may have increased traffic fatalities. In general, more vehicle miles traveled means more accidents.

The National Research Council declined to estimate traffic deaths due to CAFE standards, but said that automobile downsizing "some of which was due to CAFE standards, probably resulted in an additional 1,300 to 2,600 traffic fatalities in 1993."[40] This conclusion drew a vigorous dissent from two panel members, who argued that the data did not support such a conclusion. These panel members pointed out, for example, that younger drivers tend to both drive smaller cars and drive less safely and that relevant studies had failed to account for this.[41]

Fortunately, regulatory changes already in place mostly fix these CAFE-caused safety problems for the light truck fleet. Under CAFE reforms adopted in 2006, fuel efficiency standards for light trucks will no longer be set on a "corporate average" basis. Instead standards will be set for each vehicle depending on its "weight class." This removes a manufacturer's incentive to downsize a portion of its light truck fleet in order to keep selling larger light trucks. These changes should be applied to fuel efficiency standards for cars as well.

Several studies have found that increased costs from CAFE standards outweigh the benefits. These studies have been based upon monetized figures for traffic deaths, pollution and congestion (assuming a substantial "rebound effect").[42] To the extent that reforms to the CAFE program can successfully address safety issues, a significant amount of the costs in some of these studies would be reduced.

3. A NEW PROPOSAL—FREEDOM STANDARDS
Federal fuel efficiency standards are more than 30 years old. Three decades of experience have taught many lessons. I believe the record demonstrates that:

- fuel efficiency standards can play an important role in reducing oil consumption

- the design of current standards can be improved

Accordingly, I recommend you both strengthen and redesign fuel efficiency standards as a central part of your program for fighting oil dependence. In particular, I recommend four changes to the standards, described below. In light of these changes, the notion of a "corporate average" will no longer be a central part of the standards. For this reason, and because the changes as a whole are so extensive, I recommend discarding the old "corporate average fuel economy" label, which dates to the 1970s. I propose a new label: fuel reduction and energy efficiency or "FREEdom" standards.

Change 1: Automatic Annual Increases

Like most technologies, engine technologies improve steadily with time. Yet the current regulatory system for fuel efficiency moves in fits and starts, with extended multiyear rulemakings before standards are adjusted to reflect technological change. This is both counterproductive and wasteful, introducing uncertainty into corporate decision making and encouraging litigation over occasional new standards.

Automatic annual increases would solve these problems. If manufacturers knew fuel efficiency standards would increase by a set percentage each year, they could make long-term investment decisions accordingly. The Department of Transportation could be given authority to suspend an automatic increase, if such an increase were demonstrated to be infeasible. Reversing the presumption in this way would put the U.S. vehicle fleet on a path toward steady and sustained fuel efficiency improvements.

In January 2007, President George W. Bush suggested a 4% per year target for fuel efficiency improvements in the United States. Given the pace of technological improvements in engine design during the past several decades, this is a reasonable figure. However, President Bush's proposal was a soft, nonbinding "target." A stronger approach would be to require such improvements.

Change 2: Allow Manufacturers to Trade Credits

Emissions trading helped the United States control acid rain at costs much lower than expected. We should apply the same approach to improving fuel efficiency by allowing manufacturers to trade credits in order to meet fuel efficiency standards. The result: Costs would come down and car makers would have more incentive to innovate.[43]

Change 3: Set Standards for Cars Based on Size

Since 2005, fuel efficiency standards for light trucks have been set based on size. This solves two problems. First, manufacturers can no longer avoid improving the fuel efficiency of their large trucks by building smaller ones. (Many experts believe the incentive to build a bifurcated fleet was dangerous, increasing fatalities in two-car accidents.) Second, manufacturers who make only smaller trucks can no longer avoid improving fuel efficiency.

This same change should be applied to fuel efficiency standards for cars. The Bush administration believed it lacked statutory authority to set standards for cars based on vehicle size. You should seek such authority from Congress.

Change 4: Treat Cars and Light Trucks the Same

Under the old CAFE system, different standards applied to cars and light trucks (pickups, minivans and sport utility vehicles). This distinction dates back to 1975, when light trucks made up 10% of the vehicle fleet and were used mainly for off-road driving. Today—partly as a result of the CAFE system—light trucks make up 50% of the vehicle fleet and are typically used for trips to schools, shopping malls and the office.

With fuel efficiency standards based on size, there would be no continuing rationale for distinguishing between cars and light trucks. A car and light truck of equal size should meet the same standard. Eliminating the distinction would permit manufacturers to meet overall standards at lower cost.[44]

Key points on fuel efficiency —

- hybrid engines — huge impact in next 20 years
- clean diesel is coming
- many off-the-shelf technologies for improving fuel efficiency
- US standards weaker than Europe, Japan and <u>China</u>!

from the desk of the
SECRETARY OF LABOR

Jerome Ringo is helping bring labor, business and environmental groups together to promote clean energy. Here's an article for your speech.

★ ★ ★ ★ ★

Man with a Mission

"The energy revolution will transform our economy," Jerome Ringo tells the House Select Committee on Energy Independence and Global Warming, "creating whole new industries and millions of good new jobs."

Jerome Ringo is chair of the Apollo Alliance, a coalition of more than 100 labor unions, environmental groups and businesses. Apollo's mission, he says: to create three million new jobs, break oil addiction and cure the climate crisis. To build a clean energy economy within a decade.

Ringo speaks not just with conviction, but with specificity. He calls on Congress to invest $300 billion in clean energy programs over the next 10 years.

Funds should be used for research and development, tax credits and manufacturing incentives, he says. He urges Congress to strengthen automotive fuel efficiency standards while giving manufacturers incentives to retool U.S. factories. He emphasizes "green collar" jobs, calling on Congress to establish a new program to train workers for jobs in clean energy industries.

"The public is clamoring for action," Ringo says. "Environmentalists, working Americans, inner-city communities, technology innovators, investors, security Moms, family farmers, and more are demanding change now."

JEROME RINGO grew up in the bayous of southern Louisiana. "I grew up connected to nature," Ringo says. "Hunting and fishing were important to us."

As a teenager, Ringo became the first African-American ranger at the world's largest Boy Scout camp, in New Mexico. A few years later, he went to work as a process operator in the petrochemical industry, working in refineries and on offshore platforms for more than 20 years.

During this period, Ringo says, he first saw the impact of petrochemical plants on communities "beyond the fence line." Cancer rates in these communities were high. Respiratory diseases were common as well. Ringo had no doubt the plants were at least partly to blame.

So he became on organizer, helping communities lobby the state legislature on environmental laws even as he continued working in the industry. When his company offered an early retirement package even before he turned 40, Ringo took it and began working full time on behalf of workers, poor communities and the environment.

Ringo's organizing skills, roots in diverse communities and powerful speaking voice brought him national attention. In 1996, he joined the board of the National Wildlife Federation, a grassroots conservation group with more than four million members. In 2005, he was named board chair. The same year, he agreed to serve as President of the Apollo Alliance.

RINGO'S BACKGROUND gives him a sense of mission about his work.

"The hurricanes on the Gulf Coast were a wake-up call," he says. "The climate crisis, the war in Iraq, rising gas prices—all these factors are creating a new sense of urgency."

To solve these problems, Ringo says, it's essential to bring different communities together. He's done that for years—working both in the petrochemical industry and conservation community. "That's unusual," he says. "Usually people are involved in one or the other."

At the Apollo Alliance, he's bringing together labor unions, environmental groups and businesses, forces that have often collided. But Ringo believes there's a shared mission all can embrace.

"Don't talk to me about jobs versus the environment," he says.

"It's jobs for the environment."

"Clean energy is an issue that unites Americans," he continues. "My job is to be a Pied Piper. I'm trying to help show the way."

Ringo emphasizes that building a clean energy economy can bring far-reaching benefits.

"Most Americans don't want an easy life," Jerome Ringo says. "We want a good life. We want a life filled with purpose, with challenges, with a sense we're here for something bigger."

Ringo recalls President John Kennedy's words about sending men to the Moon and taking on other challenges "not because they easy, but because they are hard."

"If our leaders give us an easy way out, we'll take it," Ringo says. "But if our leaders give us a challenge, we'll take it in a heartbeat." Ringo believes we now have a "Sputnik moment," when Americans will respond to great challenges.

BACK IN THE HEARING ROOM, Jerome Ringo explains the policy positions of the Apollo Alliance. "We're more likely to build a new energy future with good jobs for working Americans," he says, with "an investment strategy as well as a regulatory strategy."

His powerful voice rises as he reaches his closing. "We called on the 'can do' spirit of the original Apollo program in our Alliance's name because we believe the American people are once more ready for a great challenge," Ringo says. "Energy will be the transformative issue of our generation."[1]

MEMORANDUM FOR THE PRESIDENT

FROM: CHAIR, COUNCIL OF ECONOMIC ADVISERS

SUBJECT: Gasoline Taxes

Two days ago you received a memorandum on fuel efficiency from the Secretary of Transportation. The memo recommends several sensible reforms to federal laws on that topic.

However, the memorandum simply ignores the most powerful tool for improving fuel efficiency: an increase in the federal gasoline tax.

I know taxes are controversial. Attacking elected officials who even consider changes in the Tax Code is easy and often effective.

Yet a gasoline tax increase could be a potent tool for helping the United States end oil dependence. This memo provides background and suggests several options.

1. BACKGROUND
The federal gasoline tax is 18.4 cents per gallon. Revenues from the tax are roughly $25 billion per year. Funds are dedicated to highway construction and repair (roughly 83%), mass transit (roughly 16%) and other purposes (roughly 1%).

The level of the tax has not changed since 1993. Since then, the Consumer Price Index has increased 43%. In 1993, the tax was roughly 17% of the price of a gallon of gasoline. Today it is roughly 7%.[1]

Every state taxes gasoline sales. The average state gasoline tax is roughly 20 cents per gallon. Since 1992, 28 states have increased gasoline taxes. At least four states lowered them during this period. Roughly a dozen states adjust gasoline tax rates for inflation in some way.[2]

Gasoline taxes in the United States are much lower than in other major industrialized countries. Gasoline taxes average roughly $4.50 per gallon in the United Kingdom, $4.20 per gallon in Germany, and $1.85 per gallon in Japan.[3]

2. PROPOSALS FOR REFORM

Gregory Mankiw, who served as President George W. Bush's Chair of the Council of Economic Advisers from 2003 to 2005, wrote an editorial after leaving office with the title "Raise the Gas Tax."[4] Mankiw called for raising the gasoline tax 10 cents per year for 10 years, arguing that higher gasoline taxes would improve fuel efficiency more effectively than CAFE standards, protect the environment, reduce traffic congestion, help balance the budget and promote economic growth.

Many leaders from across the political spectrum agree. Mankiw maintains a list on his website, which includes statements in favor of a gasoline tax increase by Alan Greenspan (chair of the Federal Reserve Board from 1987 to 2006), Martin Feldstein (chair of the Council of Economic Advisers under President Ronald Reagan), George Shultz (who held three Cabinet posts under Presidents Reagan and Nixon), Larry Summers (Treasury Secretary under President Bill Clinton), Joe Stiglitz (winner of the Nobel Prize in Economics), Tom Friedman (New York Times columnist) and many others.[5]

These individuals offer broadly similar arguments. In general, they believe gasoline prices fail to reflect the full costs of gasoline to society. Higher taxes would correct that, they argue, with large benefits. Higher gas taxes would make alternative fuels more attractive to drivers and investors. They would encourage conservation and promote innovation. For example, the National Research Council wrote in a 2002 report that:

> There is a marked inconsistency between pressing automotive manu-facturers for improved fuel economy from new vehicles on the one hand and insisting on low real gasoline prices on the other. Higher real prices for gasoline—for instance, through increased gasoline taxes—would create both a demand for fuel-efficient new vehicles and an incentive for owners of existing vehicles to drive them less.[6]

One interesting point, made by several experts, is that much of the cost of higher gasoline taxes would fall on foreign producers. As economist Hal

Varian has written:

> Taxes on gasoline reduce the demand for oil, thereby reducing the price received by the suppliers of oil. And most of those suppliers are foreign.... economic analysis suggests that in the long-run, a significant part of a gasoline tax increase would end up being paid by producers of oil, not consumers.[7]

3. PUBLIC ATTITUDES

Opposition to gasoline tax increases is deep and widespread. One recent poll found 85% of Americans opposed.[8] This resistance is hardly surprising. In the absence of alternative fuels, drivers have few options for minimizing the tax burden. In most situations, the only option available is to drive less, which can often cause considerable hardship.

Also not surprisingly, few members of Congress support a gas tax increase. In the words of former Congressman Phil Sharp, now president of Resources for the Future, a leading Washington think tank:

> Many experts believe that a more effective approach to reducing fuel consumption—and a more cost-effective approach for the U.S. economy—would be a stronger gasoline tax or oil tax.... These experts, of course, are not subject to popular election.[9]

Interestingly, state legislatures around the country have been much more willing to impose modest gasoline tax increases than the U.S. Congress. In recent years Indiana, Kansas, Maine, Nebraska, North Carolina and West Virginia—among others—have all raised gas levies.

Furthermore, polling data indicates that many voters may be open to gasoline tax increases tied to specific and popular purposes. For example, the same poll that found 85% of Americans opposed to a gas tax increase found 55% of respondents supported an increase when asked "What if the increased tax on gasoline would reduce the United States dependence on foreign oil?" That poll found 59% of respondents supported an increase when asked "What if the increased tax would cut down on energy consumption and reduce global warming?"[10]

4. STRUCTURAL CONSIDERATIONS
In shaping any increase to the federal gasoline tax, the most important elements would be the amount of increase, phase-in schedule and use of proceeds.

a. *Amount of Increase*
There is a large literature on externalities related to oil use, as well as on government subsidies that promote oil use.[11] This literature could serve as a guide in determining the optimal amount of a tax. However, the figures provided by this literature vary widely—from several billion to many hundreds of billions of dollars each year. The differences between small and large numbers often turn on highly subjective judgments. (What is the "cost" of a case of childhood asthma? What fraction of military and political resources in the Persian Gulf should be allocated to protecting oil flows?) There is no "correct" answer.

Furthermore, the figures provided in this literature are unlikely to play a significant role in the political dialogue on a gas tax. Although such studies may help inform the dialogue, and provide debating points for advocates, decisions on this topic are more likely to be shaped by visceral public attitudes, interest group lobbying and political rhetoric. On this topic, opinions will be strong and passions will run high.

In assessing the political acceptability of any increase, one factor to consider is the typical variability of gasoline prices. During the past several years, for example, average retail prices have risen from roughly $2.20 per gallon to roughly $3.00 per gallon within three months on at least three occasions. Price changes of more than 20 cents per gallon within a month have been typical.[12] To be sure, many drivers would strongly resist tax increases much smaller than this, even if the funds collected would help to protect them from price volatility in the medium term or long term. But an increase of (for example) 10 cents per gallon would be consistent with every driver's experience in recent years.

b. *Phase-In Schedule*
Any increase could be effective immediately or phased in over a number of years. An immediate increase would be absorbed by most drivers as a

higher cost, since adjusting driving habits is often difficult and purchasing alternatives to gasoline usually impossible. Longer phase-in periods improve the ability of drivers to adjust. Drivers can incorporate expectations about higher fuel prices into decisions about what car to buy and even where to live. Carmakers and other businesses can incorporate these expectations into capital spending decisions.

c. *Use of Proceeds*
Funds collected from a gasoline tax increase could be used to reduce the budget deficit, fund government programs or reduce other taxes. Funds could be used for general purposes or specifically to help reduce oil dependence.

Revenues from a gas tax increase could be substantial. A 10-cent-per-gallon increase would bring in roughly $14 billion in the first year. A $1-per-gallon increase would bring in roughly $140 billion. Roughly a third of these amounts would be collected from similar increases in the tax on diesel fuels.[13]

5. OPTIONS
Following are three options for your consideration. These are not intended to be a comprehensive set. The three structural elements identified above can be mixed and matched in many ways. I would be pleased to develop additional options if helpful.

Option A—Index for Inflation
One simple reform would be to index the federal gasoline tax for inflation. During the past decade, the Consumer Price Index has increased by an average of roughly 2.5% per year.[14] Increasing the current 18.4 cent federal gasoline tax by 2.5% would yield an increase of 0.46 cents. Annual increases in this range would be tiny in comparison to typical market fluctuations in gasoline prices

Pros
- Several states already do this.

- Relatively noncontroversial.

- Prevents long-term erosion of revenue base.

Cons
- Little impact on oil dependence objectives.

- Some opposition certain. (No gas tax proposal lacks controversy.)

Option B—Annual Increases with Income Tax Rebates
Another approach would be to increase the gasoline tax by a set amount each year, while rebating most of the proceeds directly to lower- and middle-income families. The remainder of the funds could be used for tax incentives and other programs to reduce oil dependence.

For example, the tax could be increased 10 cents per year for five years, with each 10-cent-increment used to mail rebate checks of $100 to households with incomes below $75,000.

Pros
- Big impact on oil dependence in the medium-term. Alternative fuels and fuel efficiency would become higher priorities for many drivers and carmakers.

- Not a financial burden for most Americans. Each 10-cent increment would raise average driving costs roughly $60 per vehicle per year (until drivers could adjust by purchasing more alternative fuels or fuel efficient cars). For drivers with incomes below $75,000, the $100 income tax rebate would offset extra costs, in whole or part.

- Indeed, disposable income of many taxpayers would increase under this proposal. For example, households with income below $75,000 and fewer than two cars would receive extra money.

- Funds not used for rebates could provide tax incentives for purchase of plug-in hybrids or support other programs to reduce oil dependence.

- Similar to a proposal offered by Gregory Mankiw, former chair of Council of Economic Advisers under President George W. Bush.

Cons
- Would be very controversial and draw strong opposition.

- Many Members of Congress might be especially reluctant to vote for a proposal that would increase the gasoline tax during election years.

- Drivers with inefficient cars and those who drive longer than average distances would bear extra costs.

Option C—One-Time Increase with Proceeds Used for Deficit Reduction
A final approach would be to increase the gasoline tax once, with funds used to reduce the federal budget deficit. For example, a $1-per-gallon increase would generate roughly $140 billion of revenue.

Pros
- Would send a strong signal about need to reduce gasoline consumption. Quickest way to promote alternatives and conservation.

- Would make a significant contribution to reducing the federal budget deficit.

Cons
- Large burden on many families. Average cost would be roughly $520 per year.

- Potential adverse impacts on inflation and growth.

- Intense political opposition.

6. RECOMMENDATION
I recommend Option B.[15] In particular, I recommend you propose to:

1. Raise the federal gasoline tax 10 cents a year for 5 years.

2. Use the funds to deliver checks to every family earning less than $75,000 per year.

   - Checks would be for $100 in Year 1, $200 in Year 2, $300 in Year 3, $400 in Year 4, and $500 in Year 5.

   - Checks would be delivered annually, just before July 4.

3. Use the remaining revenues for a dedicated fund (the "Freedom Fund") to support tax incentives and other programs to reduce oil dependence.

Such a program would help free the United States from oil dependence without imposing a financial burden on drivers. Indeed, the disposable income of many Americans would increase as a result of this proposal.

Here are some key points related to this plan:

- Each 10-cent increment in the gasoline tax adds roughly $57 to the annual cost of driving today's average vehicle.[16]

- Roughly 82 million households in the United States have incomes of $75,000 or less. (This is roughly 72% of all households.)[17] Sending a $100 check to households with income less than $75,000 would cost roughly $8.2 billion (82 million households times $100/household).

- After rebate checks were mailed, the program would generate revenues for the Freedom Fund in roughly the following amounts: year 1, $5 billion; year 2, $9.5 billion; year 3, $13.5 billion; year 4, $17 billion; year 5, $20 billion.

7. CONCLUSION

An increase in the gasoline tax would be controversial. It would also be the single most powerful step you could take to help end the nation's oil dependence. An increase could be structured in ways to eliminate the burden on many Americans and minimize the burden on others.

If you would like any additional information on this topic, please let me know.

MEMORANDUM FOR THE PRESIDENT

FROM: THE SECRETARY OF ENERGY

SUBJECT: Role for Coal

The United States is rich in coal. More than half our electric power comes from coal, but there is no risk of shortages. At current consumption rates, U.S. coal supplies will last for more than 100 years.[1]

Coal can be used to replace oil in two ways. First, coal can be turned into a liquid fuel. The technology for doing this is well-known, but expensive and significantly worse from a global warming standpoint than oil. Second, coal can be used to generate electricity for cars with electric motors. This is cheaper and cleaner than liquid coal, but depends on cars that can connect to the electric grid.

Coal can play an important role in helping reduce oil dependence, but there are many challenges. This chapter provides background and offers several recommendations.

1. BACKGROUND

Coal is formed from dead plants that have been compressed and heated beneath the Earth's surface for millions of years. The principal component of coal is carbon.[2] Coal also contains sulfur, mercury and other elements in trace amounts.

More than 27% of world's coal reserves are in the United States.[3] Coal is produced throughout the Appalachian and Rocky Mountain states, as well as in the Midwest and deep South.

Making electricity from coal is cheap. A kilowatt-hour from a coal-fired power plant generally costs half or a quarter of a kilowatt-hour from a natural gas plant.[4] Coal remains slightly cheaper than wind and much less expensive than the sun as a source of electricity.[5]

The biggest challenge in using coal is pollution. Critics argue that coal is cheap only because producers are able to impose environmental and social costs of production on society as a whole.[6] Coal mining destroys natural landscapes and pollutes waterways. Coal burning releases sulfur dioxide, mercury and other pollutants into the atmosphere. Although coal creates less pollution now than several decades ago, thanks to considerable investment in scrubbers and other pollution-control technology, coal remains one of the largest sources of pollution in the United States.

Perhaps most serious, coal is a leading cause of global warming. When coal burns, carbon in the coal bonds with oxygen in the atmosphere to form carbon dioxide, the leading heat-trapping gas. Coal contains more carbon per unit of energy than any other fuel.

Coal is found in 70 countries and mined in 50 worldwide.[7]

2. LIQUEFIED COAL

Coal exists naturally as a solid, but can be turned into a liquid. Liquefied coal can be used by cars and trucks on the road today, without modification, as a substitute for oil.

The technology for turning coal to liquid fuel is well-established. The Germans used it during World War II.[8] South Africa has been using it for decades, in part because apartheid-era embargoes limited the nation's access to oil. Today about 30% of South Africa's gasoline and diesel fuels come from coal.[9] SASOL, the leading South African producer, is currently developing several coal-to-liquid projects in China.

Federal programs to promote liquefied coal date back decades. Most of these programs ended in failure. In the 1940s, the Synthetic Liquid Fuels Act provided millions of dollars for research and development, with little impact. In the 1970s, the Synthetic Fuels Corporation launched public-private partnerships in the hopes of commercializing liquefied coal. The program was abandoned in the 1980s due to falling oil prices, environmental concerns and other factors.[10] The National Academy of Sciences described the Synthetic Fuels Corporation as "a case study of unsuccessful federal involvement in technology development," citing an overemphasis on production targets, "excessive political interference" and administrative problems among the reasons for failure.[11]

There are no operating coal-to-liquid (CTL) plants in the United States, largely because the technology is quite expensive. However, several projects are under development—in Wyoming, Illinois, Pennsylvania and elsewhere—spurred in part by high oil prices in recent years.

Several dozen "coal synfuels" plants operate in the United States. These plants produce products such as coal slurries and syngas, mainly for use in electric power plants. These "coal synfuels" plants do not make liquid fuel for use in vehicles. The terminology here can be confusing.

Under the Energy Policy Act of 2005, any liquefied coal produced in the United States would be eligible for a 50-cent-per-gallon federal excise tax credit. The credit will expire in 2009. Federal loan guarantees are available to help with construction of CTL plants. The U.S. military has shown keen interest in the technology, producing aviation fuels from coal on a trial basis.

a. *Advantages of CTL*

The principal advantage of liquid coal is that it could be produced in high volume within the United States. According to the National Coal Council, U.S. production of liquid coal could reach 2.6 million barrels per day (roughly 20% of current gasoline and diesel demand) within 20 years for an investment of roughly $200 billion. Even with conservative estimates of U.S. recoverable coal reserves, that rate of production could be sustained for many decades.[12]

Concerns about security of oil supply have led the U.S. military to begin investing in coal-to-liquid production. However, the risk the military would be unable to obtain oil in a crisis appears small. Military oil consumption is roughly 400,000 barrels per day,[13] U.S. domestic production is over 5 million barrels of oil per day, proven oil reserves in the U.S. exceed 21 billion barrels[14] and proven reserves in Canada exceed 178 billion barrels. Nevertheless, U.S. oil production peaked more than 30 years ago, reserves in the U.S. and Canada might be inaccessible for a variety of reasons and military planning requires preparation for unlikely scenarios. One or two coal-to-liquid plants could provide a margin of safety, helping to ensure fuel supply for long-range tactical aircraft and other military platforms during an extraordinary crisis.

If liquid coal were produced in the United States for commercial consumption, some of it might replace imported oil, although this is uncertain. Liquid coal would replace the most expensive oil first (unless restrictions such as tariffs or quotas were imposed on oil imports). Oil is much more expensive to produce in the United States and Canada than, for example, in the Persian Gulf. As a result, liquid coal from domestic sources might end up replacing oil from the United States or Canada, not oil from unstable regions.

b. *Disadvantages of CTL*

There are two principal disadvantages with liquid coal. First, it is expensive. Second, liquid coal is worse—potentially much worse—than oil when it comes to fighting global warming.

i. Cost

Coal-to-liquid plants are very costly. SASOL, the world's leading producer of liquefied coal, says that building a single demonstration plant in the United States would cost $8 to $9 billion. A project under development in Shaanxi Province, China, is projected to cost $6 to $8 billion.[15] Economies of scale are generally considered to require very large plants.

SASOL estimates that oil prices would need to be $50 to $70 per barrel, depending on the price of coal, for CTL plants to generate a "minimum return."[16] Some estimates are lower: One U.S. company asserts its CTL project could break even with oil prices at $40 per barrel and the World Coal Institute claims oil prices in the $35 per barrel range would make liquid coal competitive.[17] Yet a leading U.S. government expert considers hopes for coal-to-liquid production costs in the $40 per barrel range to be "far-fetched."[18]

Furthermore, dramatic declines in production costs are unlikely. The technologies for making liquid coal are mature and well-understood. (One leading technique—the "Fischer-Tropsch" process—was invented in the 1920s.) In general, the costs of mature technologies do not fall as quickly as costs of new or emerging ones. Breakthroughs are always possible, of course, but the prospects for rapid cost declines are not as good as with some other fuels (such as cellulosic ethanol).

ii. Global Warming

By far the most serious concern about liquid coal, however, is its impact on global warming. The process of mining coal and transforming it into liquid fuel creates large amounts of heat-trapping gases. (SASOL's coal-to-liquid plant in Secunda, South Africa, is the largest single source of carbon dioxide emissions in the world.[19]) The fuel produced by this process is rich in carbon—about the same as fuels made from petroleum—and creates still more heat-trapping gases when burned. Measured on a life-cycle basis, emissions of heat-trapping gases from liquid coal are roughly twice those from oil.[20]

In theory, it is possible to do better. Coal-to-liquid production facilities can be built to separate carbon dioxide from other gases in the waste stream and then pump that carbon dioxide underground for storage. However, these steps—known as "carbon capture and storage"—add considerable expense to an already expensive process. Costs will vary depending on site location and other factors, yet at many sites a rough estimate of $40 per barrel is reasonable.[21] Some of these costs will be in addition to the already high costs ($35–$70 per barrel) noted above. Carbon dioxide may have commercial value for enhanced oil recovery or other purposes at some locations, reducing these costs, but such opportunities are likely to be limited.

The technology for underground storage of carbon dioxide is well known.[22] In Beulah, North Dakota, for example, a gasification company captures carbon dioxide and transports it 200 miles by pipeline to an oil field in Saskatchewan, where the carbon dioxide helps pump oil out of the ground in a process known as "enhanced oil recovery." About 1 million tons of carbon dioxide are stored underground at this site each year.[23]

However, deploying this technology on mass scale will inevitably present challenges. Current projects do not store carbon dioxide on the scale that will be needed in the decades ahead. Different procedures are needed at different locations. Regulations addressing liability, monitoring obligations and other issues must be developed. Wide-scale deployment of carbon storage facilities will take time.[24]

Furthermore, even if "carbon capture and storage" at a coal-to-liquid plant is executed perfectly, the resulting fuel is still no better than oil when it comes to fighting global warming. If even a small percentage of the carbon dioxide at a plant is released into the atmosphere, or if some carbon dioxide leaks from underground storage years later, then replacing oil with liquid coal will make the global warming problem worse.

Despite this discouraging picture, work is under way to design facilities that could use the nation's plentiful coal resources to produce liquid fuels without negative impacts on global warming. One possibility involves selling by-products of the CTL process to coal-fired power plants in ways that would reduce emissions.[25] Another possibility involves mixing biomass with coal at the CTL facilities, also helping to reduce emissions.[26] Work in these areas should be pursued as a matter of priority.

3. COAL FOR ELECTRIC CARS

Since coal provides half the nation's electricity, coal could play a large role as a transportation fuel if our cars could connect to the electric grid.

This fact is sometimes cited as a reason to be concerned about the environmental impact of electric cars. In fact, an electric car running on coal creates less pollution than a conventional car running on petroleum. The reason: Electric motors are much more efficient than internal combustion engines.

Put differently, plug-in hybrids and other electric cars offer a way to use the United States' abundant coal resources in a way that reduces pollution.

This may seem too good to be true. But consider a new coal plant built using the most advanced technology. The technology produces far fewer conventional pollutants, such as soot, than an old-fashioned plant. Carbon dioxide is separated from other gases at the site and then stored underground. The electricity produced is used to power plug-in hybrids or other electric cars that produce no tailpipe emissions when running on their electric motors. The result—cars powered by coal that don't contribute to global warming.

To be sure, there are significant hurdles before this vision is realized. Advanced coal technologies are expensive.[27] Underground storage capacity is uncertain. Plug-in cars are not yet on the road in large numbers. But with new clean coal technologies, underground carbon storage and plug-in cars, it may be possible to use electricity from coal to move vehicles while dramatically reducing pollution.

4. POLICIES
I recommend you pursue an aggressive research program to find ways to use coal without contributing to global warming. This should be pursued through the national laboratories as well as university and private sector partners. It should include support for at least five large-scale demonstration projects for underground carbon storage at different geologies around the world. Total cost: $400 million per year.[28]

I also recommend you propose a low-carbon fuel standard, to make sure the transition away from oil helps reduce emissions of heat-trapping gases. The standard should be modeled on the one signed into law by California Governor Arnold Schwarzenegger in fall 2006.

Under the low-carbon fuel standard, fuel blenders would be required to distribute fuels with steadily decreasing carbon emissions, measured on a life-cycle basis. Credits used to implement this law would be fully tradeable. This would help ensure coal resources are used in ways fully consistent with our global warming objectives.

FROM THE DESK OF THE PRESIDENT

Key points on coal
- U.S. has 100 + year supply
- Coal-to-liquids very expensive
- Coal-to-liquids could make global warming much worse (almost twice the emissions of oil!)
- Need big investment in underground carbon storage

NOTE FOR THE PRESIDENT

FROM: SECRETARY OF THE INTERIOR

SUBJECT: Article about Jon Tester

You asked for articles about thoughtful people working on energy issues. I thought you might be interested in the attached.

★ ★ ★ ★ ★

Jon Tester, Senator-Farmer

Senator Jon Tester's office walls are bare as he walks in to greet me. He's new to Washington and has plainly had higher priorities than interior decorating. As we talk, one priority becomes clear—freeing the United States from dependence on oil.

"America needs a new energy future," says the freshman Senator from Montana. "We need to end our addiction to oil and use homegrown renewable energy."

From his seat on the Senate Energy Committee, Jon Tester could help make that happen. As he talks, it's clear energy is a topic Tester knows well.

Biodiesel. Wind energy. Renewable portfolio standards. Coal. Utility deregulation. Tester has something to say on all these and more.

Tester's words grow from a background that's no longer typical in the U.S. Senate.

Jon Tester is a working farmer. A big man with a flat-top crew-cut, he looks the part.

Tester tells me he's heading back to his farm this weekend to prepare for spring planting. His daughter and son-in-law have been helping out and may move in soon. In the meantime, he's been on the farm most weekends, staying close to the soil.

That soil, he tells me, is especially good for growing oilseeds, which can be used to make biodiesel.

Montana soils are good for growing oilseeds, such as canola, camelina and mustard. According to one Montana State University study, the potential of canola and camelina for making fuel is especially high. With a crusher and some other basic equipment, oilseeds can produce biodiesel useable in most tractors, trucks and other heavy equipment. And oilseeds can be grown year-round.

"Alternatives and choices. That's really the issue," says Tester. He can't see how it makes sense to ship oil from distant lands to states as rich in natural resources as Montana.

Oil seeds can be converted to fuel near where they're grown, he says. This could help help create thousands of new jobs. Why, he wonders, should farmers pay for petroleum diesel? If we set aside just 10% more of our agricultural land for fuel production, Tester says, it would help make a dent in the oil problem.

As we talk, the conversation keeps coming back to Montana. Tester may be sitting in an office in Washington, D.C., but it's clear a big part of him is in his hometown of Big Sandy (population 643).

The winds blow strong and steady across his farm, Tester tells me. Montana is rich in wind energy, he says. (Some people call the northern Great Plains the "Saudi Arabia of wind.")

Tester thinks the U.S. approach to wind power is too short-term. The wind industry has grown with the support of a federal tax credit, but that credit must be renewed every two years. This limits investment and makes long-term financial forecasts for wind projects difficult. Tester believes the tax credit should be extended for 15 years.

Montana is rich in another natural resource—coal. Montana mines produced $290 million of coal in 2006, providing jobs for more than 950 people.

"You cannot disregard coal," says Tester.

Tester is enthusiastic about coal, but sounds a note of caution. "Any coal development must occur in an environmentally sound manner," he says. The biggest concern is coal's contribution to global warming.

"Unless you've got your head buried in the sand," says Tester, "it's clear global warming is happening." In Montana, he says, 8 of the last 10 years have been a drought. He believes the world's scientists have spoken on global warming with a clear voice we should all heed.

Tester supports an aggressive program of federal research on clean coal technologies. He believes coal resources should be developed while finding ways to capture heat-trapping gases, remove toxins such as mercury and reclaim the land after surface mining.

Tester next raises the complex topic of utility deregulation. This is the issue that first drew him into politics. In Montana, he says, utility deregulation "simply didn't work." As we talk, it's clear that Jon Tester, Senator-farmer, is no political neophyte.

Tester served in the Montana legislature for eight years, including several terms as president of the Montana Senate. That experience taught him a lot about the legislative process.

As Montana senate president, Tester passed 26 out of 40 bills introduced. One of those bills required Montana utilities to get 15% of their energy from renewable sources by 2015. Tester thinks the United States should have a similar law and intends to push for such legislation in the U.S. Senate.

As a state legislator, Tester earned a reputation for political savvy. He also earned a reputation as a nice guy. One reporter who went looking around Big Sandy for someone to criticize Jon Tester came up empty.

But above all else, Jon Tester is a Montana farmer. He told one reporter, "I do some of my best thinking on my tractor." And during one heated campaign debate, this future member of the Senate Energy Committee said, "If I weren't here right now, I'd be out getting a vegetable press so I could press my own oil to burn in my tractors."

I'm guessing that, next time I'm back, his walls will be filled with pictures of Montana.[1]

MEMORANDUM FOR THE PRESIDENT

FROM: SECRETARY OF ENERGY

SUBJECT: Hydrogen Fuels

Hydrogen is the most abundant element in the universe. It burns cleanly, without local air pollutants or heat-trapping gases.

Hydrogen fuels could play an important role in vehicles in the long term. Yet there are few if any experts who believe such fuels could have a significant impact on U.S. oil dependence during the next 25 years.

- First, although hydrogen is abundant, it does not exist in nature in usable form. To be used in vehicles, hydrogen must be separated from the compounds in which it occurs naturally (such as water, natural gas, oil or coal). Current methods for doing this are extremely expensive, polluting or both.

- Second, hydrogen cannot be distributed in standard liquid fuel tanks. (The temperature required to convert hydrogen to a liquid is minus 423 degrees Fahrenheit, only 36 degrees above absolute zero.)[1] Massive changes in the nation's fuel distribution infrastructure would be required to accommodate hydrogen-fueled vehicles.

Research on hydrogen-fueled vehicles should be pursued. Pilot projects—such as using hydrogen to run municipal bus fleets—could pay dividends. Yet without technological breakthroughs and staggering investments, hydrogen's impact on U.S. oil dependence will be quite limited for decades to come.[2]

1. BACKGROUND
Hydrogen makes up less than 0.0001% of the Earth's atmosphere. There are no underground reservoirs of the gas. However hydrogen is found in great abundance on the Earth, bound into the molecules of other substances.[3] Hydrogen was recognized as a discrete substance in the 18th century by the British scientist Henry Cavendish, who combined acid solutions and metals to produce "inflammable air."[4]

Hydrogen's potential to move vehicles has been recognized for many years. In 1874, Jules Verne published *The Mysterious Island*, in which a character says:

> I believe that water will one day serve as our fuel, that the hydrogen and oxygen which compose it, used alone or together, will supply an inexhaustible source of heat and light, burning with an intensity that coal cannot equal. One day, in the place of coal, the coal bunkers of steamers and the tenders of locomotives will be loaded with these two compressed gases, which will burn in the furnaces with an enormous heating power. [5]

Nine decades later, the National Aeronautics and Space Administration (NASA) began using hydrogen fuel cells to power spacecraft. NASA's technology was strikingly similar to the one envisioned by Verne.

During the 1990s, the Clinton administration launched a transportation fuel cell program and several leading automakers announced substantial investments in the technology. In 1997, Daimler-Benz and Ballard Power Systems announced a $350 million program. Daimler then merged with Chrysler, and Ford later joined the venture, bringing the combined investment to more than $1 billion. Nissan, Honda and Mitsubishi launched a $1 billion fuel cell venture. GM and Toyota each announced plans to put hydrogen cars on the road by 2010. [6]

In 2002, President George W. Bush announced a partnership with automakers to conduct research on hydrogen-powered vehicles. In his 2003 State of the Union address, Bush launched a hydrogen fuels initiative, with the long-term goal of moving hydrogen-powered vehicles "from laboratory to showroom." Federal spending on these programs has been in the range of $200–$300 million per year. [7]

In 2004, California Governor Arnold Schwarzenegger announced the California hydrogen highway, with the goal of providing access to hydrogen fuel along all of California's highways by 2010. [8]

Despite this enthusiasm, several leading analyses suggest that hydrogen fuels have very limited potential to reduce oil dependence in the short or medium term. The International Energy Agency estimates that hydrogen production costs need to be reduced "3- to 10-fold" and fuel cell costs cut "10 to 50-fold" for hydrogen to play a major role in transportation systems. The IEA estimates that "a transition to hydrogen would require infrastructure investment in the range of several hundred billion to a few trillion dollars, over several decades."[9] In a 2004 study, the U.S. National Academy of Sciences concluded:

> Although a transition to hydrogen could greatly transform the U.S. energy system in the long run, the impacts on oil imports and CO_2 emissions are likely to be minor during the next 25 years.[10]

Producing, distributing, and using hydrogen in vehicles at reasonable cost would require dramatic technological advances. These are explored below.

2. PRODUCING HYDROGEN

To be used in vehicles, hydrogen must first be extracted from natural gas, water or other compounds.

Hydrogen is already used for industrial purposes in large amounts. Most of this hydrogen comes from natural gas.[11] When natural gas is combined with pressurized steam, using a process called "steam reformation," the result is hydrogen and carbon dioxide.[12]

However, there are several problems with using this process to produce hydrogen for vehicles. First, steam reforming is expensive. To compete with gasoline, costs would need to fall by at least a factor of four. Yet steam reformation is a mature technology and many experts believe cost reductions of that magnitude are unlikely.[13]

Second, natural gas is subject to supply disruptions, just like oil. Although natural gas markets are now generally regional, the long-term trend is toward global trade. Roughly 40% of the world's natural gas reserves are in the Persian Gulf.[14] Trading dependence on oil for dependence on natural gas would have uncertain national security benefits.

Third, the global warming benefits of steam reformation are modest at best. The process itself produces carbon dioxide, the leading heat-trapping gas, as a by-product. Emissions are less than from burning oil, but hardly trivial. Furthermore, it takes energy to make steam. Generating that energy usually creates emissions. Finally, leaks are a potential problem. Natural gas is a potent greenhouse gas, trapping 20 times more heat per molecule than carbon dioxide. A 2003 MIT study found that—in light of all these factors—the global warming impacts of fuel cell vehicles would likely be no better than hybrid-electric cars.[15]

Hydrogen can also be extracted from water. This can be done with a process called "electrolysis," familiar to many high school chemistry students. In electrolysis, an electric current is passed through water, producing bubbles of hydrogen and oxygen.

This process is expensive too. Costs would need to fall roughly 4 to 10 times for hydrogen from electrolysis to compete with gasoline. Electricity costs would need to fall below 2 cents per kilowatt-hour—less than a quarter of the national average.[16]

Furthermore, replacing U.S. gasoline consumption with hydrogen made from electrolysis would double electricity consumption in the United States.[17] Generating that additional electricity with coal would substantially increase emissions of heat-trapping gases. Generating that additional electricity with nuclear power would be expensive, controversial, and create nuclear waste problems the nation does not know how to solve.[18] Generating that additional electricity with wind power would require increasing capacity by more than 100 times.

Mixing and matching among these different power sources is certainly possible, but the key point is this: Replacing oil with hydrogen extracted from water would not necessarily save energy. It would require large additional amounts of electricity generation. Overall environmental and economic impacts would vary, depending on how that was done.

There are other possible sources of hydrogen, but all create similar problems. Coal is rich in hydrogen, but the process of extracting it creates carbon dioxide, which must then be released to the atmosphere or stored underground. Biomass can be used to produce hydrogen, but costs are high. Even gasoline can be used to generate hydrogen, though obviously this would have no benefits in terms of reducing dependence on oil.

Producing hydrogen for use in vehicles is not impossible. But it would be expensive, potentially polluting and would require large amounts of energy.

3. DISTRIBUTING HYDROGEN
Getting hydrogen supplies to hundreds of millions of vehicles could be an even bigger challenge.

The United States has a vast network for distributing liquid fuels, including almost 169,000 retail service stations.[19] This network can be used to distribute ethanol, biodiesel and other biofuels with little or no modification. The United States also has a vast network for distributing electricity, with wires reaching into almost every home and business. This network can be used to recharge electric cars, such as plug-in hybrids. However, the United States has no network for distributing hydrogen to vehicles. Hydrogen cannot be dispensed through the liquid fuel tanks found in current service stations. To dispense hydrogen, a service station would need new types of tanks, capable of handling pressurized gaseous material or supercooled liquids. The costs would be considerable.

A hydrogen distribution infrastructure could be built in several ways. Hydrogen could be produced at central locations and then shipped by pipeline and trucks to retail service stations. However, hydrogen pipelines are very expensive—approximately $500,000 to $1 million per mile.[20] Trucks could carry canisters of compressed hydrogen, although each truck could only carry a small amount of hydrogen (even at the maximum feasible compression). To transport the same amount of energy as contained in one gasoline tanker, 10 trucks of compressed hydrogen would be needed.[21] Trucks could carry liquid hydrogen, although supercooling to hydrogen to a liquid state requires large amounts of energy.

Hydrogen could also be produced at individual service stations. This could involve small-scale equipment for steam reformation of natural gas at each location.

Hydrogen could also be produced at homes heated with natural gas, using similar devices. Honda has built a prototype home refueling station that could be installed in a garage.[22]

Under any of the approaches, costs would be huge. Retrofitting a service station for hydrogen costs about $1 million.[23] (In contrast, retrofitting a gasoline tank for ethanol costs about $4,000.) Adding hydrogen capability to half the nation's service stations would cost almost $85 billion.

Overall infrastructure costs for a hydrogen distribution network are likely to be astronomical. A study from Argonne National Laboratory put the price tag at $600 billion.[24] As noted previously, the International Energy Agency estimates that global costs for all hydrogen infrastructure costs, including distribution networks, would be in the range of "several hundred billion to a few trillion dollars, over several decades."[25]

4. USING HYDROGEN

Hydrogen can be used to move vehicles in two ways. First, hydrogen can be injected into a fuel cell, similar to the kind NASA uses for spacecraft. Second, hydrogen can be used in a conventional (though slightly modified) internal combustion engine.

a. *Fuel Cells*

The idea behind a fuel cell is simple. Hydrogen is injected into one end of a box and oxygen is injected into the other. The hydrogen passes over a material that looks like plastic kitchen wrap. This material lets protons from the hydrogen pass through, while siphoning off the electrons. On one side of the box, protons combine with oxygen to form water. On the other side, electrons gather and become useable electricity.[26]

Fuel cells are quiet and clean, with no moving parts. They are extremely reliable, operating in some cases without disruption as much as 99.9999% of the time. (This reliability has high value to customers whose business requires uninterrupted flow of electricity.) Fuel cells are highly efficient, sometimes capturing as much as 80% of the energy in a hydrogen molecule for useful work.[27]

However, the barriers to commercial production of fuel cell vehicles are considerable. First, costs are very high. The prototype cars built so far cost roughly $1 million apiece. Costs would decline substantially with mass production, but significant technological advances are needed before fuel cell vehicles could be sold at a commercially acceptable price. Second, the water in fuel cells freezes in cold weather. Engineering advances are needed to make sure fuel cells perform well in subfreezing temperatures. Third, fuel cells are delicate. The reliability demonstrated by stationary fuel cells could not be achieved by fuel cells in a vehicle with existing technology. Engineering advances are also needed to be sure fuel cells can withstand the wear and tear of the road.[28]

Major automakers have invested several billion dollars in fuel cell research in the past decade. Results so far have been modest. In 1997, Daimler-Benz pledged to put 100,000 fuel cell cars on the road by 2010. Other automakers committed to put hydrogen cars into production between 2004 and 2010.[29] So far, however, fewer than 900 fuel cell cars have been built.[30] Today, Honda, Toyota and GM each pledge to commercialize fuel cell cars in the decade between 2010 and 2020.[31]

b. *Hydrogen Internal Combustion Engines*
Hydrogen can also be used in internal combustion engines (ICEs). The design is similar to gasoline-powered engines, although very large tanks are needed to store the hydrogen on board.

Hydrogen ICEs are much cheaper to manufacture than fuel cells. Tailpipe emissions are negligible. However, much more hydrogen is needed per mile traveled than with a fuel cell. (ICEs are much less efficient than fuel cells at converting energy into useful work.) On a life-cycle basis, running an internal combustion engine on hydrogen from natural gas would create roughly the same emissions of heat-trapping gases as running a car on gasoline.[32]

BMW is currently producing the Hydrogen 7, a gasoline-hydrogen hybrid, in small numbers. Because of the need for large tanks for hydrogen storage, the car is offered only in limo-length models.[33] Ford has announced plans to produce airport vans using hydrogen internal combustion engines.[34] The combination of large size, short distances, and central refueling make airport vans a perfect market for the hydrogen internal combustion engine.

Key points on hydrogen—
- burns clean — no tailpipe pollution
- doesn't exist in nature in usable form
- need <u>lots</u> of energy to produce it
- cannot be distributed in liquid fuel
  tanks — astronomical costs to convert
  gas stations

- no impact on oil dependence for many years

MEMORANDUM FOR THE PRESIDENT

FROM: SECRETARY OF TRANSPORTATION
               SECRETARY OF HOUSING AND URBAN
               DEVELOPMENT

SUBJECT: Smart Growth

You asked how smart growth policies could contribute to your goal of reducing oil dependence.

First, a definition. "Smart growth" means metropolitan development that emphasizes livable neighborhoods, less traffic and thriving urban centers. It is an alternative to urban sprawl.

Policies to promote smart growth can help improve the lives of millions of Americans, while reducing oil dependence. This memo provides background and offers several recommendations.

1. VEHICLE MILES TRAVELED
Americans drive almost 3 trillion miles each year. The number is difficult to grasp. To reach it, roughly 240 million vehicles drive, on average, more than 12,000 miles each.[1]

The number of "vehicle miles traveled" (VMT) in the United States has been increasing for decades, although the rate of growth is slowing. Average annual VMT increased by roughly 4.3% in the 1970s, 3.2% in the 1980s, 2.5% in the 1990s and just under 2.0% in this decade.[2]

VMT increases have significant implications for your oil dependence objectives. If the number of vehicle miles traveled continues to increase, offsetting increases in alternative fuels and/or fuel efficiency will be needed each year for oil use in vehicles simply to remain constant. Yet consider:

- The record—breaking growth of the ethanol industry during the past half-decade-at its peak—added roughly 1% to the total transportation fuel supply each year. Maintaining or increasing this rate of growth would require technological breakthroughs in biofuels production, ethanol imports and/or rapid electrification of the auto fleet.

• Recently, proposals to improve the fuel efficiency of new cars and light trucks by 4% per year have been controversial. New cars and light trucks make up roughly 1/14th of the vehicle fleet. If their fuel efficiency improves 4% annually, fleetwide fuel efficiency improvements would be much less—roughly 0.3% in Year 1, 0.6% in Year 2 and 0.9% in Year 3, reaching 2% in Year 6. Although this is a potentially powerful tool for offsetting VMT increases, significant and sustained fuel efficiency improvements would be required.[3]

To some extent, the many miles driven reflect Americans love of automobiles. Cars have been central to our culture for decades, often providing convenience, privacy and comfort. In one recent poll, 39% of Americans said they "love" their car.[4]

Yet for millions of Americans, daily driving is an unhappy burden. Complaints about long commutes and time spent driving children vast distances are regular features of modern American life. This unhappiness is widespread and growing.

Polls consistently find most drivers reporting that traffic in their area has gotten worse. Drivers report spending more time in their cars each day— up from a 49-minute average in 1990 to 62 minutes today. In a recent national poll, 36% of drivers said they disliked their daily commute. Not surprisingly, the longer the daily commute, the more drivers dislike it.[5]

In a 2005 poll in the Washington, D.C. area, 60% of commuters said they disliked their daily commute, with 23% saying they disliked it a great deal. One in five said they had left jobs or changed jobs primarily to improve their commute to work. More than one in four said they got stuck at least once a day.[6]

2. THE SPRAWL PROBLEM
"Sprawl" is a combination of low density housing subdivisions, shopping centers, office parks and roadways. It has become the dominant pattern of metropolitan development in the United States.[7]

Automobile dependence is a central feature of sprawl. Residents of subdivisions must use cars to go to shops, schools, parks and work. Distances are too great to walk. Mass transit is unavailable. Single-purpose zoning separates places people live from places they work and play.

Sprawl increases both VMT and gasoline consumption. One study analyzed the impact of moving sample households "from a city with measures of urban form and transit supply identical to those of Atlanta to a city with measures the same as those of Boston." The result: VMT fell by 25%.[8] Another study found that more than 60% of the growth in VMT during the 1980s and 1990s was due to land use factors.[9] Yet another found that, during the same period, gasoline consumption was 50% greater per person in Phoenix and Houston than Chicago or Washington, D.C.[10] One study found 2.3 billion gallons of gasoline wasted due to traffic congestion in 2005.[11]

Traffic congestion. *Source: Getty Images North America, photographer: Justin Sullivan.*

Unhappiness with sprawl is widespread. Bipartisan coalitions have been formed to promote "smart growth" as an alternative. Many cities, including Austin, Texas, Portland, Oregon and Wichita, Kansas have launched major smart growth initiatives.[12]

One popular approach is "transit-oriented development"—building mixed-use communities around transit stations. High-density development within short distances of transit stations can provide many drivers with an alternative to congested traffic and lengthy commutes. Greater investment in transit systems is also a priority. Most major metropolitan areas have new rail or rapid bus systems under development.[13]

Land use is historically a state and local function, not a federal one.[14] Much of the advocacy related to smart growth is community-based, focusing on regions and cities. One leading book says "think globally, act locally, but plan regionally."[15] Yet federal policies play a central role. One survey asked urban scholars to identify the most important influences on the American metropolis in the second half of the 20th century. Their answer: "The overwhelming impact of the federal government...especially through policies that intentionally or unintentionally promoted suburbanization and sprawl."[16]

The two most important influences, according to these scholars, were the 1956 Interstate Highway Act and Federal Housing Administration mortgages.

Quantifying the impact of smart growth policies on oil dependence presents challenges. Policies often take many years to implement, during which time other variables (such as oil prices and characteristics of the vehicle fleet) change substantially. One recent study, based on extensive statistical analyses, concludes that "...programs that alter urban form and transit supply are potentially valuable tools available to policymakers interested in reducing the social cost of driving."[17] Another recent study found that doubling ridership on mass transit nationally could save 1.4 billion gallons of gasoline per year.[18] This is roughly 1% of U.S. gasoline consumption.

Smart growth policies alone cannot end oil dependence. But they can have an impact on growth in VMT, helping reduce oil consumption while at the same time improving quality of life for millions of Americans.

3. THE ROAD BUILDING PARADOX

If a road is frequently crowded, will building more lanes help ease congestion? Surprisingly, the likely answer is no.

As Brookings economist Anthony Downs has written:

> Unfortunately, once heavy peak-hour congestion has appeared in key parts of a region's road network, building new roads or expanding existing ones there does not reduce the intensity of such congestion much in the long run. Once commuters realize the capacity of specific roads has been increased, they will quickly shift their routes, timing, and modes of travel by moving to those roads during peak periods, thereby filling up the expanded capacity.[19]

One expert summed it up by saying: "Trying to cure traffic congestion by building more roads is like trying to cure obesity by loosening your belt." One study of 30 California counties over several decades found that, for every 10% increase in road capacity, traffic increased by 9% within four years.[20]

Nevertheless, federal transportation policy often encourages new road-building, paying for 80–90% of the cost of new roads and rarely requiring rigorous assessments of land use impacts.[21]

To reduce traffic congestion, congestion pricing is a far more effective tool. A growing body of experience with these programs in cities such as London, Stockholm and Singapore is demonstrating their potential for impact. High Occupancy Vehicle lanes can also help speed traffic flow. But the standard practice in the United States for much of the past 50 years—building more roads—generally doesn't work

4. <u>POLICY RECOMMENDATIONS</u>

I recommend you propose the following as part of your oil dependence speech:

a. *Promote telecommuting*

Telecommuting means working from home. With revolutionary changes in communications and information technology, millions more Americans can telecommute than ever before. Many companies report significant improvements in worker productivity and employee job satisfaction due to telecommuting.[22]

The oil savings from growth in telecommuting could be substantial. According to one study, if every white collar worker in the United States telecommuted two days per week, total U.S. gasoline consumption would fall by roughly 8%.[23] Although that amount of telecommuting is unlikely, the analysis suggests that growth in telecommuting could play a meaningful role in offsetting VMT growth in the years ahead. Further advances in broadband and mobile telecommunications technology are likely to continue reducing barriers to telecommuting for years to come.

Federal agencies have offered employees telecommuting options for many years.[24] Programs for the early 1990s encouraged telecommuting as a tool for fighting global warming. Legislation passed in 2000 required "[e]ach executive agency [to] establish a policy under which eligible employees of the agency may participate in telecommuting to the maximum extent possible without diminished employee performance."[25]

Telecommuting continued to receive support in this decade, in part as an element of security planning. Federal managers saw telecommuting as a tool for contributing to continuity of operations after a disruption such as a pandemic or terrorist attack. In June 2007, the U.S. Office of Personnel Management reported that 6.6% of the federal workforce were regular telecommuters.[26]

However, more can be done to encourage telecommuting in both the public and private sectors. I recommend that you:

- Invite the CEOs of 20 of the nation's largest companies to a White House Conference on Telecommuting, asking each to report on steps their companies have taken to encourage telecommuting. The invitations to this event and surrounding publicity will prompt thousands of managers around the country to review the potential for telecommuting in their companies.

- Urge Congress to pass legislation to prevent double taxation of telecommuters who live in a different state than their employer's office.[27]

- Direct all federal managers to review their plans for telecommuting and provide new plans for overcoming barriers to expanding telecommuting within six months.

Using the bully pulpit of the Presidency, you can help promote this popular tool for improving worker productivity and saving oil.

b. *Promote Mass Transit*

Billions of dollars are spent on transportation projects each year by the federal government. The bias toward road construction over mass transit is extreme. From the federal gas tax, more than five times as much revenue is dedicated to the Highway Account as to the Mass Transit Account.[28]

Furthermore, the rules governing federal expenditures for road construction are more generous and lenient than those for mass transit projects. For example, the federal government typically provides 80–90% of the funds for a highway project, but only 50–60% for a transit project. The justifications required for highway projects are much less rigorous and extensive than those for transit projects. Highway projects often proceed without careful consideration of land use impacts, while evaluation of those impacts is often central to decisions on mass transit projects.[29]

I recommend you:

- Announce a historic shift in the allocation of federal transportation funding, with the goal of achieving parity between road building and mass transit expenditures in the years ahead. Federal support for repair of older roads is essential, but funding should in general be shifted from new road construction in urban areas to mass transit.

- Require oil consumption impact assessments before new roads are built in metropolitan areas. The methodology for these assessments should include a presumption that such roads will not improve traffic congestion, absent an affirmative demonstration to the contrary.

- Strengthen the Community Reinvestment Act, encouraging banks to invest in neighborhood renovation

- In major metropolitan areas, require express lanes for the most fuel efficient cars as a condition of receiving federal highway funds.

- Explore federal tax incentives (such as accelerated depreciation) for construction or renovation within one-half mile of a transit stop.

5. CONCLUSION

Americans are driving more and enjoying it less. Long commutes and crowded roads are growing problems across the nation. Your oil dependence speech provides an important opportunity to promote policies that will both improve the day-to-day lives of millions of Americans while reducing oil consumption.

Key points on smart growth—

- Americans driving more and enjoying it less
- More roads don't cure traffic congestion! ("Trying to cure traffic congestion by building more roads is like trying to cure obesity by loosening your belt.")
- Federal policies favor road-building over mass transit. Need to level the playing field.
- Telecommuting can cut oil use while improving productivity and quality of life.

from the desk of the
SECRETARY OF AGRICULTURE

I thought you might be interested in this, for your oil dependence speech.

★ ★ ★ ★ ★

A Visit to Biotown, USA

I arrive in the Indianapolis Airport, on my way to Reynolds, Indiana. At the rental car counter, here in the heart of ethanol country, I ask for a flex fuel car—the kind that takes either gasoline or ethanol.

"Sorry sir, we don't carry them," I'm told.

Which reminds me of the problem the good people of Reynolds, Indiana, are trying to solve.

Reynolds is a town of 547 people 100 miles north of Indianapolis. The drive there is an unbroken expanse of straight roads and corn fields. Reynolds is a farm town, like thousands around the nation. But in one way, Reynolds stands out.

Reynolds is trying to become the first community to meet all its energy needs with renewable resources. The sign on the way into town says "Welcome to Biotown." The people of Reynolds want to become a model for the nation.

One afternoon in May, I sit at the Country Crossroads restaurant in Reynolds with the town president, Charlie van Voorst, and two officials from the Energy Office of the Indiana state government.

Van Voorst is a big, friendly man. "We're a farm town," he tells me. "Mainly hogs and corn. Also some cattle."

Several years ago Charlie agreed to serve as a member of the town board. It was a low-key position and didn't involve much time. Then some folks from Indianapolis came calling.

One was Brandon Seitz. Seitz, who worked for Republicans in the state legislature and then on the campaign of Gov. Mitch

Daniels, sits across from me, dressed in jeans and a plaid shirt, telling his part of the story.

The idea had kicked around for years, Seitz tells me. Find a town in Indiana. See whether it could meet all its energy needs with renewable resources.

It might not be easy. But you'd learn a lot trying. And it could become a model for the nation.

The project took off in early 2005 when the new governor, Mitch Daniels, enthusiastically gave it his blessing. Seitz was appointed to a position in the new administration. He and his colleague started looking for the perfect town.

It had to be rural. It needed lots of "biomass"—plants or animal waste—that could be turned into fuel. Perhaps most important, the people of the town needed to be enthusiastic.

In spring 2005, Seitz and several colleagues went to a town meeting in Reynolds. At first, there were lots of skeptical questions. As Charlie van Voorst says, "it's hard to get people to believe in something that's never happened before."

But the more the people of Reynolds heard, the more they liked the idea. In September 2005, Gov. Daniels announced the first "Biotown USA." The goal: meet all Reynolds' energy needs with "biorenewable resources."

The first phase of the project was about vehicles. What would it take for Reynold's vehicles to run on biofuels?

First, cars and trucks that could take the stuff. Second, pumps that could dispense it. Third, a dependable source of the fuel itself.

Someone contacted General Motors. The company's "Live Green Go Yellow" advertising campaign highlights GM's commitment to flex fuel technology. More than 2 million flex fuel GM cars are already on the road. The company promises that half its new cars and trucks will be flex fuel by 2012.

GM agreed to donate 20 flex fuel cars to the Reynolds community for two years. A lottery was held, with anyone in the Reynolds zip code eligible. GM also agreed to sell anyone in Reynolds a flex fuel car or truck at deeply discounted rates.

Today, Reynolds has more than 150 flex fuel vehicles—

almost half the cars and trucks on the road (which may be the highest percentage of any community in the nation.)

Someone else starting working on fuel pumps. Soon, a pump for E85 (85% ethanol fuel) was built in the middle of town, with support from the state government.

Another team started talking with ethanol producers. Indiana already had a half dozen ethanol plants under construction. VeraSun, one of the country's largest ethanol producers, decided to build one in Reynolds.

The second phase of the project is about electricity.

Like almost every community in the nation, Reynolds draws electricity from the grid, relying on power plants hundreds of miles away. Could Reynolds really disconnect from the grid? If so, where would its energy come from?

Some energy experts came to town and gave a surprising answer: hog waste.

With more than 150,000 hogs, Reynolds has struggled with waste disposal problems for years. But as the experts pointed out, it's not difficult to turn manure into energy. Why not solve two problems at once, helping to manage the waste problem while freeing the citizens of Reynolds from dependence on the grid?

In November 2006, Rose Energy began construction on a closed-loop system for taking animal waste, municipal waste, and crop residues and turning them into electricity. The same process will produce fertilizer and biodiesel as well.

Today, almost two years after the first conversations, Reynolds is on the way to getting all its energy from renewable sources. But it still has a long way to go.

I ask Charlie van Voorst what the people of Reynolds think about the project at this point. They like it, he says. If anything, they're impatient. They want to see more progress quickly.

"We want to be able to showcase Reynolds," says Charlie. "That is the whole idea—to change the country. To make a difference."

"When you buy E85," he says, "that money goes right to a farmer, not overseas to buy bullets to kill a neighbor's boy."

I ask Charlie what he thinks about the state government team that's been lending a hand. Charlie sings their praises. "They're here to help," he says. "We have a great relationship."

As I leave, I thank Charlie for his time. I tell him I may write a profile of him for a project I'm working on.

"Don't talk just about me," says Charlie. "Talk about the community."

I get back in the car to drive to the airport. As I do, I turn on the small black box I picked up for $10 per day at the rental car counter. This remarkable machine, constantly beaming signals to Global Positioning System satellites far above, not only finds the best way to the airport, it talks to me as I drive, telling me which way to turn.

I never even imagined such a machine when I was a child. Since then, new information and communications technologies have changed the world.

Can new energy technologies do the same? The people of Reynolds, Indiana, are working on it.[1]

MEMORANDUM TO THE PRESIDENT

FROM: SECRETARY OF ENERGY

SUBJECT: Strategic Petroleum Reserve

The federal government maintains a strategic petroleum reserve (SPR) of
approximately 700 million barrels of oil, equivalent to roughly 33 days of
U.S. consumption.[1] The oil is stored in underground caverns in Texas and
Louisiana. The President is authorized to release oil from the SPR in
response to disruptions in energy supply.

The strategic petroleum reserve can help manage several problems created
by oil dependence. However, the SPR was not established to solve the full
range of these problems, nor could it do so even with far-reaching
reforms. This memorandum explores the background of the SPR, its
benefits and limitations and some sensible proposals for modifying it. The
memorandum recommends several reforms to the SPR you could propose
in connection with your upcoming oil dependence speech.

1. BACKGROUND
  a. *History of the Strategic Petroleum Reserve*
The Strategic Petroleum Reserve was established by the Energy Policy
and Conservation Act of 1975. Initial plans called for storing enough oil to
replace imports for 90 days. The President was authorized to draw down
reserves completely, in response to a "severe energy supply disruption," and
partially, in response to less serious shortages.

Oil from the SPR has been sold on the open market twice in response to
supply disruptions. In January, 1991, 21 million barrels were sold as
hostilities were launched in Operation Desert Storm. In September 2005,
11 million barrels were sold in the wake of Hurricane Katrina. Oil from
the SPR has been exchanged with individual oil companies to help
manage short-term supply problems on roughly a dozen occasions.

The physical limit on withdrawals from the strategic petroleum reserve is
approximately 4.4 million barrels per day. The Department of Energy can

deliver oil from the SPR into the marketplace within 13 days of on order from the President for an emergency sale.

The Strategic Petroleum Reserve stores crude oil only, not refined products such as gasoline. This limits the benefits of the SPR in the event of widespread problems with refinery operations, such as occurred following Hurricane Katrina. Refined products in general cannot be stored indefinitely, unlike crude oil.

At $60 per barrel, the total value of oil in the SPR is more than $40 billion. If that were converted to financial assets paying 5% annual interest, the return would be $2 billion per year.

The Energy Policy Act of 2005 required the Secretary of Energy to increase the amount of oil in the strategic petroleum reserve to 1 billion gallons. This exceeds the current capacity of caverns dedicated to the SPR. Work is under way to increase this capacity as well as to build a new site—a process projected to take roughly 10 years. In his 2007 State of the Union address, President George W. Bush called for doubling the size of the SPR.[2]

b. *Other Reserves*
Roughly 1.5 billion barrels of oil are held in strategic reserves by governments around the world. European governments hold more than 400 million barrels and Japan holds 300 million. China is just beginning to develop strategic reserves, but plans to increase them significantly in the years ahead.[3]

Commercial oil inventories are several times larger than government stockpiles. In early 2007, commercial stockpiles in the United States and Europe each held roughly one billion barrels of oil. These inventories fluctuate, sometimes significantly, depending on the price of oil.[4]

Members of the International Energy Agency (IEA) are required to maintain petroleum reserves equal to 90 days of net imports. This requirement can be met with a combination of government and private sector reserves.[5]

IEA member states agree to work cooperatively in the event of a significant oil supply disruption. Possible steps include releasing oil from strategic stocks, restraining demand, switching to other fuels, or increasing domestic production. The IEA has acted pursuant to these provisions twice—once in 1991 in response to the Gulf War and once in 2005 in response to Hurricane Katrina. In September 2005, IEA member states made 60 million barrels of oil and refined product available.[6]

2. LIMITATIONS OF THE STRATEGIC PETROLEUM RESERVE

The Strategic Petroleum Reserve is designed to address one specific problem related to oil dependence: the risk of short-term disruptions in crude oil supply. This risk is certainly real, as the world discovered during the 1970s.

However, several observations are in order.

First, the SPR is not intended to address other problems related to oil dependence, such as:

- Short-term price spikes related to psychological factors (e.g., concern among traders that international tensions might cause a disruption in supply)

- Short-term price spikes related to disruptions in refinery capacity (as occurred after Hurricane Katrina)

- Price increases related to demand growth (as during 2003–2006)

- Global warming and other pollution related to oil use

- Accumulation of vast wealth by leaders of oil-exporting nations that wish us ill

- Disruptive impact of oil revenues on democracy

- Casualties sustained by U.S. combat troops while securing oil supply lines in combat

Second, even with reforms, the SPR could not address most of the foregoing problems. The SPR is at most a palliative, designed to replace disrupted crude oil supplies and thereby dampen short-term price volatility. This is an important function. Yet the SPR cannot, by its nature, address problems such as long-term mismatches between supply and demand, pollution caused by oil consumption or some of the disruptive impacts of oil on both political development and geopolitics.

Third, electrification of the vehicle fleet would provide benefits similar to those provided by the SPR. U.S. utilities already maintain substantial reserve generating capacity. (This "peaking power" is used when electricity demand is unusually high, such as on hot summer days.) If the vehicle fleet could connect to the electric grid, this reserve electric generating capacity would become, in effect, an additional "strategic reserve." A driver of a plug-in hybrid, for example, could adjust driving habits if oil supplies were disrupted, relying somewhat more on electricity.

3. PROPOSED REFORMS

Nevertheless, the Strategic Petroleum Reserve plays an important role. Short-term oil supply disruptions are a problem, disrupting the economy when they occur and enhancing the power of oil-exporting nations even when they don't.[7] Electrification of the vehicle fleet—which could provide significant protection against oil supply disruptions—will take many years.

Unfortunately, the SPR as currently designed is inadequate to address these problems. It cannot respond to disruptions in the supply of refined oil products such as gasoline. It often sparks political controversy. Coordination with other nations is inadequate.

I recommend two changes to the SPR:

1. The SPR should ensure that enough distilled product is available to protect against refinery disruptions. These distilled products need not be maintained in government reserves. Commercial inventories or excess refinery capacity in Europe or elsewhere may be sufficient. But widespread disruptions to refinery capacity due to weather or terrorism are possible in the years ahead, as demonstrated by Hurricane Katrina. The SPR should take on the function of ensuring readily available reserves are at hand.

2. Authority for day-to-day management of the SPR should be transferred to an independent body, similar to the Federal Reserve.[8] Managing a body with such a sensitive mandate requires independence and substantial market expertise. The President would retain authority to order a release in the event of a threat to national security, but routine releases would be handled by the independent body.

In addition, the United States should seek to change the terms of agreement on this topic at the International Energy Administration, which requires member countries to maintain reserves equal to 90 days of net imports. Two changes are appropriate:

1. China, India and other major oil-consuming countries that are not part of the IEA should be brought into the agreement.[9]

2. The requirement should be calibrated in terms of a country's total oil consumption, not net imports. Because oil prices are set on a global market, net imports are of secondary importance in determining a country's vulnerability to price spikes. Total consumption is a more important measure.

The Strategic Petroleum Reserve cannot solve the full range of problems created by oil dependence, but it is an important tool for managing some of them. The SPR should be improved and modernized in the years ahead.

MEMORANDUM TO THE PRESIDENT

FROM: SECRETARY OF STATE

SUBJECT: Oil Dependence—Diplomatic Strategy

This memo responds to your request for a diplomatic strategy in connection with your oil dependence speech.

After careful review, I believe two points merit your particular attention:

- First, some of the national security, environmental and economic benefits anticipated from reducing U.S. oil dependence depend in part on trading partners reducing their oil dependence as well. I elaborate on this and suggest approaches for addressing it below.

- Second, the policies announced in your speech could have significant impacts on oil-exporting nations, many of whom are historic friends and allies. This memo suggests three principles for managing relationships with those countries in the months ahead.

I believe the steps recommended here will be central to the success of your oil dependence policies. Oil is traded globally. Events anywhere can influence oil markets everywhere. No policy related to oil proceeds in isolation from the rest of the world.

1. GLOBAL OIL DEPENDENCE
The United States is the world's largest oil consumer, using 24% of global production each year. Yet we are just one part of a larger global market. Europe uses roughly 18%, Japan uses 6% and China uses 9%. China's percentage is growing each year.[1]

Oil is important in every corner of the globe. In almost every country, oil provides more than 95% of the fuel used by motor vehicles. In some countries, oil is still used to generate electricity. There are wide variations in how much oil is used per person, but oil plays an important—often central—role in the economy of every nation. In the past two decades, global oil production has grown by more than a third.[2]

At the same time, the global economy is rapidly becoming more integrated. According to Federal Reserve Board Chair Ben Bernanke:

> [B]y most economically relevant measures, distances are shrinking rapidly. The shrinking globe has been a major source of the powerful wave of worldwide economic integration and increased economic interdependence. . .

Bernanke notes that global merchandise exports rose from less than 15% of global GDP in 1990 to more than 20% today, stating that this data "understate[s] the magnitude" of the economic integration we are now experiencing due to the emergence of China, India and former Communist-bloc countries.[3]

The foregoing has important implications for your oil dependence policies.

For example, one objective often cited for reducing U.S. oil dependence is greater strategic flexibility in the Persian Gulf. The political and military resources we devote to securing oil flows from the Persian Gulf make it more difficult to accomplish other important objectives, such as defeating Islamic jihadism.[4] After two wars in two decades, many Americans want the freedom to disengage from the region.

However, the global nature of oil markets and interdependence of the global economy make that more challenging. Consider a scenario in which U.S. oil dependence drops sharply but the rest of the world remains dependent on oil. A disruption in supplies from the Persian Gulf—producer of more than a quarter of the world's oil—could still send oil prices skyrocketing and trigger a global recession.[5] Yet more than 5 million U.S. jobs depend on manufacturing exports. U.S. exports to Europe and Japan alone total more than $260 billion per year.[6] Would stable oil supplies from the Persian Gulf remain a vital U.S. interest in such a scenario? In all likelihood, yes.

Another objective for reducing oil dependence is to reduce the flow of funds to unfriendly regimes. Yet if cuts in U.S. oil consumption are matched barrel for barrel with increases elsewhere, revenues to these regimes might not change. Money, like oil, is fungible. Of course, all things being equal, oil prices will be lower if the United States reduces consumption than if it doesn't. A drop in U.S. consumption might help reduce the flow of funds from what it would be otherwise, but it's unlikely to be enough.

Yet another objective in reducing oil dependence—one of the most important—is to fight global warming. Here, too, the actions of others matter greatly. Emissions reductions from U.S. vehicles are an essential part of any strategy for protecting the climate system. Yet rapidly growing oil-dependent vehicle fleets elsewhere pose a big threat as well.

In short, the problem is bigger than simply U.S. oil dependence. The problem extends to the world as a whole.

To achieve some of our objectives with respect to oil dependence, the extent of oil dependence in other countries matters greatly.

Broadly speaking, I believe there are two kinds of activities you can undertake to help the world as a whole become less dependent on oil.

First, you can launch an aggressive program to reduce U.S. oil dependence. The United States is a global leader in technology innovation, as well as the world's largest market. A bold plan to reduce oil dependence in the United States would unleash a wave of technological change that would have impacts on oil dependence around the world.

Second, you can transform oil diplomacy. Traditional oil diplomacy focuses on securing adequate and reliable supplies.[7] This will remain a necessary element of U.S. diplomacy for years to come. But the focus on oil supply could be supplemented by another: reducing oil dependence in all consuming nations.

I have consulted with the Secretary of Energy and recommend the following specific steps:

1. The Secretary of Energy could convene a conference on electrification of the auto fleet in Detroit. The Secretary would invite

energy and transportation ministers, business leaders and others. The purpose of the conference would be to highlight advances in electric vehicle technology and speed its deployment around the world.

2. You could hold an "energy summit" with the Chinese premier. Any meeting you hold with the Chinese premier will include dialogue on a wide range of topics. However, a focus on energy would highlight a topic on which many of our interests coincide and on which there is an important cooperative agenda. Such a focus could have benefits not only for your energy policy agenda, but for U.S.-China bilateral relations as well. Subject to your approval, Embassy Beijing will explore whether the premier would welcome an invitation from you to attend such a summit in your speech.

3. The Agency for International Development could launch a major program to promote sustainable biofuels programs in the least developed countries. U.S. Executive Directors at the World Bank and regional development banks could support such programs as a matter of priority. For many of the world's poorest countries, increasing costs for imported oil have dwarfed the benefits of debt relief in recent years. Indigenous biofuels production can help fight poverty while reducing global oil dependence.[8]

4. The Secretary of Energy could propose measures to modernize the International Energy Agency (IEA). The IEA was established in the 1970s, in the wake of the Arab oil embargoes. Membership is limited to members of the Organization for Economic Cooperation and Development (OECD), all of whom are industrialized countries. With the rise in energy consumption by China, India and others, this structure is outdated. You should propose measures to bring major new oil consumers within the IEA, either as full members if they are willing or in a formalized partnership.

5. The U.S. Export-Import Bank could give priority to projects that help reduce oil dependence, with improved financing terms for export of fuel efficiency and alternative fuel technologies.

Two more general steps are also key. You should give top priority to new international climate change negotiations, which can help to reduce oil dependence in the decades ahead. You can also make oil dependence a centerpiece of your personal diplomacy, raising it in all bilateral meetings, at the G–8 and other multilateral fora as well.

2. MANAGING RELATIONSHIPS WITH OIL EXPORTERS

The world's top five oil exporters are Saudi Arabia, Russia, Norway, Iran and the UAE.[9] The top five exporters to the United States are Canada, Mexico, Saudi Arabia, Venezuela and Nigeria.[10] A high-profile initiative to reduce oil dependence will have implications for all these countries.

Our relationships with these countries differ greatly, of course. So does each country's reliance on oil exports. Saudi Arabia depends on oil for roughly 90% of its export earnings, as do Nigeria and Iran. For Venezuela, the figure is 75%–80%. At the other end of the spectrum, oil provides roughly 9% of export earnings for Canada.[11]

Of particular interest is Saudi Arabia, the world's largest oil exporter. Saudi Arabia's willingness to maintain substantial spare production capacity has played an important role in managing world oil markets for decades. Despite its extraordinary oil wealth, Saudi Arabia faces considerable economic challenges, including high unemployment and one of the world's fastest growing populations. Our relationship with Saudi Arabia is complex, with multiple crosscurrents.[12]

By itself, a major speech on oil dependence might not be a big source of concern to the Saudis (or other oil exporters). Such speeches have been delivered by Presidents before you, with little impact. Yet I believe you place substantially higher priority on this topic than your predecessors. The U.S. public is ready to be mobilized on this issue. As your program to reduce oil dependence proceeds, our relationships with oil exporters could undergo changes.

Saudi Arabia might respond to a serious program to reduce oil dependence in several ways. It could withhold production, sending oil prices higher in the short term in order to dissuade political leaders from adopting such a program. I consider such a response unlikely. Were this to happen, political support for reducing oil dependence would skyrocket along with oil prices. The Saudis are unlikely to see this as being in their long-term interest.

Instead, the Saudis may be more likely to build additional production capacity, with the aim of keeping world oil prices low enough in the short term to make development of alternatives difficult. In 2005, with world oil prices reaching record highs, the Saudis undertook a major investment program in part with this objective.[13]

I recommend three principles to guide our relationships with Saudi Arabia during a period of transition:

1. *Avoid vilification.* Saudi Arabia is widely resented in this country. Attacks focused on it could help generate political support for your program. I urge you to resist that temptation.

   Saudi Arabia is of course a central player in the difficult politics of the Middle East. If the Saudi government were seeking some form of retaliatory action, it could look the other way as Saudi nationals fund surrogates to frustrate U.S. interests in Iraq, Lebanon or other parts of the Middle East. It could decide to shift dollar-denominated assets to Euros. Public criticism might not provoke such responses. However, the relationship should be managed with a clear eye toward mutual interests, not shaped by public invective.

2. *Maintain high-level communication.* Pending your approval, I will travel to Saudi Arabia on the eve of your speech. My objective will be to explain fully your policy agenda when it comes to oil dependence. I will plan to proceed from there to China with a similar objective.

3. *Promote economic diversification.* Saudi Arabia's nonoil exports have been growing at double digit rates in recent years. There is considerable interest in the Kingdom in economic diversification. Ready access to cheap natural gas could provide the basis for a highly competitive manufacturing base in the country. This is a trend we should encourage through any tools available.[14]

In general, these principles should guide our changing relations with other oil exporters as well. Additional country-specific analyses will follow.

3. <u>CONCLUSION</u>

Some of the benefits anticipated from reducing U.S. oil dependence depend in part on trading partners reducing their oil dependence as well. In addition, your oil dependence policies could have significant impacts on oil-exporting nations. For these reasons, a well-designed diplomatic strategy will be central to the success of your oil dependence policies. Such a strategy can contribute to meeting your broader foreign policy objectives as well.

PART III

Decision

MEMORANDUM FOR THE PRESIDENT

FROM: CHIEF OF STAFF

SUBJECT: Oil Dependence—Options Memo

The memos you've received contain dozens of individual policy proposals. This memo seeks your guidance on the most important items.

With the help of your advisers, I organized the proposals into six categories. They are:

- Transforming the vehicle fleet

- Transforming the fuel supply

- Improving traffic

- Investing in research

- Implementing a "tax and rebate" program

- Transforming oil diplomacy

Your advisers agree on most of the proposals summarized in this memo. There is sharp disagreement on several items, however. Those disagreements are noted below.

This memo provides very brief assessments of the pros and cons of each proposal. More detailed memos will be developed for any item if you would find that helpful.

1. TRANSFORMING THE VEHICLE FLEET
The proposals you received include:

a. *Federal Leadership*
The Secretary of Transportation recommends you issue an open order for 30,000 plug-in hybrid electric vehicles (PHEVs), offering to pay an $8,000 premium for each vehicle. You would commit to repeat this order every year following delivery of the first 30,000 vehicles, with the premium declining over time. All vehicles would meet basic performance

requirements. You would state a formal policy that half of all vehicles purchased by the federal government will be plug-in hybrids, once they become commercially available.

Legislation to amend federal procurement statutes may be necessary. Total program costs would be $1 billion, spread out over roughly a decade. The timing of expenditures would depend on the pace at which PHEVs are delivered.

_____Approve   _____Disapprove   _____More Information

b. *Grand Bargain with Detroit*
The Secretary of Transportation proposes a federal program to help pay for retooling manufacturing facilities to produce vehicles that reduce oil dependence. The Secretary recommends these payments be provided by reimbursing manufacturers for retiree health care expenses.

The Secretary of Health and Human Service is evaluating this proposal for its impact on your broader health care agenda. Costs of this program are difficult to predict, but could be capped at any level with payments allocated to the most productive investments in terms of oil savings or other factors. The recommended budget authority is $500 million a year.

_____Approve   _____Disapprove   _____More Information

c. *Consumer Tax Credits*
The Secretary of Transportation proposes consumer tax credits of up to $8,000 for purchasers of the first million plug-in hybrids and $4,000 for purchasers of the second million. Credits would be fully refundable (so Americans could benefit regardless of income) and exempt from the Alternative Minimum Tax. Cars would meet strong fuel efficiency standards when operating on their internal combustion engines to be eligible.

This program would provide a powerful incentive for growth of the plug-in hybrid market. Total cost would be $12 billion (starting out small and then building up over several years).

_____Approve   _____Disapprove   _____More Information

d. *Fuel Efficiency Standards*

The Secretary of Transportation proposes a new set of Fuel Reduction and Energy Efficiency ("FREEdom") standards. These would replace the 1970s-era Corporate Average Fuel Efficiency Standards (widely known as CAFE). Under the new standards, companywide fuel efficiency levels would no longer be relevant. Fuel efficiency requirements for new cars would be (1) based entirely on vehicle weight and other attributes, and (2) fully tradable among manufacturers. Standards would increase automatically by 4% each year.

A requirement for continuous improvement of the new car fleet would help reduce oil consumption significantly over the long term. Because improvements are incremental and the fleet turns over so slowly, short-term benefits would not be large. Previous fuel efficiency standards were plagued by unintended consequences, including the rise of sport utility vehicles.

The Secretary of Commerce and Chair of the Council of Economic Advisers object to this proposal, for somewhat different reasons. The Secretary believes this proposal would hurt U.S. automakers. The Chair of the Council of Economic Advisers believes a gasoline tax increase would be a superior tool for achieving the same results. Your other advisers support this proposal.

_____Approve   _____Disapprove   _____More Information

e. *Federal Battery Guarantee Corporation*

The Secretary of Transportation proposes establishing a Federal Battery Guarantee Corporation (FBGC). The FBGC would help spread the risk that batteries in plug-in hybrids do not last for the full life of the vehicle. It would reimburse car makers 100% of any costs incurred under extended battery warranties for the first 20,000 electric cars sold; 80% of costs under extended battery warranties for the second 20,000 sold; 60% of costs for the third 20,000; 40% of costs for the fourth 20,000; and 20% of costs for the fifth 20,000. It could adjust this schedule, within limits.

The program would directly address a core concern of auto manufacturers reluctant to bring PHEVs to market. It would stimulate improvements in battery technology, making the program itself less important over time.

According to the Secretary, costs are difficult to estimate, but no more than $500 million over 10 years.

_____Approve   _____Disapprove   _____More Information

2. TRANSFORMING THE FUEL SUPPLY

a. *E85 Pumps*
The Secretary of Agriculture recommends legislation requiring all major oil companies to retrofit tanks for E85 at 50% of their owned or branded stations. The Secretary also recommends legislation prohibiting franchise agreements that limit pumps for biofuels at service stations.

Lack of a retail fuel distribution network is a critical barrier limiting growth of biofuels. However, some second-generation biofuels (such as biobutanol) might be compatible with existing, overcoming this problem without retrofits. Costs of retrofits to oil companies would be roughly $300 million. Federal budget costs would be minimal.

The Secretary of Commerce does not support this proposal, expressing concern about interference with core business operations of the oil companies. Your other advisers support this proposal.

_____Approve   _____Disapprove   _____More Information

b. *Ethanol Tax Credit*
The Secretary of Agriculture recommends making the ethanol tax credit variable, depending on the price of oil. (If oil prices decrease, the credit would increase, and vice versa.) The Secretary also recommends a 30-cent-per-gallon additional credit for the first 50 billion gallons of cellulosic ethanol and other advanced biofuels produced in the U.S. The Secretary recommends these credits be put in place for 10 years.

The cost of making the tax credit variable depends on the future price of oil and is therefore uncertain. The additional credit for advanced biofuels would cost $15 billion total, spread out over roughly the next decade.

_____Approve   _____Disapprove   _____More Information

c. *Ethanol Tariff*

The U.S. Trade Representative recommends phasing out the 54-cent-per-gallon tariff on ethanol imports. In connection with this, the Trade Representative recommends restructuring the ethanol excise tax credit so it is paid directly to domestic ethanol producers, instead of to fuel blenders. (This would eliminate the rationale for the tariff, which is to make sure the tax credit does not benefit foreign producers.)

This proposal could contribute to ending oil dependence, helping provide drivers with billions of gallons of biofuels soon. It could help reduce emissions of heat-trapping gases, since ethanol made from sugar (the most likely feedstock for imported ethanol) produces far fewer emissions than either gasoline or ethanol made from corn. It could help reduce poverty in some developing nations. The current price difference between domestic and imported ethanol would be mostly maintained.

However, this proposal would generate considerable political controversy. Farm state members of Congress from both parties would be strongly opposed. If the proposal led to additional clearing of tropical rainforests, either directly or indirectly, that would increase emissions of heat-trapping gases and threaten biodiversity.

The Secretary of Agriculture and Counselor strongly oppose lifting the tariff. The EPA Administrator and the Chair of the Council on Environmental Quality express concern about the potential impact on tropical rainforests of lifting the tariff, but could support lifting it subject to certain conditions. The U.S. Trade Representative, the Secretary of Energy, the Secretary of Commerce, the chair of the National Economic Council and the chair of the Council of Economic Advisers support lifting the tariff.

_____Approve   _____Disapprove   _____More Information

d. *Low-Carbon Fuel Standard*
The Secretary of Energy recommends you propose a low-carbon fuel standard. Under the standard, fuel blenders would be required to distribute fuels with steadily decreasing carbon emissions, measured on a life-cycle basis. Credits used to implement this law would be fully tradeable.

The standard would be modeled on the one signed into law by California Governor Arnold Schwarzenegger in fall 2006. The objective is to ensure the transition away from oil helps reduce emissions of heat-trapping gases.

_____Approve _____Disapprove _____More Information

3. IMPROVING TRAFFIC
The Secretary of Transportation and Secretary of Housing and Urban Development recommend you announce a historic shift in federal funding away from new road construction and toward mass transit. Federal funding for road repair would not change. The Secretaries also recommend you launch a campaign to promote telecommuting, highlighting its benefits to private employers and adopting new rules for the federal workforce.

_____Approve _____Disapprove _____More Information

4. INVESTING IN ADVANCED RESEARCH
You received several proposals related to research and development. The Secretary of Transportation recommends additional spending on battery research. The Secretary of Agriculture recommends additional spending on biofuels research. The Secretary of Energy recommends additional spending on underground carbon storage. We have requested additional budget detail from each agency. Total costs are $1 to $2 billion per year.

_____Approve _____Disapprove _____More Information

5. TAX AND REBATE PROGRAM
No topic provoked more disagreement among your advisers than possible increases in the gasoline tax. The Chair of the Council of Economic

Advisers recommends you propose a 10-cent-per gallon increase each year for 5 years, with most of the revenues rebated to families earning $75,000 or less. Rebate checks would be for $100 in Year 1, $200 in Year 2, $300 in Year 3, $400 in Year 4 and $500 in Year 5. The balance of the revenues would be dedicated to a "Freedom Fund" used for programs to reduce oil dependence.

This proposal would be very controversial. The Counselor, Secretary of Commerce and your Political Director strongly oppose it, arguing it would overwhelm and potentially threaten other parts of your agenda. Your other advisers believe that public concern about oil dependence (on national security, environmental and economic grounds) is sufficiently great to manage such controversy. They believe a proposal to increase the gasoline tax would demonstrate seriousness and play an important substantive role in moving the nation beyond oil.

After rebate checks, the proposal would generate revenues for the Freedom Fund in roughly the following amounts: Year 1, $5 billion; Year 2, $9.5 billion; Year 3, $13.5 billion; Year 4, $17 billion; Year 5, $20 billion.

_____Approve   _____Disapprove   _____More Information

6. TRANSFORMING OIL DIPLOMACY

The Secretary of State and Secretary of Energy recommend a new approach to oil diplomacy, focusing not just on securing supply but on limiting demand. They recommend cooperative action with other oil-consuming nations to diversify fuel supply and deploy fuel-efficient technologies. They recommend you make this a centerpiece of your personal diplomacy.

_____Approve   _____Disapprove   _____More Information

7. CONCLUSION

If you would like additional options or more information, please let me know.

NOTE FROM THE PRESIDENT

TO: CHIEF OF STAFF

SUBJECT: Oil Dependence and Big Government

Thank you for pulling together the policy package for my oil dependence speech.

Is it too "big government"? Individually, many of these items make sense. Together, do they interfere too much in the free market? Will they be perceived as doing so?

As you know, my own view is that government has an important role in helping solve many problems, but the entrepreneurial spirit of the American people is ultimately the most powerful tool. I want to be sure our oil dependence policies reflect that.

Could you collect thoughts on these questions? Thanks.

MEMORANDUM FOR THE PRESIDENT

FROM: SECRETARY OF ENERGY

SUBJECT: "Big Government" and Oil

You asked whether the Chief of Staff's policy package amounts to a "big government" solution to the problem of oil dependence.

I understand why you're concerned. For the past half century, debates about the size and role of government have shaped the presidency. Lyndon Johnson and Richard Nixon aggressively expanded the role of the federal government, with programs like the Great Society (under Johnson) and wage and price controls (under Nixon). Partly in response, Ronald Reagan sought mostly to restrain the role of government. Bill Clinton, in the wake of the Republican takeover of Congress, declared that "the era of big government is over." In the past several years, a rift opened between George W. Bush and some of his conservative base, who objected to the record growth in federal spending on his watch.

You have charted a course between two extremes on this issue. I have heard you say on several occasions that "government has an important role in helping solve problems, but the entrepreneurial spirit of the American people is our most powerful tool." This, broadly speaking, is the view shared by most Americans.

I believe the policy package shaped by the Chief of Staff is consistent with your general approach. However, I would like to make a more basic point:

Oil's dominance as a transportation fuel is the result of decades of help from "big government."

In making this point I offer no value judgments, but simply state a fact. For much of the past century, securing oil flows has been a top priority of presidents and Cabinet secretaries. For much of the past century, public lands have been used for oil production. For much of the past century, federal tax policy has given oil producers special benefits.

During World War II, for example, Secretary of the Interior Harold Ickes warned that the United States was running out of oil and worked to secure oil from the Middle East. During this period, according to oil historian Daniel Yergin, "even private-enterprise Republicans were calling for direct government involvement in foreign oil concessions." Henry Cabot Lodge, the prominent Republican senator, said, "History does not give us confidence that private interest alone would adequately safeguard the national interest." On Ickes' recommendation, President Roosevelt authorized assistance to King Ibn Saud under the Lend Lease program, even though Saudi Arabia plainly did not meet the program's requirements (including a democratic government).[1]

In 1950, President Truman wrote to inform King Saud that "No threat to your Kingdom could occur which would not be a matter of immediate concern to the United States." In November 1956, with the Suez Crisis threatening oil supplies to Europe, President Eisenhower said he would exempt oil companies from the antitrust acts in order to allow them to cooperate in the supply effort.[2]

In 1980, President Carter declared that:

> An attempt by any outside force to gain control of the Persian Gulf region will be regarded as an assault on the vital interests of the United States of America, and such an assault will be repelled by any means necessary, including military force.[3]

This declaration of U.S. interests in the Persian Gulf—known as the "Carter Doctrine"—has been embraced by all presidents since.

In 1991, President George H.W. Bush told Congress that war with Iraq was necessary because "[v]ital economic interests are at stake," citing the fact that Iraq and Kuwait together controlled 20% of the world's proven oil reserves.[4] Today, protecting oil shipments through the Straits of Hormuz remains an important mission for the U.S. Central Command (CENTCOM).

For generations, the resources and influence of the U.S. government has been used to secure oil flows around the world. This has included not just military assets but political and diplomatic leverage, including frequent interventions by presidents, secretaries of state and other senior officials.

Could the oil industry have prospered without such help from the world's largest and most powerful government? Perhaps. But without confidence the U.S. government would help secure supplies of oil, many businesses would surely have pursued alternatives with considerably more priority than they have to date. Oil's dominance as a transportation fuel would not have been possible without continuing assistance from government.

In addition, public lands have been used to produce oil. This has been controversial since at least the 1920s, when the Teapot Dome scandal erupted over use of an oil field in Wyoming. Favorable rates and lease terms have helped the industry.

Special tax preferences have been provided for domestic oil production. The "oil depletion allowance," which gives oil producers special preferences, dates to 1909.

If you were really intent on removing "big government" from the oil business, you would forswear further effort to secure supply from the Persian Gulf, renounce the Carter Doctrine, adjust CENTCOM's mission, redefine our relationship with Saudi Arabia (now dominated by the desire to secure cooperation in managing world oil markets), eliminate special preferences for domestic production and probably take other steps as well.

A few people might advocate this. But most would be concerned that short-term costs would substantially exceed the benefits. In particular, the consequences of removing big government from the oil business in this manner would be to increase volatility in world oil markets. Speculative pressures would probably drive oil prices higher—possibly much higher—than they are today.

Unless you are prepared to adopt such an approach, you do not face a choice between policies that involve "big government" and those that do not. You face a choice between continuing the current "big government" policies and adopting a different set to manage the transition away from oil dependence. My own view is you should do the latter.

In doing so, you should not "pick technologies." Government's track record at doing so is abysmal. In general government should establish an objective that serves the public interest and let the private sector figure out how best to achieve that goal.

However, the proposals summarized by the Chief of Staff are no more "big government" than those that have been pursued by presidents of both parties for many years.

MEMORANDUM FOR THE PRESIDENT

FROM: THE COUNSELOR

SUBJECT: A Scarce Resource

You have now received almost a dozen memos on the topic of oil dependence. The information you've received so far is helpful. However, I thought it might be helpful to stand back from specifics and make a more general point.

As you know, the presidency is a resource-rich environment. You have motorcades, airplanes, a mansion and a huge staff available for your use at any time. If you want to speak with anyone in the world, your staff gets that person on the phone promptly. If you want to go anywhere in the world, a jumbo jet with the world's most advanced communications equipment takes you there.

Waiting at your immediate beck and call are hundreds of hard-working and ambitious aides. For many, the chance to work for you fulfills lifelong dreams. Beyond them lie the federal agencies, led by extraordinary individuals who serve at your pleasure and filled with hundreds of thousands of civil servants for whom a tasking from the President takes top priority.

You command the attention of the media every day. When you say or do something, tens of millions of Americans will notice.

You are, of course, commander-in-chief of the greatest military of all time.

However, there is one resource any U.S. President finds in short supply—time.

As President, the pressures on your time are extraordinary and unrelenting. Dozens of issues vie for your attention daily. Crises you can neither predict nor control burst into your office, requiring immediate attention without notice.

Foreign leaders, members of Congress, the media, your own staff and countless others compete for small slivers of your time. Many more of these people consider themselves entitled to your time, by virtue of their stature or prior relationship with you, than you can possibly accommodate.

If you consider oil dependence to be a priority, the most important resource you can devote to it is your time.

You have reached this office because of a combination of political skills, strategic sophistication and sound judgment. (To your credit, you have retained the perspective to realize that good fortune also played a role.) For you to achieve transformational change on any issue, you will need to draw on all these strengths.

Based on the memos I've seen, I believe any effort to wean the United States from oil dependence will require far more than a single speech. It will require a sustained conversation with the American people. It will require dialogue with leaders from the business world and advocacy groups. It will require close cooperation with the Congress. It will require you to build bipartisan coalitions that stand the test of time.

Ending oil dependence will require many decisions, big and small. Some can be delegated, but not all. On the really big issues, decisions must be made by you alone.

You have a superb team in place. Their work on this topic will be essential. But to command public attention, break logjams and forge lasting coalitions, their most powerful weapon in many cases will be you.

If this issue is a priority, one of the most important resources you can commit to it is your time.

NOTE FROM THE PRESIDENT

TO: DIRECTOR, OFFICE OF SPEECHWRITING

SUBJECT: The Phrase "Oil Addiction"

For my speech on oil dependence, please consider carefully whether or not to use the phrase "oil addiction." Oil companies are filled with many thousands of good, hard-working people. I want to take bold steps to solve this problem, but don't want to vilify them in the process.

Could you please look into the history of this phrase and consult with the experts to determine whether we should include it in my speech? Thanks.

MEMORANDUM FOR THE PRESIDENT

FROM: DIRECTOR, OFFICE OF SPEECHWRITING

SUBJECT: "Oil Addiction"

You asked whether the phrase "oil addiction" should be used in your upcoming speech on oil dependence. My staff examined the history of the phrase and consulted with energy experts. We found:

  i. The phrase "oil addiction" dates back decades and is in widespread use across the political spectrum.

 ii. The dictionary definition of "addiction" fits patterns of oil use in the United States during the past 30 years.

iii. The word "addiction" is often applied to oil, fast food and BlackBerry mobile devices, as well as to tobacco and narcotics.

I believe that using the phrase "oil addiction" in your speech would be appropriate and recommend it. I will explain this a bit more below.

1. HISTORY OF THE PHRASE "OIL ADDICTION"
The phrase "oil addiction" has been in common parlance for decades. Newspaper editorialists, business magazines, activists and others have used it. Although President Bush's use of the phrase in his 2006 State of the Union address prompted a flurry of commentary, the phrase has been in common use across the political spectrum for many years.

A search of the Nexis database reveals the phrase "oil addiction" as early as 1974. On March 6, 1974, the *New York Times* published a piece by Dr. Thomas Szasz arguing that the American motorist's need for gasoline is equivalent to a drug user's need for narcotics. The phrase was used in several news stories and articles during the 1980s.

During the 1990s, the phrase "oil addiction" was used by magazines, newspapers and commentators across the political spectrum. An August 20, 1990 *Business Week* editorial carried the title "Weaning the U.S. from its Oil Addiction." A February 17, 1991 *New York Times* editorial begins with the sentence "The energy policy now taking shape within the Bush administration is distressingly blind to the oil addiction that underlies the dispatch of 500,000 American troops to the Persian Gulf." A September 8, 1996 editorial by the *Atlanta Journal and Constitution* argues that "We will continue to be vulnerable to madmen until we get our oil addiction under control." There are many other examples.

The Nexis database contains more than 650 references to "oil addiction" during the period January 2000–December 2005. Among these is an article in *Fortune* magazine on August 23, 2004, with the title "How to Kick the Oil Habit," which refers to "our longtime oil addiction."

In January 2006, President Bush declared that "America is addicted to oil" in his State of the Union address. That sentence led many news stories about the speech the next day. Most attention focused not on the merits of the phrase, but on the fact that Bush would use it. For example, CNN.com reported that: "'America is addicted to oil, which is often imported from unstable parts of the world,' the former oil executive said."

Since then, the phrase "oil addiction" has been in widespread use by commentators and speakers across the political spectrum, including by centrist, mainstream commentators.

Nexis reports almost 2,000 "hits" on the phrase "oil addiction" during 2006.

2. DICTIONARY DEFINITIONS
The *Merriam-Webster's Medical Dictionary* (Merriam-Webster, 2002) defines "addiction" to include "persistent compulsive use of a substance known by the user to be physically, psychologically or socially harmful.

U.S. oil use patterns fit this definition Oil use is certainly "persistent," having grown for decades. Oil use has resisted countless policy interventions and public exhortations designed to minimize its use, and in that sense its use is "compulsive." (*American Heritage Dictionary*: "compulsive—caused or conditioned by compulsion; compulsion—an irresistible impulse to act. . . .") Large majorities of Americans declare that current oil use is a serious national problem, suggesting that oil use is "known by the user to be . . . socially harmful."

The American Heritage Dictionary (Houghton Mifflin 2006) defines "addiction" to include "The condition of being habitually or compulsively occupied with or involved in something . . . [and] An instance of this: *had an addiction for fast cars*." The automotive reference is especially striking.

Because there is little fuel diversity in the United States, and because mobility is a central feature of modern life, many if not most people are "habitually . . . involved in" using oil. Within the dictionary definition of the term, they can reasonably be considered "addicted."

3. OTHER ISSUES
The word "addiction" is frequently applied today to oil, fast food, Blackberries, tobacco and narcotics. Nexis reports more than 100 articles during the past year in which the phrase "fast food" appeared within two words of a word starting with "addict." It reports more than 500 articles on BlackBerry "addiction" within the past year.[1]

Oil, fast food, and BlackBerries each provide considerable benefits. Oil provides heat, light, and mobility, among other services. It is an important chemical feedstock. Fast food helps control hunger and delivers some nutrition. BlackBerries provide portable e-mail and phone services.

Yet, applying the dictionary definition, these benefits don't affect whether use of the word "addiction" is appropriate. An addiction is a "habitual or compulsive" use, known by the user to be harmful. The fact that there may also be benefits isn't relevant.

Is use of the word "addiction" so stigmatizing to those who work for oil companies that discretion dictates it must be avoided? Use of the term by President George W. Bush, Secretary of State Condoleezza Rice (who has an oil tanker named after her!), leading business magazines, and others strongly suggests otherwise.

4. CONCLUSION
The phrase "oil addiction" has been widely used for decades. It is fully justified by patterns of oil usage in the United States. The phrase has a powerful resonance. I recommend using it in your upcoming speech.

MEMORANDUM TO THE PRESIDENT

FROM: THE VICE PRESIDENT

SUBJECT: <u>Oil Dependence Speech</u>

When you asked me to be your running mate, you urged me always to provide my candid counsel. You invited my views on all decisions. You encouraged me always to step back and consider the big picture.

I recall that conversation tonight, as I write this memo.

For more than three weeks, I have been reading memoranda from around the government on the topic of oil dependence. They provide a wealth of information and opinions. Rather than participate in the exchange of views, I have waited to offer thoughts on the main choices posed by these memos as a whole.

These memos point to dozens of smaller decisions that must be made as you shape a program to free our nation from oil dependence. Yet there are four questions I believe will, above all others, determine the success of your efforts. These decisions will have especially far-reaching consequences, not just for your work on oil dependence but on your presidency as a whole.

The first question is whether to deliver a major speech on oil dependence at all.

There are several good reasons not to do so.

First, real success will be all-consuming. A presidency can have only a few priorities. You can accomplish a great deal in many areas, with the help of your talented Cabinet and staff, but you will be fortunate if you are a transformational figure in even one. Do you wish to devote time and attention to this issue?

If you believe the time is right for a major speech, there are two clear alternatives. The first is Iraq. Managing the difficult situation we face there will be a defining feature of your presidency. It will command your attention, day in and day out. You could update the American people on events there and, in light of the most recent events, share your vision on how to respond to growing threats from the Persian Gulf more broadly.

The second alternative is global warming. Many people accurately call this the greatest challenge of our time. In the past several years, public attention to global warming has skyrocketed. I know you hope to lead the nation toward a historic response to this epic issue. A major speech would help do that.

Perhaps the best reason to deliver a major speech on oil dependence is that it would help lay the foundation for addressing both these issues. We cannot solve the web of problems related to our role in the Persian Gulf without serious steps to reduce oil dependence. We cannot reverse the rising concentrations of heat-trapping gases in the atmosphere without doing the same.

To be sure, ending oil dependence alone would not solve either problem. Even if you lead the nation in historic steps to reduce oil dependence, events in the Gulf will continue to present extraordinary challenges for years to come. Even if global oil consumption drops sharply, measures to address other causes of global warming, such as coal combustion and tropical deforestation, will still be essential. But steps to reduce oil dependence are a central part of the strategy for addressing both problems.

In your tasking memo a month ago, you asked others to "Make no small plans, for they have no power to stir the soul." Those words have been credited at different times to Niccolo Machiavelli, Daniel Burnham (the architect who oversaw Chicago's 1893 World's Fair) and Winston Churchill. If you decide to take up this challenge, you will need Machiavelli's keen understanding of power, Burnham's visceral appreciation of the American heartland and Churchill's eloquent determination.

I think your reference to these words signals your intentions. I applaud you for it.

The second question is whether to propose a gasoline tax increase.

Four of your five immediate predecessors proposed increases in gasoline or other energy taxes. Presidents Clinton, George H. W. Bush, Reagan, and Carter each decided—at different stages of their presidencies—that such tax increases were important and appropriate.[1]

Their record in this regard is one of almost unbroken failure. Each of these proposals provoked considerable controversy. Each was opposed by members of the President's own party. Each took a toll on the President's political standing. None were enacted in the form they were proposed.

In some regards, the proposal from the Chair of the Council of Economic Advisers is attractive. It will make many Americans better off in the short term. It gives many drivers a chance to avoid the tax if they choose. Costs will be borne by those best able to do so. It will no doubt have a powerful impact in reducing our nation's dependence on oil.

Yet opposition will be strong. When a politician promises to raise your taxes and return money in another form, many voters doubt that second step will ever happen. Suspicions will be very high.

Indeed many members of Congress have signed pledges never to support a "tax increase." These pledges are typically construed quite narrowly, so a package of measures that includes both increases in one tax and equal reductions in another is considered an "increase." These pledges significantly reduce the ability of some members of Congress to support a plan to free the United States from oil dependence that includes changes in tax policy.

I derive small comfort from the long list of distinguished individuals who believe a gasoline tax increase is the most intellectually defensible solution to this problem. Many are remarkable people and their analysis may be compelling. But you were elected by the public, not them.

Politicians who are several steps ahead of the public are leaders. Politicians who are utterly out of step with the people they serve are not.

One lesson from recent experience—taxes dedicated to a specific purpose are more acceptable than those used for general revenues. President Reagan saw himself as an opponent of tax increases, but nevertheless supported a 5-cent per gallon increase in the gasoline tax in 1982, labeling it a "user fee." Revenues were dedicated to improving the nation's transportation infrastructure. If you approve a measure of the type proposed, any new revenue should be placed in a separate fund and dedicated to programs for reducing the nation's oil dependence.

If you wish to make transformational change on this issue, I recommend you approve the CEA chair's proposal. But proceed cautiously. The stakes are high.

The third question is whether to court controversy on other topics. Many of the issues described in the memos you received are technical, without political significance. But two topics—the ethanol tariff and coal-to-liquid fuels—could spark heated debate.

The U.S. Trade Representative argues for ending the ethanol tariff. I believe I can count 40 senators strongly opposed to such a proposal from Day 1. The politics of this issue are more regional than partisan, with members of Congress from farm states opposed and members of Congress from the east and west coasts more likely to be in favor. Yet even on the coasts, where drivers would most likely benefit, environmental concerns (such as the impact of ending the tariff on tropical rainforests) and skepticism about hemispheric free trade create doubts about ending the tariff. The intensity of opponents of this proposal will far outweigh the intensity of supporters.

Coal-to-liquid fuels will also present political challenges, as you move forward with this agenda. Coal is produced in more than 20 states and most regions of the country. The political forces pushing to subsidize liquefied coal will be strong. They will collide, however, with the concerns of the growing number of Americans focused on fighting global warming. To some extent these differences can be bridged with measures all can embrace, such as research programs and demonstration projects aimed at deploying clean coal technologies. But the potential for controversy is high.

To move forward in reducing oil dependence, you will need to build bipartisan coalitions. Our constitutional system is designed to require high levels of consensus before any significant legislation is passed. (In the modern era, the consensus required has become even greater, with the emergence of a de facto 60-vote requirement to enact major legislation in the U.S. Senate.) I recommend you pick priorities carefully.

A fourth question perhaps the most central—is how to offer an optimistic vision of the future. Leadership is about inspiration. You must rise above the many details in the memos you solicited to offer a vision.

If you believe ending oil dependence is a central challenge of our time, you must convey that to the American people in a way that focuses on the bright future, not the dark past. You must relate it to broader themes that touch all our lives.

With that in mind, I recommend you find ways to relate this to the great yearning for bipartisanship felt throughout the country. Americans are disgusted with the poisonous political culture in Washington, D.C., and for good reason. As several of the memos you received pointed out, oil dependence is a topic that unites Americans. If you can make this part of a unifying mission, overcoming partisan divides, you can change history.

In light of that, I recommend you deliver this speech to a Joint Session of Congress, not from the Oval Office. To succeed, the Congress must be a full partner in your program. The changes you're considering will take sustained support over the course of many years. You cannot do this alone. I recommend you signal that fact, as well as the historic significance of your proposals, by seeking an invitation to speak to the Congress on this topic.

NOTE FOR THE PRESIDENT

FROM: CHIEF OF STAFF

SUBJECT: <u>Oil Dependence Speech</u>

Attached is the announcement we will distribute in connection with your speech tomorrow.

As you can see, it sets forth an aggressive agenda for the months ahead. I recommend we begin with a bipartisan meeting of congressional leaders here the day after tomorrow, as well as calls to a half dozen heads of state. A more detailed outreach and work plan is on the way.

THE WHITE HOUSE
OFFICE OF THE PRESS SECRETARY

For Immediate Release

ENDING OIL DEPENDENCE

The President's Plan to Free the United States from Oil Dependence

Today, the President announced an historic plan to free the United States from oil dependence. The plan includes policy changes, Executive Orders and proposed legislation.

I. <u>TRANSFORMING THE VEHICLE FLEET</u>

   a. <u>Federal Leadership</u>. The President will issue a Clean Vehicles Executive Order to put the purchasing power of the federal government behind the rapid deployment of alternative fuel vehicles. Under the Executive Order, the U.S. government will offer to purchase 30,000 plug-in hybrid electric vehicles (PHEVs) at a premium of $8,000 each. Once these vehicles are delivered, half the vehicles purchased by the federal government each year will be PHEVs. The Clean Vehicles Executive Order will also require that, within one year, all new gasoline vehicles purchased by the federal government will have flex-fuel engines. Within six months, all official vehicles in presidential motorcades will be flex-fuel plug-in hybrids, capable of running on gasoline, ethanol or electricity from the grid.

   b. <u>Modernizing U.S. Auto Factories</u>. The President will propose legislation authorizing the federal government to help pay for retooling U.S. factories to produce plug-in hybrid and highly efficient new vehicles. Funds will be provided by reimbursing manufacturers for the cost of retiree health care.

   c. <u>Consumer Tax Credits</u>. The President will propose tax credits of up to $8,000 for purchasers of the first million plug-in cars and $4,000 for purchasers of the second million plug-ins.

d. <u>FREEdom Standards</u>. The President will propose Fuel Reduction and Energy Efficiency (FREEdom) standards to replace the 1970s–era Corporate Average Fuel Efficiency (CAFÉ) standards. FREEdom standards will set requirements for the fuel efficiency of new vehicles based on weight and other attributes, not company-wide averages. These requirements will increase automatically by 4% each year. FREEdom standards will require that half of all new gasoline vehicles sold in the United States be flex fuel by 2012 and all new vehicles sold be flex fuel by 2015.

e. <u>Federal Battery Guarantee Corporation</u>. The President will propose legislation to establish a Federal Battery Guarantee Corporation. The FBGC will help manufacturers pay for 10-year full warranties on batteries in the first two million plug-in cars sold.

II. <u>TRANSFORMING THE FUEL SUPPLY</u>

a. <u>E85 Pumps</u>. The President will propose legislation requiring all major oil companies to retrofit pumps for E85 at 50% of their owned or branded stations. The legislation will prohibit franchise agreements that restrict or discourage pumps for biofuels at service stations.

b. <u>Ethanol Tax Credit</u>. The President will propose legislation to extend the ethanol tax credit for 10 years. The credit would be variable, depending on the price of oil. The legislation will propose an additional 30-cent-per-gallon credit for advanced biofuels, including cellulosic ethanol.

c. <u>Low-Carbon Fuel Standard</u>. The President will propose a Low-Carbon Fuel Standard. Under the standard, fuels in the United States will have 5% less carbon by 2015 and 10% less carbon by 2020 (measured on a life-cycle basis).

III. <u>IMPROVING TRAFFIC</u>

The President will propose legislation to shift federal funding from new road construction to mass transit. He will direct federal agencies to take additional steps to promote telecommuting and urge all private employers to do the same.

IV. INVESTING IN RESEARCH

The President will launch the Reynolds Project, named after the Indiana town that several years ago set a goal of obtaining all its energy from renewable sources. The Reynolds Project will be a multibillion dollar research program focused on transformational energy technologies. Initial priorities will be research on batteries, advanced biofuels, and carbon capture and storage. The President will seek $1 billion for the next fiscal year and more in the years ahead.

V. TAX AND REBATE PROGRAM

The President will propose a "tax and rebate" program to help end oil dependence. Under this proposal, the federal gasoline tax will be increased 10 cents per gallon each year for five years. Most of the money collected will be returned in the form of rebate checks that arrive each year just before July 4, Independence Day. Families earning $75,000 and less will receive checks for $100 in the first year of the program, $200 in the second year, $300 in the third year, $400 in the fourth year and $500 in the fifth year. Revenues remaining after rebates will be placed in a new Freedom Fund, dedicated solely to tax incentives and other programs to reduce oil dependence.

VI. TRANSFORMING OIL DIPLOMACY

The President announced that promoting clean fuels and energy efficiency will be among the U.S. government's top diplomatic priorities. The President will host the Chinese premier for an energy summit later this year. The Secretary of Energy will host a global conference on electrification of the vehicle fleet, to be held in Detroit next year.

WHITE HOUSE
OFFICE OF THE PRESS SECRETARY

The President's
Speech to the Nation

Official Transcript

Members of Congress, members of my Cabinet, assembled guests, my
fellow Americans.

I am humbled to appear here. History fills this hall. From this podium,
Presidents before me have called our nation to battle and summoned our
ancestors to greatness.

We gather here today, a free and prosperous people, because those who
came before us met great challenges with wisdom, courage and
determination.

Tonight I've come to speak about one of the great challenges of our time.
I've come to talk about our nation's dependence on oil.

For more than a century, oil has shaped our lives. Long ago, oil gave us
light. In a few states today, oil provides heat. But mostly, oil moves us
about—from home to work, from home to school, from town to town,
from place to place.

We are a nation on the move. Many of us travel 20, 30, even hundreds of
miles each day.

And since our grandparents were young, the cars, trucks and trains we
depend on have depended on oil.

For this, we have paid a price. The thirst for oil has left us vulnerable to
our enemies, polluted the planet and cost us dearly when oil prices rise.

Today, oil keeps us tethered to distant lands where people wish us ill. In
the past two decades we have fought two wars in the Persian Gulf. The

reasons for those wars are complex. But the proximity of half the world's oil reserves is no coincidence.

Today, oil fouls the air and heats the planet. The buildup of heat-trapping gases in the atmosphere creates an epic threat we must address as a matter of urgency. These gases have many sources, but none more important than oil.

Today, oil exposes Americans to misery whenever world prices rise. Just a few years ago, oil prices doubled within 21 months. International tensions or natural catastrophes could send prices still higher at any time. The unpredictable swings of an unforgiving global market hurt business and family budgets alike.

Why do we tolerate these problems? Why have earlier efforts to solve them failed?

There are many reasons, but none more important than this: Last year, oil provided more than 96% of the fuel for our cars and trucks. For most Americans, in most situations today, there are no substitutes for oil available.

We grew up with this. So did our parents and grandparents. We consider it normal.

But it is deeply abnormal.

If you're thirsty and don't want orange juice, you can drink water, milk or soda.

If you're hungry and don't want meat, you can eat fish, vegetables or pasta.

But if you need to travel beyond your neighborhood and don't want to use oil, you're almost certainly out of luck. Perhaps you can walk or ride a bicycle, but in almost all situations, you'll need oil.

Oil has a proper place in our lives and economy. It is not evil. But our dependence on it makes us weak.

Today I stand before you to declare that our addiction to oil must end.

The twentieth century was the Age of Oil. But this is a new era.

Ending our nation's dependence on oil will not be quick or easy. Oil is everywhere. More than 240 million cars and trucks on the road today depend on it. Many of those cars stay on the road for 15 years and more. Ending our dependence on oil will take time.

Yet those who came before us did not shrink from great challenges.

Tonight I recall two Presidents.

John Kennedy was a charismatic leader who summoned the nation to greatness. When he set a goal of sending a man to the Moon, he said, "now is the time to take longer strides" Those words guide us today. Now is the time to take longer strides.

Ronald Reagan was another charismatic leader—one who spoke to the American people with simplicity, clarity and style. In his Second Inaugural Address, President Reagan asked two questions I believe should guide us today.

President Reagan asked: "*If not us, who? If not now, when?*"

In the past year, I've visited many communities across this great nation. I visited Hazelwood, Missouri, where a factory that once made sports utility vehicles closed recently, leaving many good people without jobs. I visited Soperville, Georgia, where a plant will be built to turn wood chips into ethanol, creating jobs and helping reduce oil dependence.

These two cities tell a story. Our old way of doing business isn't working. But there are new ways of doing business that create jobs, cut pollution and make us stronger.

The road to reducing oil dependence is rich with opportunity. America's entrepreneurial spirit makes us great. To solve the problem of oil dependence, our most important natural resource is the American people.

On a recent trip to California, I met Martin Eberhard, who's launching a new company to build electric sports cars. I also met Chelsea Sexton, who has been fighting tirelessly to promote electric cars since her first job in a car dealership many years ago. Both of them are here with us tonight.

Ladies and gentlemen, we need electric cars on the road, soon. The United States has a vast infrastructure for generating electricity, reaching into every home. But that infrastructure is essentially useless for reducing oil dependence, because our cars can't connect to it. To solve the problem of oil dependence, we need cars that can connect to the electric grid.

Electric cars are fast. They're quiet. At today's electricity prices, they cost the equivalent of 75 cents per gallon to drive. Electric motors can be combined with an old-fashioned gasoline engine to produce a "plug-in hybrid"—a perfect choice for many drivers.

For most Americans, electric cars are still too expensive. This must change.

Tonight I am proposing three measures to transform our auto fleet and put millions of electric cars on the road.

First, the federal government will lead. Tomorrow I will sign an Executive Order that puts the purchasing power of the federal government behind these efforts. As soon as possible, half the cars purchased by the federal government each year will be plug-in hybrids. I urge state and local governments, along with owners of other large fleets, to do the same.

Within six months, every car I ride in will be a "plug-in hybrid."

Second, I am proposing a grand bargain with America's automakers. If you invest in advanced technologies, we'll invest in you.

Today, American automakers pay the cost of health care for their retirees, which can add more than $1,500 to the cost of each car. In other countries governments pay these costs, giving manufacturers in those countries a competitive edge. It's time we got smarter about the way we do this. Tonight, I propose a deal: When a company invests in oil-saving technology at a U.S. auto factory, the federal government will help pay health care costs for that company's retirees. This simple step will reduce oil dependence, improve U.S. industrial competitiveness and provide a more secure retirement for millions of American.

Third, I am proposing tax credits of up to $8,000 for the purchase of electric cars. These credits will be available for the first million electric cars sold—either all-electric or plug-in hybrids. The computer industry teaches a simple lesson: The price of a new product declines rapidly as more are sold. The best way to bring down the costs of electric cars is to get them into mass production, soon.

But electricity is not the only alternative fuel that can help us kick the oil habit. Ethanol and other biofuels are important too.

Last May, I was thrilled to attend the Indianapolis 500. That race is now run entirely on ethanol. When I was there, I met with Buddy Rice, who won the race in 2004 and has become an advocate for ethanol. Recently, I also met with Vinod Khosla, an entrepreneur who made a fortune in the computer industry and is now using it to invest in advanced biofuels. Both Buddy and Vinod are with us tonight too.

Ladies and gentlemen, we need to transform America's fuel supply. Already, ethanol is leading a renewal of rural America. Farm communities across this country have been revitalized by the explosion of demand for ethanol in recent years.

This is just the beginning. To reduce oil dependence, we must make ethanol not only from corn, as we do today, but from switchgrass, wood chips, and other sources as well. We must expand production of other biofuels, such as biodiesel, as well.

Tonight, I am proposing several measures to make sure every American who wants to buy biofuels can do so.

First, I am urging every auto company to make flex-fuel technology, standard in all new cars, immediately. This technology—which allows cars to take both gasoline and ethanol, costs roughly $100 per vehicle. Already, most car makers are moving quickly to do this, but they can move quicker.

Here's one way to make sure they do: If you're buying a new car, insist that it be "flex fuel." No tool is more powerful than the market. If everyone listening tonight starts insisting on flex-fuel cars, car makers will respond.

Second, I will propose legislation to require every major oil company to install an ethanol pump in at least 50% of their stations. The same legislation will make sure that any service station owner who wants to install an ethanol pump is legally able to do so. At present, some oil companies use franchise agreements to restrict the ability of service station owners to sell ethanol and other biofuels. That must end.

Third, I am proposing changes to the federal tax credits for ethanol. The main purpose of these changes is to prevent OPEC from wreaking havoc with our industry by manipulating oil prices. This type of conduct has happened in the past. To protect against it, I will propose tax credits for ethanol that vary depending on the price of oil.

In the past few years, concerns have been raised about the impact of ethanol and other biofuels on both food prices and the environment. I take these concerns very seriously. In the years ahead, all government biofuels programs will be shaped with these concerns as a top priority. Biofuels that have the least impact on food prices and the best impact on the environment will receive the strongest support.

Electricity and ethanol are both important. But ending oil dependence requires three "E's"—electricity, ethanol and efficiency.

Ladies and gentlemen, we waste an astonishing amount of fuel in our cars and trucks. It's not good for national security, it's not good for the environment and it's not good for business.

Many Americans have been working for years to end energy waste. One who stands out is Fred Smith, who founded and built Federal Express. Few companies have a greater stake in fuel efficiency than FedEx and Fred has worked tirelessly on this issue. Another is Jerome Ringo, who grew up in New Orleans and now runs a coalition of unions and environmental groups dedicated to promoting a clean energy future. Fred and Jerome are with us tonight.

More than 30 years ago, Congress passed and the President signed corporate average fuel efficiency standards, known as "CAFE." At first, CAFE standards worked, but for decades they have been the topic of bitter political disputes. I propose we replace them with new rules to promote "Fuel Reduction and Energy Efficiency." I call them "FREEdom standards."

FREEdom standards will provide tough new rules to be sure that automakers continually improve the fuel efficiency of their cars. At the same time FREEdom standards will scrap the basic requirement of the old system—that each manufacturer meet certain fuel efficiency targets across its entire fleet. FREEdom standards will also scrap the distinction in the old rules between cars and light trucks. The standards will automatically become stronger each year, so automakers can plan years in advance, knowing what standards will need to be met.

FREEdom standards will improve the efficiency of our vehicles and help free us from dependence on oil.

Cutting back on traffic jams will do the same.

I recently visited Atlanta, where hundreds of people told me how crowded highways and long commutes are a constant frustration. On a recent trip to Phoenix, I heard the same. And right here in the Washington, D.C. area, too many parents are missing Little League games and family dinners as they sit in traffic jams that stretch for miles.

For too long, federal policies have promoted new road building over mass transit. In recent years, federal spending on new roads has exceeded funding for mass transit by four to one. This has not made people happier or lives better. It must end. Tonight I am proposing a complete overhaul of federal transportation programs, with the objective of supporting mass transit in metropolitan areas where it will improve people's lives.

I also urge every employer to use telecommuting whenever possible. The experience from the past few years is clear: Telecommuting improves productivity and worker satisfaction. It cuts down on traffic and helps save oil. Already more than 6% of the federal workforce are regular telecommuters. During the next six months, every federal agency will take steps to expand telecommuting options still further.

To end oil dependence, we must harness the innovative spirit and technological know-how of the American people.

Tonight I am proposing a major new research program to help free the United States from dependence on oil. Next year we will commit $1 billion to this program. Most of these funds will be provided directly to universities and private research institutions. Funding will increase significantly in the years ahead.

Many people have called for such a program, labeling it a new "Manhattan Project"—after the program that led to the invention of the atom bomb—or a new "Apollo Project," recalling the race to the Moon. The program I'm launching tonight will be called the "Reynolds Project," after the town of Reynolds, Indiana.

Ladies and gentlemen, several years ago Reynolds became the first town in the United States to set a goal of getting all its energy from renewable resources. Charlie van Voorst, president of the Reynolds Town Council, is with us tonight. Along with many others, he's working hard to turn this dream into a reality.

When I met with Charlie in Reynolds, he had many words of wisdom but one thought stood out. He told me, "It's hard to get someone to believe in something that's never happened before."

Charlie's right. Whenever our country has faced great challenges in the past, some have said that a solution was impossible. But the innovative spirit and relentless determination of the American people can overcome great odds. The Reynolds Project can change the world. I believe it will.

Ladies and gentlemen, there's one other proposal I will make tonight. I've saved it for last, because I know it will be the most controversial.

Tonight, I am proposing a tax and rebate program, to help us kick our dependence on oil. Here's how it will work. The federal gasoline tax will be increased 10 cents per gallon each year for five years. Most of the money collected will be returned to American families, in the form of rebate checks that will arrive each year just before July 4, Independence Day.

The first year, every family that earns $75,000 or less will receive a $100 check. The second year, $200. Amounts will keep getting bigger until the fifth year, when checks will be for $500.

Any revenues not used for rebates will be placed in a Freedom Fund, dedicated to tax incentives and other programs to help us declare independence from oil.

The average family making $75,000 or less will break even under this proposal. But millions of families will save money. If you start buying ethanol, or if you buy a plug-in car with one of the new $8,000 tax credits, or if you buy a more fuel-efficient car of any kind or if you own fewer than two cars, you'll probably save money under this program.

You'll also be helping your country break its oil habit.

It's true that Americans with higher incomes who keep driving the same cars the same way and filling up with nothing but gasoline will pay more under this proposal. But this new program will encourage all Americans to shift toward alternative fuels and fuel-saving technologies. We'll all be better off.

Believe me, I do not make this proposal lightly. There's no better way for an elected official to become a former elected official than to start tinkering with the gasoline tax.

I know that some of you will be opposed to this from the start and never change your mind. But I hope most of you will keep an open mind and consider whether this is worth it.

For decades, we've talked about oil dependence without making progress. Now is the time to act.

To succeed, we're going to have to do things differently. And for that reason, tonight I am departing from tradition.

Tonight I am inviting Senator X to the podium to join me. As you know, Senator X and I are from different political parties. We disagree on many issues. But the need to end the nation's oil dependence is not among them. Before going further, I'd like to ask Senator X to say a few words.

<u>Senator X:</u>
Thank you. To our President, I say: I am honored to join you here tonight. I welcome your invitation to speak together to the American people.

We have many differences. But concern—indeed alarm—about U.S. oil dependence is not among them. This is not a partisan issue. It is a vital national security issue for us all.

As you know, joining you tonight on this podium was not an easy decision for me. Although I was honored by your invitation, I was concerned my presence would be interpreted as support for your proposals. And so I insisted, and you agreed, that I might say the following words.

[Mr./Madame] President, I cannot commit to support every one of your proposals. Some are far-reaching. Some may be insufficient. Some, including the one we just heard, may be unwise.

However, I will commit to this: Your proposals will have a fair hearing with members of my party. We will consider them in a spirit of openness, dedicated to solving the problems of the American people.

We will also offer proposals of our own. I hope and trust you will extend us the same courtesy. I expect the package that emerges will be not just yours, but ours.

In his First Inaugural Address, Franklin Roosevelt spoke of the "warm courage" of national unity.

In his Second Inaugural Address, which you have already quoted tonight, Ronald Reagan spoke about coming together "not as Democrats or Republicans, but as Americans."

[Mr/Madame] President, we are from different political parties. We have different beliefs and backgrounds. But above all, we are Americans. If we work together, if you respond to our proposals in the same spirit we'll respond to yours, we can solve this problem.

The President:
Thank you Senator X. You have my commitment. I will do so.

For too long, this country has been plagued by a poisonous political culture. This did not start in our time, but in recent decades it has become especially acute. Working to solve the problem of oil dependence can have broader benefits, restoring a sense of community and common purpose.

So tonight I ask all of you to join with me.

In the days ahead, some experts will say this is too difficult. Or too expensive. Or impossible. They are wrong.

Clean energy can help fuel our future. Reducing oil dependence can make us safer, cleaner and richer.

Please join with me in imagining a better future.

Imagine a world in which your family's budget does not depend on decisions in a distant land.

Imagine a world in which global warming is on its way to being controlled.

Imagine a world in which our auto industry is thriving.

Imagine a world in which rural communities are bursting with good jobs and opportunity.

Imagine a world in which you can choose the fuels for your car.

Imagine a world in which the clean energy is an engine of innovation.

Imagine a world in which our soldiers are not sent to far away, oil-rich lands.

Can we work together to build this world?

With your help, with your commitment, with your dedication, with your determination, we can.

God bless you, God bless America and good night.

Notes

Introduction

1 Daniel Yergin, *The Prize: The Epic Quest for Oil, Money and Power* (Free Press 1991) at p. 14.

PART I: THE PROBLEM

Memorandum from the Counselor

1 See, generally, David Abshire, ed., *Triumphs and Tragedies of the Modern Presidency: Seventy-Six Case Studies in Presidential Leadership* (Praeger 2001); Michael Beschloss, ed., *Power and the Presidency* (Public Affairs 1999); Richard Neustadt, Presidential Power and the Modern Presidents: *The Politics of Leadership from Roosevelt to Reagan* (Maxwell Macmillan 1990).

Memorandum from the Secretary of Energy: Ten Facts about Oil

1 Energy Information Administration, *Electric Power Annual* (November 2006)-http://www.eia.doe.gov/cneaf/electricity/epa/epa_sum.html; EIA Petroleum Products (2005 data)—http://www.eia.doe.gov/neic/infosheets/petroleumproducts.html. A barrel of oil is equal to 42 gallons.

2 See *BP Statistical Review of World Energy 2007* (Historical Data Workbook)—http://www.bp.com/productlanding.do?categoryId=6848&contentId=7033471.

3 See Nationmaster.com, "Energy Statistics-Oil Consumption (per capita)"—http://www.nationmaster.com/graph/ene_oil_con_percap-energy-oil-consumption-per-capita.

4 See Energy Information Administration, "World Proved Reserves of Oil and Natural Gas, Most Recent Estimates" (January 9, 2007)—
http://www.eia.doe.gov/emeu/international/reserves.html.

5 See Peter Huber and Mark Mills, "Oil, Oil Everywhere...," *The Wall Street Journal* (January 27, 2005); Ian W. H. Parry and Joel Darmstadter, "The Costs of U.S. Oil Dependency" Resources for the Future Discussion Paper 03-59 (December 2003), at note 8.

6 Energy Information Administration, "International Energy Annual-Table 3.1, World Petroleum Supply and Disposition"—
http://www.eia.doe.gov/pub/international/iea2004/table31.xls.

7 Energy Information Administration, "Persian Gulf Oil and Gas Exports Fact Sheet" (September 2004) at p. 5—
http://commercecan.ic.gc.ca/scdt/bizmap/interface2.nsf/vDownload/CABS_0059/$file/p gulf.pdf.

8 Energy Information Administration, "U.S. Carbon Dioxide Emissions from Energy Sources 2006 Flash Estimate" at p. 11—
http://www.eia.doe.gov/oiaf/1605/flash/pdf/flash.pdf.

9 Energy Information Administration, "Basic Petroleum Statistics"—
http://www.eia.doe.gov/neic/quickfacts/quickoil.html.

10 See Energy Information Administration, "Refining"—
http://www.eia.doe.gov/pub/oil_gas/petroleum/analysis_publications/oil_market_basics/r efining_text.htm.

11 See Oak Ridge National Laboratory, *Transportation Energy Data Book 2007*, Table 3.3. U.S. Department of Transportation; Bureau of Transportation Statistics Table 1-11: Number of U.S. Aircraft, Vehicles, Vessels, and Other Conveyances (243 million registered highway vehicles in 2004)—
http://www.bts.gov/publications/national_transportation_statistics/html/table_01_11.html ; Plunkett Research, "Automobiles and Trucks Statistics" (260 million cars and truck on the road in 2006)—
http://www.plunkettresearch.com/Industries/AutomobilesTrucks/AutomobilesandTrucks Statistics/tabid/90/Default.aspx.

12 See Sperling's Best Places, "High Gas Prices - Which Cities are Hit the Hardest?" (September 29, 2005)—http://www.bestplaces.net/docs/studies/gasprices.aspx; Mark Cooper, "Impact of Rising Prices on Household Gasoline Expenditures" (Consumer

Federation of America (September 2005) at note 1—
http://www.consumerfed.org/pdfs/CFA_REPORT_The_Impact_of_Rising_Prices_on_
Household%20Gasoline_Expenditures.pdf; Linda Bailey, "Public Transportation and
Petroleum Savings in the U.S," (American Public Transportation Association January 2007)—
http://www.apta.com/research/info/online/documents/apta_public_transportation_fuel_
savings_final_010807.pdf.

13 Energy Information Administration, Household Vehicles Energy Use: Latest Data &
Trends (November 2005)—http://www.eia.doe.gov/emeu/rtecs/nhts_survey/2001/;
Testimony of Geoff Sundstrom, AAA Director Public Affairs, before House Committee on
Energy and Commerce (May 10, 2006)—
http://energycommerce.house.gov/reparchives/108/Hearings/05102006hearing1869/Sun
dstrom.pdf; ABC News/Time Magazine/Washington Post Poll: Traffic (January 31, 2005)—
http://abcnews.go.com/images/Politics/973a2Traffic.pdf; Sperling's Best Places, "High Gas
Prices-Which Cities Are Hit the Hardest?" (September 29, 2005) —
http://www.bestplaces.net/docs/studies/gasprices.aspx.

14 "Yale Center for Environmental Law and Policy: "Environmental Poll," March 2007—
http://www.yale.edu/envirocenter/environmentalpoll.htm.

15 New York Times/CBS News Poll (February 22–26, 2006)—
http://www.nytimes.com/packages/pdf/national/20060228_poll_results.pdf; "Confidence
in U.S. Foreign Policy Index," *Foreign Affairs* website—
http://www.publicagenda.org/foreignpolicy/index.cfm.

Memorandum from the National Security Adviser

1 See, generally, Daniel Yergin, *The Prize: The Epic Quest for Oil, Money and Power* (Free
Press 1991); Ken Pollack, *Persian Puzzle: The Conflict Between Iran and America* (Random
House, 2004) ; President Jimmy Carter, State of the Union Address" (January 23, 1980).

2 President George H.W. Bush, Speech to Joint Session of Congress (September 11, 1990).

3 See Amy Myers Jaffe, "U.S. and the Middle East: Policies and Dilemmas" (National
Commission on Energy Policy 2004) at p.7 (quoting from *Frontline* series, January 9, 1996)—
http://energycommission.org/files/finalReport/O82F4877.pdf.

4 William Wechsler and Lee Wolosky, *Terrorist Financing* (Council on Foreign Relations
2002).

5 See James Woolsey, "The High Cost of Crude," Testimony before the Senate Foreign Relations Committee (November 16, 2005)—http://lugar.senate.gov/energy/hearings/pdf/051116/Woolsey_Testimony.pdf; Amy Myers Jaffe, note 3 this chapter. See also Thomas Friedman, "No Mullah Left Behind," *New York Times* (February 13, 2005).

6 For estimates of risk premium in the range of $4-$13/barrel, see John Schoen, "Oil Prices Include a Growing 'Risk Premium'" (May 12, 2004)—http://www.msnbc.msn.com/id/4962032/.

7 See Michael O'Hanlon and David Sandalow, "Iran: Regaining Energy Leverage," *The Washington Times* (January 31, 2006).

8 See David Victor, *National Security Consequences of US Oil Dependency* (Council on Foreign Relations, 2006) at p. 26.

9 See Energy Information Administration, Top World Oil Producers and Consumers (2006)—http://www.eia.doe.gov/emeu/cabs/topworldtables1_2.html.

10 See Maj. Gen. Richard Zilmer (USMC), "Joint Staff Rapid Validation and Resourcing Request" (July 25, 2006).

11 Amory Lovins, *Winning the Oil Endgame* (Rocky Mountain Institute 2004) at p. 85.

12 John Young and Philip Grone, Joint Statement before the Subcommittees on Terrorism, Unconventional Threats and Capabilities and Readiness, House Armed Services Committee (September 26, 2006).

13 Michael Lewin Ross, "Does Oil Hinder Democracy?," *World Politics* (April 2001) at pp. 325-361; Kevin Tsui, "More Oil, Less Democracy?: Theory and Evidence from Crude Oil Discoveries" (November 2005)—http://are.berkeley.edu/courses/envres_seminar/s2006/KTsuijobmarketpaper.pdf. See also Jeffrey D. Sachs, and Andrew M. Warner, "Natural Resource Abundance and Economic Growth," (National Bureau of Economic Research Working Paper 1995)

14 Kevin Tsui, *ibid.*, at p. 21; Thomas L. Friedman, "First Law of Petropolitics," *Foreign Policy* (May/June 2006).

15 Michael Lewin Ross, note 13 this chapter.

"General Fights for Renewable Energy" (Profile: General Richard Zilmer)

1 Article written by David Sandalow for this book. Sources: Conversation between Gen. Richard Zilmer and Sandalow (2007); Gen. Richard Zilmer (USMC), "Joint Staff Rapid Validation and Resourcing Request" (July 25, 2006); Official Biography for Richard C. Zilmer— http://www.usmc.mil/genbios2.nsf/0/81D1866C13EA3C4B8525699E006FEE16?opendoc ument; Mark Clayton, "In the Iraqi War Zone, US Army Calls for 'Green' Power," *Christian Science Monitor* (September 7, 2006); Greg Grant, "Renewable Energy Demand Reaches U.S. Front Lines," *DefenseNews.com*, Aug. 14, 2006; "Renewable Energy Systems Wanted in Iraq," *InsideDefense.com* (August 11, 2006). On military platforms and energy efficiency, see generally Amory Lovins, *Winning the Oil Endgame* (Rocky Mountain Institute 2004); Col. Gregory Lengyel USAF, "Department of Defense Energy Strategy: Teaching an Old Dog New Tricks," Federal Executive Fellow Research Paper, The Brookings Institution (April 2007).

Memorandum from the Chair, Council on Environmental Quality

1 Carbon dioxide is responsible for approximately 80% of the human contribution to global warming. Methane, nitrous oxide and some other gases also have an impact. See "Climate Change Science," Environmental Protection Agency website— http://www.epa.gov/climatechange/science/recentac.html.

2 Intergovernmental Panel on Climate Change (IPCC) Working Group 1, *The Physical Science Basis of Climate Change—Summary for Policymakers* (2007) at p. 3—http://ipcc-wg1.ucar.edu/wg1/wg1-report.html. See also Al Gore, *An Inconvenient Truth: The Planetary Emergency of Global Warming and What We Can Do about It* (Rodale Books 2006).

3 IPCC Working Group 1 (2007), *Ibid*, at pp. 5, 7 and 10.

4 IPCC Working Group 1 (2007), *Ibid*, at pp. 3 and 10.

5 IPCC Working Group 1 (2007), *Ibid*, at p. 13.

6 Intergovernmental Panel on Climate Change (IPCC) Working Group 2, *Climate Change Impacts, Adaptation and Vulnerability-Summary for Policymakers* (2007)— http://www.ipcc-wg2.org/index.html.

7 IPCC Working Group 1 (2007), note 2 this chapter, at p. 9.

8 Donald Kennedy, "An Unfortunate U-turn on Carbon," *Science* (March 2001); See also Al Gore, *An Inconvenient Truth*, note 2 this chapter.

9 "Joint Science Academies Statement: Global Response to Climate Change" (June 7, 2005)—http://nationalacademies.org/onpi/06072005.pdf.

10 See Energy Information Administration, *International Energy Outlook 2007* at p. 73 (oil 40%, coal 39%)—http://www.eia.doe.gov/oiaf/ieo/pdf/emissions.pdf; International Energy Agency, *World Energy Outlook 2006* at p. 5 ("Coal overtook oil in 2003 as the leading contributor to global energy-related CO_2 emissions").

11 Joyce Dargay, Dermot Gately and Martin Sommer, "Vehicle Ownership and Income Growth Worldwide: 1960-2030" (January 2007)—http://www.econ.nyu.edu/dept/courses/gately/DGS_Vehicle%20Ownership_2007.pdf.

12 Data from World Resources Institute Climate Analysis Indicators Tool—http://cait.wri.org/cait. See also Energy Information Administration, "U.S. Carbon Dioxide Emissions from Energy Sources, 2006 Flash Estimate" at p. 11 (US CO_2 emissions from petroleum in 2005 were 2575 million metric tons)—http://www.eia.doe.gov/oiaf/1605/flash/pdf/flash.pdf; Bureau of Transportation Statistics, U.S. Dept. of Transportation—http://www.bts.gov/publications/national_transportation_statistics/2002/html/table_04_4 9.html (U.S. CO_2 emissions from petroleum in 2000 equal to 502 million tons of carbon—equivalent to 1,840 tons of carbon dioxide).

13 See U.S. Environmental Protection Agency, "Emission Facts: Average Carbon Dioxide Emissions Resulting from Gasoline and Diesel Fuel"—http://www.epa.gov/otaq/climate/420f05001.htm; John DeCicco and Freda Fung, "Global Warming on the Road: The Climate Impact of America's Automobiles (Environmental Defense, 2006)"—http://www.environmentaldefense.org/documents/5301_Globalwarmingontheroad.pdf; "Dave Chameides, "Help the Planet: Offset Your Car's Emissions," Edmunds.com (February 2007)—http://www.edmunds.com/advice/fueleconomy/articles/119580/article.html.

14 American Lung Association, "Car Care for Clean Air"—http://www.lungusa.org/site/pp.asp?c=dvLUK9O0E&b=36085. See also Union of Concerned Scientists, "How Oil Works"—http://www.ucsusa.org/clean_energy/fossil_fuels/offmen-how-oil-works.html.

15 See American Lung Association, "Outdoor Air Pollutants"—http://www.lungusa.org/site/apps/lk/links.aspx?c=dvLUK9O0E&b=35364.

16 Environmental Protection Agency, "Mobile Source Emissions-Past, Present, and Future"—http://www.epa.gov/otaq/invntory/overview/solutions/milestones.htm.

17 American Lung Association, "State of the Air: 2004"—
http://www.lungusa.org/site/pp.asp?c=dvLUK9OoE&b=50752.

18 National Association of Clean Air Agencies, "Vehicles and Fuels"—
http://www.4cleanair.org/TopicDetails.asp?parent=27.

19 See George Draffan, "Major Oil Spills"—http://www.endgame.org/oilspills.htm.
Environment Canada, "Tanker Spills"—http://www.etc-cte.ec.gc.ca/databases/
TankerSpills/Default.aspx?Path=\Website\river\http://www.etc-cte.ec.gc.ca/databases/
TankerSpills/Default.aspx.

20 *Ibid.* See also David Sandalow, Statement at Hearing on Phaseout of Single-Hull Tank Vessels, U.S. Senate Committee on Commerce, Science and Transportation (January 9, 2003).

21 National Oceanic and Atmospheric Administration, "Response to the Exxon Valdez Spill"—http://archive.orr.noaa.gov/intro/valdez.html.

22 National Research Council, *Oil in the Sea III: Inputs, Fates and Effects,* National Academies Press (2003).

23 *Ibid.*

Memorandum from the Administrator, Environmental Protection Agency

1 Michael Wang, "The Debate on Energy and Greenhouse Gas Emissions Impacts of Fuel Ethanol" (Argonne National Laboratory August 2005) at p. 21—
http://www.transportation.anl.gov/pdfs/TA/347.pdf.

2 *Ibid.*

3 See Electric Power Research Institute and Natural Resources Defense Council,
Environmental Assessment of Plug-In Hybrid Electric Vehicles, Volume 1: Nationwide Greenhouse Gas Emissions (2007)—http://www.epri-reports.org/PHEV-ExecSum-vol1.pdf; Michael Kintner-Meyer et al., "Impact Assessment of Plug-In Hybrid Vehicles, Part I: Technical Analysis" (Pacific Northwest National Laboratory, 2007)—

http://www.pnl.gov/energy/eed/etd/pdfs/phev_feasibility_analysis_combined.pdf; Mark Duvall, Testimony before the Subcommittee on Energy, House Science Committee (May 17, 2006).

4 Robert Williams and Eric Larson, "Comparison of Direct and Indirect Liquefaction Technologies for Making Fluid Fuels from Coal," *Energy for Sustainable Development* (December 2003).

"Messenger from the North" (*Profile: Sarah James*)

1 Article written by David Sandalow for this book. Sources: Conversation between Sarah James and Sandalow (2007); "Fun and James," www.grist.org (December 15, 2006); Conversation between Robert Corell and Sandalow (2007); Robert Corell (chair), *Impacts of a Warming Arctic - Arctic Climate Impact Assessment* (2004).

Memorandum from the Chair, Council of Economic Advisers

1 See Energy Information Administration, "Petroleum Navigator-Product Supplied" (average 20.8 million barrels per day consumed)— http://tonto.eia.doe.gov/dnav/pet/pet_cons_psup_dc_nus_mbblpd_a.htm; Energy Information Administratin, "Petroleum Navigator-Domestic Crude Oil First Purchase Prices by Area" (roughly $60 per barrel average price), available at http://tonto.eia.doe.gov/dnav/pet/pet_pri_dfp1_k_a.htm.

2 See Bureau of Economic Analysis, U.S. Department of Commerce, "National Income Accounts" ($13.2 trillion GDP for 2006)—http://www.bea.gov/national/xls/gdplev.xls.

3 Energy Information Administration, "Basic Petroleum Statistics"— http://www.eia.doe.gov/neic/quickfacts/quickoil.html.

4 Energy Information Administration, *International Energy Annual*, Table 3.1, "World Petroleum Supply and Disposition 2003"— http://www.eia.doe.gov/pub/international/iea2004/table31.xls.

5 See Energy Information Administration, *Monthly Energy Review* (March 2007), Table 3.4 (finished motor gasoline imports rose from 511,000 barrels per day in August 2005 to 644,000 barrels per day in September 2005 to a high of 866,000 barrels per day in October 2005)—http://tonto.eia.doe.gov/FTPROOT/multifuel/mer/00350703.pdf.

6 Energy Information Administration, "Selected Crude Oil Spot Prices"—
http://www.eia.doe.gov/emeu/international/crude1.html. See also, Ian W. H. Parry and
Joel Darmstadter, "The Costs of U.S. Oil Dependency," Resources for the Future
Discussion Paper 03-59 (December 2003) at page 4 and figure 4.

7 Energy Information Administration, "Selected Crude Oil Spot Prices"—
http://www.eia.doe.gov/emeu/international/crude1.html.

8 See George Perry, "The War on Terrorism, the World Oil Market and the U.S.
Economy," Brookings Analysis Paper No. 7 (2001) at p. 7 (0.05 in first year)—Patrick
Anderson et al., "Price Elasticity of Demand" (Nov. 1997)—
http://www.mackinac.org/article.aspx?ID=1247.

9 See Cooper, John C.B., "Price Elasticity of Demand for Crude Oil: Estimates for 23
Countries," *OPEC Review* (March 2003)— http://ssrn.com/abstract=416815; International
Monetary Fund, *World Economic Outlook 2007* at p. 31.

10 See Noureddine Krichene, "A Simultaneous Equations Model for World Crude Oil
and Natural Gas Markets" IMF Working Paper 05/32(2005)—
http://www.imf.org/external/pubs/ft/wp/2005/wp0532.pdf.

11 See Alan Greenspan, Statement before the U.S. Senate Committee on Foreign
Relations (June 7, 2006) at p. 4; Ian Parry and Joel Darmstadter, note 6 this chapter, at p. 6;
Jad Mouawad, "Saudi Officials Seek to Temper the Price of Oil," *The New York Times*
(January 28, 2007) (quoting a former OPEC President saying, "High prices are not in the
interest of Saudi Arabia" because they "attract . . . alternatives.")

12 National Commission on Energy Policy, "Collaborative Development of Petroleum
Sector Performance Indicators" (January 2007) at slide 10—
http://www.energycommission.org/site/page.php?report=29.

13 See Peter Huber and Mark Mills, "Oil, Oil Everywhere...," *The Wall Street Journal*,
January 27, 2005; Ian Parry and Joel Darmstadter, note 6 this chapter, at note 8.

14 See "Really Big Oil," *The Economist* (August 10, 2006); Justin Blum, "National Oil
Firms Take Bigger Role," *The Washington Post* (August 3, 2005).

15 Organization of the Petroleum Exporting Countries, "Who Are OPEC Member
Countries?"—http://www.opec.org/library/FAQs/aboutOPEC/q3.htm.

16 EIA, "Petroleum Navigator-U.S. Crude Oil and Petroleum Products Supplied"—
http://tonto.eia.doe.gov/dnav/pet/hist/mttupus2a.htm

17 See Alan Greenspan, note 11 this chapter, at p. 8; Parry and Darmstadter, note 6 this chapter, at p. 3.

18 Energy Information Administration, "Petroleum Navigator-U.S. Crude Oil Field Production"—http://tonto.eia.doe.gov/dnav/pet/hist/mcrfpus2a.htm.

19 Energy Information Administration, "Petroleum Navigator-Crude Oil Production"—http://tonto.eia.doe.gov/dnav/pet/pet_crd_crpdn_adc_mbblpd_a.htm.

20 Energy Information Administration, "Overview of U.S. Petroleum Trade"—http://www.eia.doe.gov/emeu/mer/pdf/pages/sec1_15.pdf.

21 Energy Information Administration, "Overview of U.S. Petroleum Trade" (2006 total imports, 13,612 barrels per day; 2006 net imports,12,278 barrels per day)—http://www.eia.doe.gov/emeu/mer/pdf/pages/sec1_15.pdf. Energy Information Administration, "Petroluem Navigator-Landed Costs of Imported Crude by Area" (2006 average landed cost of imported crude oil, $59 per barrel)—http://tonto.eia.doe.gov/dnav/pet/pet_pri_land1_k_a.htm.

22 The order presented is for calendar year 2005. Canada consistently exports more to the United States than any other country. Other rank orderings vary somewhat month to month. See Energy Information Administration, "Petroleum Navigator, U.S. Imports by Country of Origin"—http://tonto.eia.doe.gov/dnav/pet/pet_move_impcus_a2_nus_ep00_im0_mbblpd_a.htm.

23 Energy Information Administration, "Global Consumption of Oil per Capita 2003,"—http://www.eia.doe.gov/pub/oil_gas/petroleum/analysis_publications/oil_market_basics/dem_image_cons_per_cap.htm#Consumption%20of%20Oil%20Per%20apita. See also Nationmaster.com, "Energy Statistics—Oil Consumption (per capita)—http://www.nationmaster.com/graph/ene_oil_con_percap-energy-oil-consumption-per-capita.

24 Energy Information Administration, "World Proved Reserves of Oil and Natural Gas, Most Recent Estimates (Jan 9, 2007)"—http://www.eia.doe.gov/emeu/international/reserves.html

25 Bureau of Economic Analysis, U.S. Department of Commerce, "Gross Domestic Product—Percent Change from Preceding Period." Available online at http://www.bea.gov/national/xls/gdpchg.xls; Alan Greenspan, note 11 this chapter, at p. 8 ("To date, it is difficult to find serious erosion in world economic activity as a consequence of sharply higher oil prices.")

26 See Alan Greenspan, note 11 this chapter; Parry and Darmstadter, note 6 this chapter.

27 See Robert Rasche and John Tatom, "Energy Resources and Potential GNP," Federal Reserve Bank of St. Louis (June 1977)— http://research.stlouisfed.org/publications/review/77/06/Resources_Jun1977.pdf; John Burbidge and Alan Harrison, "Testing for the Effects of Oil-Price Rises Using Vector Autoregressions," *International Economic Review* (June 1984).

28 James Hamilton, "What Is an Oil Shock?" *Journal of Econometrics* (April 2003); James D. Hamilton, "Oil and the Macroeconomy since World War II," *Journal of Political Economy* Vol. 91 (April 1983); James Hamilton, "This Is What Happened to the Oil Price-Macroeconomy Relationship," *Journal of Monetary Economics* vol. 38 issue 2 (1996).

29 James Hamilton, "What Is an Oil Shock?," *ibid.*, at p. 364.

30 Ben Bernanke et al., "Systematic Monetary Policy and the Effects of Oil Price Shocks," *Brookings Papers on Economic Activity* (1997).

31 See John Fernald and Bharat Trehan, "Why Hasn't the Jump in Oil Prices Led to a Recession?", *Federal Reserve Board of San Francisco Economic Letter* 2005-31 (November 18, 2005) —http://www.frbsf.org/publications/economics/letter/2005/el2005-31.html.

32 *Ibid.* The U.S. imports roughly 5 billion barrels of oil per year. Every $10 increase in the price of oil, therefore, adds roughly $50 billion of foreign payments.

33 Robert Westcott, "What Would $120 Oil Mean for the Global Economy?" (April 2006)—http://www.secureenergy.org/reports/westcott_report.pdf.

34 Energy Information Administration, "Petroleum Navigator-U.S. All Grades All Formulations Retail Gasoline Prices"— http://tonto.eia.doe.gov/dnav/pet/hist/mg_tt_usM.htm.

35 U.S. Census Bureau, *Income, Poverty and Health Insurance Coverage in the United States* 2005 at Table 1—http://www.census.gov/prod/2006pubs/p60-231.pdf.

36 See "U.S. Consumer Spending Rises by Slowest Amount in 5 Months," *International Herald Tribune* (April 30, 2007)— http://www.iht.com/articles/ap/2007/04/30/business/NA-FIN-ECO-US-Economy.php.

37 Robert Westcott, note 33 this chapter, at p. 5.

"Fred Smith on the Move" (*Profile: Frederick W. Smith*)

1 Article written by David Sandalow for this book. Sources: Conversation between Frederick W. Smith and Sandalow (2007); FedEx Web site at www.fedex.com; Environmental Defense Web site at www.environmentaldefense.org; Forbes.com, "400 Richest Americans" (Sept. 21, 2006)—
http://www.forbes.com/lists/2006/54/biz_06rich400_Frederick-Wallace-Smith_44U5.ht ml; Vance Trimble, *Overnight Success: Federal Express and Frederick Smith, Its Renegade Creator* (Crown Publishers, 1993).

Memorandum from the Secretary of Energy: Trapped in the 1970s

1 Daniel Yergin, *The Prize: The Epic Quest for Oil, Money and Power* (Free Press 1991) at pp. 393, 567ff.

2 Alan Greenspan, Statement before the U.S. Senate Committee on Foreign Relations (June 7, 2006) at page 7.

3 *BP Statistical Review of World Energy* 2007 (Historical Data Workbook)—
http://www.bp.com/productlanding.do?categoryId=6848&contentId=7033471.

4 See generally Daniel Yergin, *The Prize*; Ben Bernanke et al., "Systematic Monetary Policy and the Effects of Oil Price Shocks," *Brookings Papers on Economic Activity* (1997).

5 Imports climbed from 1.1 million barrels per day in 1967 to 6.5 million barrels per day in 1979. Energy Information Administration, "Petroleum Navigator-U.S. Crude Oil Imports from All Countries"—http://tonto.eia.doe.gov/dnav/pet/hist/mcrimus1A.htm.

6 David Goldwyn and Michelle Billig, "Building Strategic Reserves," in David Goldwyn and Jan Kalicki, eds., *Energy and Security: Toward a New Foreign Policy Strategy* (Woodrow Wilson Press 2005); David Victor and Josh House, "Politics Dog the Oil Reserve," *LA Times*, August 22, 2004. See generally Philip Verleger, *Adjusting to Volatile Energy Prices* (Institute for International Economics 1993).

7 Energy Information Administration, "Net Import Share of Petroleum Consumption"—
http://www.eia.doe.gov/oiaf/economy/images/figure_3.gif; Energy Information Administration, "Overview of U.S. Petroleum Trade"—
http://www.eia.doe.gov/emeu/mer/pdf/pages/sec1_15.pdf.

8 U.S. Census Bureau, "Exports, Imports, and Balance of Goods, Petroleum and Non-Petroleum End-Use Category Totals"—
http://www.census.gov/foreign-trade/Press-Release/current_press_release/exh9.pdf.

9 Economists debate the importance of reducing the trade deficit. See, e.g., Walter Williams, "Trade Deficits: Good or Bad" (January 17, 2007)—
http://www.townhall.com/columnists/WalterEWilliams/2007/01/17/trade_deficits_good_or_bad.

10 Energy Information Administration, "Petroleum Navigator-U.S. Imports by Country of Origin"—
http://tonto.eia.doe.gov/dnav/pet/pet_move_impcus_a2_nus_ep00_im0_mbblpd_a.htm.

11 Energy Information Administration, "Persian Gulf Oil and Gas Exports Fact Sheet" (September 2004) at p. 5—
http://commercecan.ic.gc.ca/scdt/bizmap/interface2.nsf/vDownload/CABS_0059/$file/p gulf.pdf.

12 Ron Minsk, "Ending Oil Dependence As We Know It: The Case for National Action," Progressive Policy Institute report (January 30, 2002)—
http://www.ppionline.org/documents/ending_oil.pdf.

13 See generally: EIA, "Voluntary Reporting of Greenhouse Gases Program."—
http://www.eia.doe.gov/oiaf/1605/coefficients.html; EIA, "Uncertainty in Emissions Estimates"—http://www.eia.doe.gov/oiaf/1605/87-92rpt/appb.html; and EPA, Emission Facts: Average Carbon Dioxide Emissions Resulting from Gasoline and Diesel Fuel"—
http://www.epa.gov/otaq/climate/420f05001.htm.

14 Parliamentary Debates, House of Commons (July 17, 1913) at pp. 1474–1477.

15 See Amy Raskin and Saurin Shah, "The Emergence of Hybrid Vehicles: Ending Oil's Stranglehold on Transportation and the Economy" (AllianceBernstein June 2006)—
http://www.calcars.org/alliance-bernstein-hybrids-june06.pdf.

PART II: SOLUTIONS

Memorandum from the Secretary of Energy: Plug-in Hybrids

1 U.S. Department of Energy, "History of Electric Vehicles" —
http://www1.eere.energy.gov/vehiclesandfuels/avta/light_duty/fsev/fsev_history.html;

John Rae, "The Electric Vehicle Company: A Monopoly That Missed"—
http://sloan.stanford.edu/EVonline/rae.htm.

2 U.S. Department of Energy, "History of Electric Vehicles"—
http://www1.eere.energy.gov/vehiclesandfuels/avta/light_duty/fsev/fsev_history.html.

3 The first hybrids first went on sale in Japan in 1997 (Toyota Prius) and in the United
States in 1999 (Honda Insight). See Alex Taylor, "The Birth of the Prius," *Fortune Magazine*,
(February 24, 2006)—
http://money.cnn.com/magazines/fortune/fortune_archive/2006/03/06/8370702/.

4 *Ibid.*

5 See Toyota News Release, "Toyota Worldwide Hybrid Sales Top 1 Million Units"—
http://www.toyota.co.jp/en/news/07/0607.html.

6 See generally Sherry Boschert, *Plug-in Hybrids: The Cars That Will Recharge America* (New
Society Publishers, 2006). See also the CalCars website (www.calcars.org), Plug-In America
website (www.pluginamerica.org) and Plug-In Partners website (www.pluginpartners.org).

7 A PHEV can be designed to rely entirely on its electric motor until the battery is
depleted and then switch to its internal combustion engine. Alternatively, a PHEV can be
designed to switch back and forth between its electric motor and internal combustion
engine, much like a conventional hybrid. There are advantages and disadvantages to each
configuration. See Tony Markel and Andrew Simpson, "Plug-in Hybrid Vehicle Energy
Storage System Design," National Renewable Energy Laboratory Conference Paper (May
2006)—http://www.nrel.gov/vehiclesandfuels/vsa/pdfs/39614.pdf.

8 See Danilo Santini, "Fuel Consumption, Operational Attributes and Potential Markets for
Plug-in Hybrid Technologies" Argonne National Laboratory (October 5, 2006) at slide 21—
http://www.ccap.org/domestic/Domestic%20Dialogue%20October%2006%20Presentations
/Santini%20-%20Plug-in%20Hybrid%20Technology%20Overview%20.pdf; Mark Duvall,
Testimony before the Energy Subcommittee, Science Committee, U.S. House of
Representatives (May 17, 2006) at p. 4—
http://science.house.gov/commdocs/hearings/energy06/May%2017/Duvall.pdf; Cal Cars,
"All About Plug-in Hybrids"—http://www.calcars.org/vehicles.html. National average
retail electricity prices in 2005 were 8.14 cents per kilowatt hour. EIA, "Electric Power
Annual" (November 2006)—
http://www.eia.doe.gov/cneaf/electricity/epa/epa_sum.html.

9 See Leonora Oppenheim, "Plug-In Hybrids" (May 6, 2006)—
http://www.treehugger.com/files/2006/06/treehuggertv_plug_in_prius.php

10 Tony Markel et al., "Plug-In Hybrid Vehicle Analysis," National Renewable Energy Laboratory Milestone Report (November 2006) at p. 2— http://www.nrel.gov/docs/fy07osti/40609.pdf.

11 See Mark Duvall, "Advanced Batteries for Electric Drive Vehicles," Electric Power Research Institute (May 2004)— http://www.evworld.com/library/EPRI_adv_batteries.pdf.

12 See Menahem Anderman, Testimony before U.S. Senate Committee on Energy and Natural Resources (January 30, 2007)— http://energy.senate.gov/public/_files/andermantestimony.pdf.

13 See Amy Raskin and Saurin Shah, "The Emergence of Hybrid Vehicles: Ending Oil's Stranglehold on Transportation and the Economy" (AllianceBernstein June 2006) at p. 2— http://www.calcars.org/alliance-bernstein-hybrids-june06.pdf.

14 See Tony Markel et al., note 10 this chapter, at p. 3.

15 See Ahmad Pesaran, "Battery Choices for Different Plug-in HEV Configurations" National Renewable Energy Laboratory (July 12, 2006) at slide 31— http://www.aqmd.gov/tao/ConferencesWorkshops/PHEV_Forum-07-12-06/4-AhmadPe saran-NREL-revised.pdf.

16 Today's best-selling hybrid-the Toyota Prius-gets 46 mpg (combined city and highway). See U.S. Department of Energy, Fuel Economy Guide— http://www.fueleconomy.gov/feg/calculatorSelectEngine.jsp?year=2007&make=Toyota& model=Prius.

17 See Danilo Santini, note 8 this chapter, at p. 5; Ahmad Pesaran, note 15 this chapter at slide 31; Tony Markel et al., note 10 this chapter, at p. 3.

18 See Michael Kintner-Meyer et al., "Impacts Assessment of Plug-in Hybrid Vehicles on Electric Utilities and Regional U.S. Power Grids" (Pacific Northwest National Laboratory 2007)— http://www.pnl.gov/energy/eed/etd/pdfs/phev_feasibility_analysis_combined.pdf.

19 Oil is not used to generate electricity in the United States, except in very small amounts. Energy Information Administration, *Electric Power Annual*, November 2006, at http://www.eia.doe.gov/cneaf/electricity/epa/epa_sum.html; EIA Petroleum Products (2005 data) at http://www.eia.doe.gov/neic/infosheets/petroleumproducts.html. The electricity used to recharge PHEVs will make up only a small portion of the nation's electricity consumption, even when PHEVs are in widespread use. A substantial rise in electricity rates in response to an oil supply disruption is unlikely, even with PHEVs on the road in large number. In many jurisdictions, electricity rates remain regulated, further dampening potential price shocks.

20 Michael Kintner-Meyer et al., note 18 this chapter, at p. 12. See also Electric Power Research Institute (EPRI) and Natural Resources Defense Council (NRDC), *Environmental Assessment of Plug-In Hybrid Electric Vehicles, Volume 2: United States Air Quality* (2007)—http://www.epri-reports.org/PHEV-ExecSum-vol2.pdf.

21 U.S. Environmental Protection Agency, "Mobile Source Emissions-Pollutants"— http://epa.gov/otaq/invntory/overview/pollutants/index.htm.

22 See National Research Council, *Effectiveness and Impact of Corporate Average Fuel Economy (CAFE) Standards* (National Academies Press, 2002) at p. 31— http://www.nap.edu/catalog/10172.html; Colorado State University Engines and Energy Conversion Lab, "Heat Transfer"— http://www.engr.colostate.edu/~allan/heat_trans/page2/page2.html; Perrin Quarles Associates, "Review of Potential Efficiency Improvements at Coal-Fired Power Plants" (April 17, 2001)— http://www.cier.umd.edu/RGGI/documents/Stakeholder%20Comments/Data_coaleff_epa_2001.pdf.

23 See U.S. Environmental Protection Agency, "Emission Facts: Average Carbon Dioxide Emissions Resulting from Gasoline and Diesel Fuel"— http://www.epa.gov/otaq/climate/420f05001.htm.

24 See U.S. Environmental Protection Agency, "Light-Duty Automotive Technology and Fuel Economy Trends: 1975 Through 2006—Executive Summary" at Highlight #1— http://www.epa.gov/otaq/cert/mpg/fetrends/420s06003.htm; David Gerard and Lester Lave, "The Economics of CAFE Reconsidered: A Response to CAFE Critics and a Case for Fuel Economy Standards," AEI-Brookings Joint Center for Regulatory Studies (September, 2003) at p. 18, Figure 1.

25 See U.S. Department of Energy, "Carbon Dioxide Emissions from the Generation of Electric Power in the United States" (July 2000) at p. 2— http://tonto.eia.doe.gov/FTPROOT/environment/co2emiss00.pdf.

26 See Danilo Santini, note 8 this chapter, at p. 21 (citing figure of roughly 3 miles/kWh); Doug Korthof, "Why Not Switch to Electric Cars? *EVWorld* (Sept. 2, 2005), citing figures of 4 miles/kwH and above—http://www.evworld.com/news.cfm?newsid=9376.

27 See Joe Romm, "Energy Expert Joe Romm on CO2 Emissions of Gas and Electric Cars" (June 13, 2005)—http://www.calcars.org/calcars-news/65.html.

28 Michael Kintner-Meyer et al., note 18 this chapter; Mark Duvall, testimony, note 8 this chapter. See also Electric Power Research Institute (EPRI) and Natural Resources Defense Council (NRDC), *Environmental Assessment of Plug-In Hybrid Electric Vehicles, Volume 1: Nationwide Greenhouse Gas Emissions* (2007)—http://www.epri-reports.org/PHEV-ExecSum-vol1.pdf.

29 Michael Kintner-Meyer et al., note 18 this chapter; EPRI and NRDC, Volume 2: U.S. Air Quality, note 20 this chapter.

30 Robert L. Mitchell, "Lithium Ion Batteries: High-Tech's Latest Mountain of Waste," *Computerworld* (August 22, 2006)—http://www.computerworld.com/blogs/node/3285.

31 See, generally, Rechargeable Battery Recycling Corporation website—http://www.rbrc.org/call2recycle/corporate/index.html ; Environment, Health and Safety Online—http://ehso.com/ehshome/batteries.php; Battery Council International website—http://www.batterycouncil.org/recycling.html.

32 See Mark Duvall testimony, note 8 this chapter; Michael Kintner-Meyer et al., note 18 this chapter at p. 10 (84% of existing fleet could be supported with generating, transmission and distribution capacity currently available); Bureau of Transportation Statistics, U.S. Department of Transportation, "Table 1-11: Number of U.S. Aircraft, Vehicle, Vessels, and Other Conveyances (247 million registered highway vehicles in 2005)—http://www.bts.gov/publications/national_transportation_statistics/html/table_01_11.html.

33 See Amy Raskin and Saurin Shah, note 13 this chapter, at p. 37; Lucy Sanna, "Driving the Solution," *EPRI Journal* (Fall 2005)—www.calcars.org/epri-driving-solution-1012885_PHEV.pdf.

34 With "time-of-day metering," electricity costs vary depending on the time of day. Rates are usually lowest at night, when electricity demand is low, and highest in the afternoon. See, generally, AC Propulsion, "Electric Drive Vehicles as Distributed Power Generation Systems" (2000)—http://www.acpropulsion.com/Veh_Grid_Power/Veh_grid_power.htm.

35 See, generally, Ahmad Pesaran, note 15 this chapter.

36 See AllAboutBatteries.com, "Battery Energy—What Battery Provides More?"—http://www.allaboutbatteries.com/Battery-Energy.html.

37 See Damon Darlin and Barnaby J. Feder, "Need for Battery Power Runs Into Basic Hurdles of Science," *The New York Times* (August 16, 2006); CalCars, "Thinking About Lithium Batteries and Safety" (September 18, 2006)—http://www.calcars.org/calcars-news/521.html. Another concern is that lithium shortages may develop in the years ahead. See Jack Lifton, "Investing in U.S. Natural Resources, Part 1: A Lithium Supply Crisis," *Resource Investor* (December 13, 2006)— http://www.resourceinvestor.com/pebble.asp?relid=27139.

38 See Tony Markel et al., note 10 this chapter, at p. 2; Darlin and Feder, "Need for Battery Power Runs Into Basic Hurdles of Science," *The New York Times* (August 16, 2006).

39 *Ibid.*; Sebastian Blanco, "ECTA Conference," AutoblogGreen (Nov. 29, 2006)— http://www.autobloggreen.com/2006/11/29/edta-conference-altair-nanotechnologies-na nosafe-batteries-in-p/; A123 Systems website at www.a123systems.com

40 U.S. General Services Administration, *Federal Fleet Report 2005* at Table 2-9 (over 68,000 in 2005 and 65,000 in 2004)— http://www.gsa.gov/gsa/cm_attachments/GSA_DOCUMENT/FFR2005_R2K-g6_0Z5 RDZ-i34K-pR.pdf.

41 On January 24, 2007, President George W. Bush issued an executive order (E.O. 13423) on federal environmental and energy management that requires federal agencies to buy PHEVs when "commercially available at a cost reasonably comparable, on the basis of life-cycle cost" to other cars. Text at http://a257.g.akamaitech.net/7/257/2422/01jan20071800/edocket.access.gpo.gov/2007/ pdf/07-374.pdf. This provision, while unobjectionable, will do little to accelerate commercialization of PHEVs, since first-generation PHEVs will cost more than similar cars.

42 See www.pluginpartners.org. (A "soft order" is a declaration of strong interest in buying a PHEV.) See also Miguel Llanos "Cities to Seek Plug-in Hybrids," MSNBC (January 24, 2006)—http://www.msnbc.msn.com/id/10990145/.

43 See Peter Orszag, Fred Goldberg, Jr. and Lily Batchelder, "Reforming Tax Incentives into Uniform Refundable Tax Credits," Brookings Policy Brief (August 2006)— http://www.brookings.edu/comm/policybriefs/pb156.htm.

44 See Bracken Hendricks et al., *Health Care for Hybrids: Investing in Oil Savings, Retiree Health Care and a Revitalized Auto Industry for a Stronger America*— *http://*www.thebreakthrough.org/PDF/HealthCareHybrids.pdf; Stephen Cooney and Brent Yacobucci, *U.S. Automotive Industry: Policy Overview and Recent History* (Congressional Research Service) April 25, 2005).

45 *Ibid.*

46 See generally, National Research Council, *Effectiveness of the United States Advanced Battery Consortium as a Government-Industry Partnership* (National Academy Press , 1998).

47 See National Research Council, *Energy Research at DoE: Was It Worth It? Energy Efficiency and Fossil Energy Research 1978 to 2000* (National Academies Press 2001)— http://books.nap.edu/execsumm_pdf/10165.pdf; American Council for Energy Efficient Economy, "Energy Efficiency Research, Development and Deployment: Why Is Federal Support Necessary?"—http://www.aceee.org/energy/rdd.pdf.

"From Showroom to the Big Screen" (*Profile: Chelsea Sexton*)

1 Article written by David Sandalow for this book. Sources: Conversations between Chelsea Sexton and Sandalow (2007); Sebastian Blanco, "Exclusive Q&A with Chelsea Sexton about the EV1," *AutoblogGreen* (June 22, 2006)— http://www.autobloggreen.com/2006/06/22/exclusive-qanda-with-chelsea-sexton-about-the-ev1-why-the-priu/; Chelsea Sexton, "Why I Think GM Killed the EV-1" *EVWorld* (July 15, 2005)—http://www.evworld.com/article.cfm?storyid=875.

"Electric Entrepreneur" (*Profile: Martin Eberhard*)

1 Article written by David Sandalow for this book. Sources: Conversation between Sandalow and Martin Eberhard (2007); Tesla Motors Web site at www.teslamotors.com; Interview with Martin Eberhard, *Plenty TV*— http://www.plentymag.com/tv/2006/11/2_minutes_with_tes.php; Martin Eberhard, Testimony before U.S. Senate Finance Committee (May 1, 2007)— http://www.senate.gov/~finance/hearings/testimony/2007test/050107testme.pdf.

Memorandum from the Secretary of Agriculture: Biofuels

1 Bill Kovarik, "Henry Ford, Charles F. Kettering and the Fuel of the Future," *Automotive History Review* (Spring 1998) at pp. 7-27 — http://www.radford.edu/~wkovarik/papers/fuel.html.

2 See National Biodiesel Board, "News Events" (March 17, 2006)— http://www.biodiesel.org/news/07clicktrhrus/20070318_biodieselday.shtm. See also Gerhard Knothe, "Historical perspectives on vegetable oil-based diesel fuels," *Inform* (November 2001) (similar quote with slightly different wording)— http://www.biodiesel.org/resources/reportsdatabase/reports/gen/20011101_gen-346.pdf.

3 See Renewable Fuels Association, "Industry Statistics" (2007)—
http://www.ethanolrfa.org/industry/statistics/#B; Energy Information Administration,
"Renewable Energy, Consumption, by Sector and Source" (February 2007)—
http://www.eia.doe.gov/oiaf/aeo/excel/aeotab_17.xls.

4 David Bransby, "Switchgrass Profile"—
http://bioenergy.ornl.gov/papers/misc/switchgrass-profile.html.

5 The gasoline in E85 helps ignite the fuel in cold weather. See National Ethanol Vehicle
Coalition, "Frequently Asked Questions"—
http://www.e85fuel.com/e85101/faqs/types.php.

6 See Ron Miller, Testimony before Agriculture, Nutrition and Forestry Committee, U.S.
Senate (January 10, 2007)—
http://www.ethanolrfa.org/objects/documents/924/aventine_ron_miller_testimony_1-10-
07.pdf.

7 See Ken Thomas, "Flex Fuel Vehicles Touted," *USA Today.com* (May 5, 2007)—
http://www.usatoday.com/money/autos/environment/2007-05-05-ethanolvehicles_N.ht
m; Mark Clayton, "Gas Substitutes Boost the Flex Fuel Car *Christian Science Monitor*
(January 26, 2007)—http://www.csmonitor.com/2007/0126/p01s04-sten.html.

8 See ZFacts.com, "Ethanol" (116,000 BTU/gallon in gasoline; 76,000 BTU/gallon in
ethanol)—http://zfacts.com/p/436.html; Gene Johnston, "E85 and Gas Mileage,"
Agriculture On-line (May 8, 2006)—
http://www.agriculture.com/ag/story.jhtml?storyid=/templatedata/ag/story/data/114709
8565893.xml; SaabUSA website, "Ethanol-fueled Saab 9-5 Bio-Power honored with
Popular Science 'Best of What's New' award," (November 9, 2005)—
http://www.saabusa.com/saabjsp/about/pr_051109.jsp.

9 The literature on this point is sparse. See Farzad Taheripour and Wallace Tyner, "Ethanol
Subsidies, Who Gets the Benefits?" (Purdue University, April 2007) (providing a theoretical
analysis which suggests that, in the current environment, the ethanol industry likely
captures most of the benefit of the excise tax credit)—
http://www.farmfoundation.org/projects/documents/TaheripourandTyner_St_Louis.pdf.
See also Bruce Gardner, "Fuel Ethanol Subsidies and Farm Price Support: Boon or
Boondoggle?" (University of Maryland October 2003)—
http://www.arec.umd.edu/publications/papers/Working-Papers-PDF-files/03-11.pdf.

10 See Bob Dineen, Testimony before the Subcommittee on Select Revenue Measures, Committee on Ways and Means, U.S. House of Representatives (April 19, 2007)— http://waysandmeans.house.gov/hearings.asp?formmode=view&id=5797.

11 See generally David Luhmow and Geraldo Samor, "As Brazil Fills Up on Ethanol, It Weans Off Energy," *Wall Street Journal* (January 16, 2006); David Sandalow, "Ethanol: Lessons from Brazil," in *A High Growth Strategy for Ethanol* (Aspen Institute, 2006); National Association of Automakers of Brazil (ANFAVEA), "Tabela 11-Vendas Atacado Mercado Interna por Tipo e Combustivel" (2007)— http://www.anfavea.com.br/tabelas/autoveiculos/tabela11_vendas.pdf.

12 Martin von Lampe, "*Agricultural Market Impacts of Future Growth in the Production of Biofuels* (OECD, February 2006)—http://www.oecd.org/dataoecd/58/62/36074135.pdf.

13 See National Biodiesel Board estimates— http://www.biodiesel.org/pdf_files/fuelfactsheets/Biodiesel_Sales_Graph.pdf.

14 BP Press Office, "BP and DuPont Announce Partnership to Develop Advanced Biofuels" (June 20, 2006)— http://www.bp.com/genericarticle.do?categoryId=2012968&contentId=7018942.

15 See, e.g., Dennis Avery, "Biofuels, Food, or Wildlife: The Massive Land Costs of U.S. Ethanol" (Competitive Enterprise Institute, September 21, 2006)— http://www.cei.org/pdf/5532.pdf.

16 See, e.g., Khosla Ventures website—http://www.khoslaventures.com/resources.html.

17 Current gasoline usage is roughly 140 billion gallons per year. EIA, "Petroleum Navigator, Product Supplied"— http://tonto.eia.doe.gov/dnav/pet/pet_cons_psup_dc_nus_mbbl_a.htm.

18 Based on historical trends without significant technological breakthroughs, the ethanol produced from an acre of corn could increase from roughly 460 gallons today to roughly 640 gallons by 2025. This is based on yields of 200 bushels of corn per acre and 3.2 gallons of ethanol per bushel by 2025. See, generally, Hosein Shapouri, "Comparative Advantage in Ethanol Production: U.S. Grains versus Sugar" (USDA December 2005)— http://www.farmfoundation.org/projects/documents/HoseinShapouri.pdf; Vinod Khosla, "Imagining the Future of Gasoline: Separating Reality from Blue-sky Dreaming?" (September 2006 draft)— http://www.khoslaventures.com/presentations/ImaginingTomorrowSept2006a.doc.

19 See Vinod Khosla, "Is Ethanol Controversial? Should it be?" (September 2006 draft)—http://www.khoslaventures.com/presentations/KhoslaEthanolControversySept2006.doc; Henrique Oliveira, "Learning Curve: Ethanol Production Costs Decrease 75% in 25 Years," *Ethablog* (August 6, 2006)—http://ethablog.blogspot.com/2006/08/learning-curve-ethanol-production.html.

20 See Nathaniel Green, *Growing Energy: How Biofuels Can Help End America's Oil Dependence* (December 2004)—http://www.nrdc.org/air/energy/biofuels/biofuels.pdf; Energy Future Coalition, *Biofuels* for Our Future: A Primer at note 178—http://www.unfoundation.org/staging/biofuelsprimer/Biofuel_Primer.doc; Vinod Khosla, "Is Ethanol Controversial? Should It Be?", note 19 in this chapter.

21 See generally Timothy Egan, "Life on the Ethanol-Guzzling Prairie," *The New York Times* (February 11, 2007)

22 See National Corn Growers Association, *Taking Ownership of Grain Belt Agriculture* (February 2005) at p. 11—http://ncga.com/public_policy/takingOwnership/index.htm; John M. Urbanchuk, "Contribution of the Ethanol Industry to the Economy of the United States" (Renewable Fuels Association, February 2006)—http://www.ncga.com/ethanol/pdfs/031506Urbanchuk.pdf; Vern Pierce et al., "Employment and Economic Benefits of Ethanol Production in Missouri" (Missouri Corn Growers Association, February 2007)—http://agebb.missouri.edu/commag/ethanolreport2007.pdf; Energy Future Coalition, *Biofuels for Our Future: A Primer*, note 20 this chapter, at p. 35.

23 National Corn Growers Association, "Future Structure of Agriculture Task Force"—http://www.usda.gov/oce/forum/2006%20Speeches/PDF%20speech%20docs/Tumbleson 229.pdf.

24 See State Energy Conservation Office, State of Texas, "Ethanol"—http://www.seco.cpa.state.tx.us/re_ethanol_plants.htm.

25 Energy Information Administration, U.S. Carbon Dioxide Emissions from Energy Sources 2006 Flash Estimate, p.11. Available online at http://www.eia.doe.gov/oiaf/1605/flash/pdf/flash.pdf.

26 Michael Wang, "The Debate on Energy and Greenhouse Gas Emissions Impacts of Fuel Ethanol" (Argonne National Laboratory August 2005) at p. 21—http://www.transportation.anl.gov/pdfs/TA/347.pdf.

27 *Ibid.*

28 See generally Energy Future Coalition, "Comments on U.S. EPA's Proposed Rule: Control of Hazardous Air Pollutants from Mobile Sources" (submitted May 30, 2006)— http://www.energyfuturecoalition.org/pubs/EFC_Aromatics.pdf; Energy Future Coalition, Comments on U.S. EPA's Proposed Rule: Regulation of Fuel and Fuel Additives-Renewable Fuel Standard Program (submitted November 12, 2006)— http://www.energyfuturecoalition.org/pubs/EFC_RFSCommentNov.2006.pdf.

29 Nathaniel Green, "Ethanol and the Environment" in *A High Growth Strategy for Ethanol* (Aspen Institute, 2006); Gary Z. Whitten, "Air Quality and Ethanol in Gasoline," (Renewable Fuels Association 2004)— http://www.ethanolrfa.org/objects/documents/69/nec_whitten.pdf.

30 See Tom Lovejoy, "Biofuels," *Foresight* (July 2007).

31 See David Tilman et al., "Carbon-Negative Biofuels from Low-Input High-Diversity Grassland Biomass," *Science* (December 8, 2006)— http://www.sciencemag.org/cgi/content/abstract/314/5805/1598.

32 See J. Hettenhaus, "Achieving Sustainable Production of Agricultural Biomass for Biorefinery Feedstock" (Biotechnology Industry Organization November 2006)— http://www.bio.org/ind/biofuel/SustainableBiomassReport.pdf.

33 See U.S, Department of Agriculture, "Feeds Grain Datase"— http://www.ers.usda.gov/data/feedgrains/; Iowa Department of Agriculture and Land Stewardship, "Grain Report Archive"—http://www.agriculture.state.ia.us/historic.html.

34 See Michael Pollan, *The Omnivore's Dilemma* (Penguin 2006); Michael Pollan, "What's Eating America," *Smithsonian Magazine* (July 2006)— http://www.smithsonianmagazine.com/issues/2006/july/presence.php.

35 Economic Research Service, U.S. Department of Agriculture, "Farm to Retail Price Spreads for Individual Food Items" (July 28, 2006)— http://www.ers.usda.gov/briefing/foodpricespreads/spreads/table1a.htm.

36 See Keith Collins, A Status Report on Biofuels (USDA, April 12, 2007)— http://www.farmfoundation.org/projects/documents/CollinsEnergyStatusofBiofuels4-12-07.pdf; National Corn Grower's Association, "Have Higher Corn Prices *Really* Driven Consumer Food Prices Higher in the Last Six Months?"— http://www.ethanolrfa.org/objects/documents/1072/042307highercornpricesfoodprices.pdf.

37 See Lester Brown, Testimony before Senate Committee on Environment & Public Works (June 13, 2007)—http://www.earth-policy.org/Transcripts/SenateEPW07.htm; Lester Brown, "Ethanol Could Leave the World Hungry," *Fortune* (August 16, 2006).

38 Ford Runge and Benjamin Senauer, "How Biofuels Could Starve the Poor," *Foreign Affairs* (May/June 2007)—http://www.foreignaffairs.org/20070501faessay86305/c-ford-runge-benjamin-senauer/how-biofuels-could-starve-the-poor.html.

39 See John Podesta, "Fueling the Future," Remarks to Harvard University Center for the Environment (March 23, 2006)—http://www.americanprogress.org/kf/jdp_harvard.pdf; Center for American Progress, "Africa's Oil Emergency" (June 2006)— http://www.americanprogress.org/kf/hipc_energypoverty_chart.pdf; Energy Future Coalition, "Biofuels FAQs"—http://www.energyfuturecoalition.org/biofuels/.

40 See Ted Turner, "Breaking the WTO Logjam with Biofuels, Remarks to WTO Public Forum" (September 25, 2006); Jake Caldwell, *Fueling a New Farm Economy: Creating Incentives for Biofuels in Agriculture and Trade Policy* (Center for American Progress 2007)— http://www.americanprogress.org/issues/2007/01/pdf/farm_economy.pdf.

41 See David Nilles, "U.S. E85 Availability Reaches Milestone," *Ethanol Producer Magazine* (October 2006)—U.S. Department of Energy, "E85 Toolkit" (including copies of invoices for E85 tank conversions)—http://www.eere.energy.gov/afdc/e85toolkit/pdfs/bh_cost.pdf and http://www.eere.energy.gov/afdc/e85toolkit/pdfs/west_side_cost.pdf; Anu Prasad telephone interview with Roger Listenberger, Director of E85 Fuel Networking, National Ethanol Vehicle Coalition (November, 2006); Laura Meckler, "Big oil rules may keep ethanol out of some stations," *Wall Street Journal* (April 2, 2007).

42 See Energy Information Administration, "A Primer on Gasoline Prices" (May 2006)— http://www.eia.doe.gov/bookshelf/brochures/gasolinepricesprimer/eia1_2005primerM.html; Association for Convenience and Petroleum Retailing, "2006 Gas Price Kit."

43 See Alan Greenspan, Statement before the U.S. Senate Committee on Foreign Relations (June 7, 2006) at page 4— http://www.senate.gov/~foreign/testimony/2006/GreenspanTestimony060607.pdf; Ian W. H. Parry and Joel Darmstadter, "The Costs of U.S. Oil Dependency," Resources for the Future Discussion Paper 03-59 (December 2003) at p. 6; Jad Mouawad, "Saudi Officials Seek to Temper the Price of Oil," *The New York Times* (January 28, 2007), quoting a former OPEC President saying, "High prices are not in the interest of Saudi Arabia because they "attract . . . alternatives."

44 These include the extraordinary political and military resources devoted to securing and protecting oil flows worldwide.

Memorandum from the U.S. Trade Representative: Ethanol Tariff

1 Lore Serra and Subhojit Daripa, "Sugar and Ethanol Prices—BiWeekly Data Sheet," (Morgan Stanley Research July 27, 2007) at p. 6; Christopher Palmeri and Aaron Pressman, "Let the Ethanol Flow," *BusinessWeek*, May 4, 2006.

2 Joel Severinghaus, "Why We import Brazilian Ethanol" (Iowa Farm Bureau, July 2005)— http://www.iowafarmbureau.com/programs/commodity/information/pdf/Trade%20Matt ers%20column%2020050714%20Brazilian%20ethanol.pdf.

3 See Lore Serra and Subhojit Daripa, note 1 this chapter.

4 James Hoare, "Jeb Bush Urges End to Ethanol Tariff," *Environment News* (August 2006)—http://www.heartland.org/Article.cfm?artId=19470.

5 See Office of Senator Diane Feinstein, "Senators Feinstein and Kyl Call for Eliminating Ethanol Import Tariff" (press release May 5, 2006)— http://feinstein.senate.gov/06releases/r-ethanol-tariff.htm.

6 Renewable Fuels Association, "Ethanol Facts: Trade"— http://www.ethanolrfa.org/resource/facts/trade/.

"I Am Indy" (*Profile: Buddy Rice*)

1 Article written by David Sandalow for this book. Sources: Conversation between Sandalow and Buddy Rice (2007); Indy Car Web site at http://www.indycar.com/tech/ethanol.php; Ethanol Promotion and Information Council, "Motorsports"—http://www.drivingethanol.org/motorsports/motorsports.aspx; Roland James, "Ethanol Boosters Hoping for Indy 500 Win" (MSNBC.com May 28, 2006)— http://www.msnbc.msn.com/id/12740848/.

"From High Tech to Ethanol" (*Profile: Vinod Khosla*)

1 Article written by David Sandalow for this book. Sources: Conversations between Vinod Khosla and Sandalow (2006 and 2007); Khosla Ventures website— http://www.khoslaventures.com; Vinod Khosla, "My Big Biofuels Bet," *Wired Magazine* (October 2006); Justin Hibbard, "Catching up with Vinod Khosla," *BusinessWeek* (May 31, 2005); Robert Rapier, "R-Squared Energy Blog"—http://i-r-squared.blogspot.com.

Memorandum from the Secretary of Transportation: Fuel Efficiency

1 See Toyota News Release, "Toyota Worldwide Hybrid Sales Top 1 Million Units" (June 7, 2007)—http://www.toyota.co.jp/en/news/07/0607.html.

2 Figures are for the 2007 model year, combined city and highway, using the new EPA ratings system. See U.S. Department of Energy, Fuel Economy Guide—http://www.fueleconomy.gov.

3 Amy Raskin and Saurin Shah, "The Emergence of Hybrid Vehicles: Ending Oil's Stranglehold on Transportation and the Economy" (AllianceBernstein June 2006) at p. 18—http://www.calcars.org/alliance-bernstein-hybrids-june06.pdf.

4 Unlike internal combustion engines, electric motors produce instantaneous torque upon ignition. As a result, hybrids have better torque than standard cars at low engine speeds.

5 Mahesh Lunani, "What Is Your Hybrid Strategy?" *Automotive Design & Production* (July 2005)—http://findarticles.com/p/articles/mi_moKJI/is_7_117/ai_n14932628.

6 Amy Raskin and Saurin Shah, note 3 this chapter, at p.1.

7 Amy Raskin and Saurin Shah, note 3 this chapter, at p.8.

8 Amy Raskin and Saurin Shah, note 3 this chapter, at p.10 (projecting a *decline* in global oil consumption in vehicles to 16 million barrels per day in 2030 due to improved fuel efficiency).

9 See James Healey, Toyota Hopes to Cut Hybrid Premium in Half, *USA Today* (September 12, 2005)—http://www.usatoday.com/tech/news/techinnovations/2005-09-12-toyota-hybrid_x.htm; *Consumer Reports*, "The Dollars and Sense of Hybrid Cars" (ConsumerReports.org, September 2006).

10 Amy Raskin and Saurin Shah, note 3 this chapter, at p. 20; James Healey, note 9 this chapter.

11 National Commisson on Energy Policy (NCEP) staff, "The Potential Role of Diesel Technology" (NCEP Background Paper February 2003)—http://www.energycommission.org/files/finalReport/I.5.a%20-%20Diesel%20Technology.pdf; Matt Vella, "Diesels Come Clean," *BusinessWeek* (March 26, 2007)—http://www.businessweek.com/autos/content/mar2007/bw20070326_220157.htm?chan=autos_autos+index+page.

12 See European Automobile Manufacturers Association, "Press Release" (8 November 2006)—http://www.acea.be/files/20061978att01.pdf; Diesel Technology Forum, "Cars, Trucks and SUVs"—http://www.dieselforum.org/where-is-diesel/cars-trucks-suvs.

13 Kevin Bullis, "How Diesel Technology Could Cut Oil Imports," *MIT Technology Review* (Oct. 13, 2006)—http://www.technologyreview.com/read_article.aspx?id=17615.

14 National Commission on Energy Policy staff, note 11 this chapter.

15 National Commission on Energy Policy staff, note 11 this chapter.

16 Matt Vella, note 11 this chapter.

17 Peter Schmidt, "Diesel Car Prospects to 2011" (October 27, 2006)—at http://www.eagleaid.com/.

18 National Research Council, *Effectiveness and Impact of Corporate Average Fuel Economy (CAFE) Standards* (National Academies Press 2002) at p. 3— http://www.nap.edu/catalog/10172.html.

19 *Ibid.* at chapter 3.

20 Union of Concerned Scientists, "Clean Vehicles"— http://www.ucsusa.org/clean_vehicles/cars_pickups_suvs/nas-report-cafe-effectiveness-and-impact.html.

21 David Gerard and Lester Lave, "The Economics of CAFE Reconsidered: A Response to CAFE Critics and a Case for Fuel Economy Standards," *AEI-Brookings Joint Center for Regulatory Studies* (September, 2003) at pp.2 and 18

22 Pietro Nivola and Robert Crandall, *The Extra Mile: Rethinking Energy Policy for Automotive Transportation* (Brookings Institution 1995) at p.24.

23 Paul Portney et al., "The Economics of Fuel Economy Standards," (Resources for the Future Discussion Paper November 2003) at p. 2.

24 See, generally, Robert Bamberger, "Automobile and Light Truck Fuel Economy: The CAFE Standards" (Congressional Research Service, June 19, 2003) at Table 2— http://www.ncseonline.org/NLE/CRSreports/03Jul/IB90122.pdf.

25 See U.S. Environmental Protection Agency, "Light-Duty Automotive Technology and Fuel Economy Trends: 1975 Through 2006 - Executive Summary" at Highlight #1— http://www.epa.gov/otaq/cert/mpg/fetrends/420s06003.htm; David Gerard and Lester Lave, note 21 this chapter, at pp. 4 and 18.

26 See, generally, Keith Bradsher, *High and Mighty: The Dangerous Rise of the SUV* (Public Affairs 2003); Gregg Easterbrook, "Turn On: Why Kerry's Great on Energy," *The New Republic* (October 18, 2004); Gregg Easterbrook, "Axle of Evil: America's Twisted Love Affair with Sociopathic Cars" (*The New Republic*, January 10, 2003).

27 David Gerard and Lester Lave, note 21 this chapter, at p. 3.

28 See, generally, William Pizer, Testimony before Committee on Energy and Commerce, U.S. House of Representatives (May 3, 2006) at p. 5— http://www.rff.org/rff/Documents/Pizer%20CAFE%20testimony%205-3-06.pdf; John Dernbach, "Stabilizing and Then Reducing U.S. Energy Consumption," *Environmental Law Review* (January 2007).

29 Feng An and Amanda Sauer, "Comparison of Passenger Vehicle Fuel Economy and Greenhouse Gas Emissions Standards Around the World" (Pew Center on Global Climate Change December, 2004)— http://www.pewclimate.org/docUploads/Fuel%20Economy%20and%20GHG%20Standards%5F010605%5F110719%2E.pdf.

30 National Research Council, note 18 this paper, at pp. 19-20.

31 National Research Council, note 18 this paper, at p. 3.

32 See David Greene, Testimony before Committee on Commerce, Science and Transportion, U.S. Senate (March 6, 2007).

33 See Bureau of Economic Analysis, U.S. Department of Commerce, "Current Dollar and 'Real' Gross Domestic Product"—http://www.bea.gov/national/xls/gdplev.xls; Energy Information Administration, "International Petroleum Monthly-OECD Countries and World Petroleum Demand 1970–2006"—http://www.eia.doe.gov/emeu/ipsr/t46.xls.

34 3.2 million barrels/day$\times$42 gallons/barrel$\times$19.6 pounds CO_2/gallon gasoline$\times$365 days/year$\times$1 metric ton/2204 pounds=436 million metric tons CO_2. Total U.S. CO_2 emissions in 2005 were just over 6,000 million metric tons. Energy Information Administration, "Emissions of Greenhouse Gases in the United States 2005"— http://www.eia.doe.gov/oiaf/1605/ggrpt/carbon.html. See also National Research Council, note 18 this chapter, at p. 20 ("improvements in light duty fuel economy have reduced overall U.S. emissions by about 7%").

35 Paul Portney et al., note 23 this chapter.

36 See National Automobile Dealers Association, "The New Vehicle Department," *AutoExecMag.com* (May, 2007) (16.5 million new vehicles sales in 2006)— http://www.nada.org/NR/rdonlyres/C18D7380-0175-4D46-BC65-AF2AA8A2C268/0/ NADA_DATA_2007_NewVehicle_Department.pdf; see also Bureau of Transportation Statistics, U.S. Department of Transportation, "Table 1-11: Number of U.S. Aircraft, Vehicles, Vessels, and Other Conveyances" (more than 247 million registered vehicles in 2005)— http://www.bts.gov/publications/national_transportation_statistics/html/table_01_11.html . See, generally, Pietro Nivola and Robert Crandall, note 22 this chapter.

37 National Research Council, note 18 this chapter, at p.19 ("a 10% increase in fuel economy is likely to result in roughly a 1 to 2 percent increase in vehicle travel, all else being equal").

38 See David Gerard and Lester Lave, note 21 this paper, at p.3.

39 Variation in weight among vehicles contributes to traffic fatalities. See R. M. Van Auken and J. W. Zellner, "An Assessment of the Effect of Vehicle Weight on Fatality Risk" (Dynamic Research February, 2002)— http://www.citizen.org/documents/Dynamic_Research_study_on_Weight_and_Safety_ex ec_summary.pdf; Hans Joksch, Dawn Massie and Robert Pichler, *Vehicle Aggressivity: Fleet Characterization Using Traffic Collision Data.* (National Highway Traffice Safety Administration, U.S. Department of Transportation, 1998)—http://www-nrd.nhtsa.dot.gov/pdf/nrd-11/aggress1.pdf; C. J. Kahane, "Relationships between Vehicle Size and Fatality Risk in Model Years 1985–93: Passenger Cars and Light Trucks" (U.S. Department of Transportation January 1997).

40 National Research Council, note 18 this chapter at p. 3.

41 National Research Council, note 18 this chapter at Appendix A, p. 117.

42 See Randall Lutter and Troy Kravitz (2003), "Do Regulations Requiring Light Trucks to Be More Fuel Efficient Make Economic Sense?" (AEI-Brookings Joint Center for Regulatory Studies February 2003)— http://www.aei.brookings.org/admin/authorpdfs/page.php?id=244.

43 See William Pizer, note 28 this chapter, at p. 6. Under the old CAFE program, manufacturers can earn credits for superior performance and use these credits themselves in future years. FREEdom standards would retain this feature.

44 William Pizer, note 28 this chapter, at p. 6.

"Man with a Mission" (Profile: Jerome Ringo)

1 Article written by David Sandalow for this book. Sources: Conversation between Jerome Ringo and Sandalow (2007); Jerome Ringo, Testimony before Select Committee on Energy Independence and Global Warming, U.S. House of Representatives (May 22, 2007); Erik Kancler, "The Pioneer," *Mother Jones* (April 25, 2005); Alison Grant, "Turning American Industry Green," *Cleveland Plain Dealer* (June 7, 2007); Jerome Ringo, Remarks at Take Back America Conference (June 12, 2006)— http://home.ourfuture.org/tba06/agenda.html.

Memorandum from the Chair, Council of Economic Advisers: Gasoline Taxes

1 Bureau of Labor Statistics, U.S, Department of Labor, "Inflation Calculator," http://www.bls.gov/cpi ; Energy Information Administration, "Petroleum Navigator, U.S. All Grades All Formulations Retail Gasoline Prices" (average retail price of gas was $1.07 in 1993 and $2.62 in 2006)—http://tonto.eia.doe.gov/dnav/pet/hist/mg_tt_usA.htm.

2 See Robert Puentes and Ryan Prince, "Fueling Transportation Finance: A Primer on the Gas Tax" (Brookings Institution Series on Transportation Reform March 2003); Craig Hansen and David Sandalow, "Greening the Tax Code" (Brookings/World Resources Institute Policy Brief April 2006).

3 International Energy Agency, "End User Petroleum Product Prices and Average Crude Oil Import Costs" (July 2007) at p. 5—http://www.iea.org/textbase/stats/surveys/mps.pdf.

4 Gregory Mankiw, "Raise the Gas Tax," *Wall Street Journal* (October 30, 2006).

5 Gregory Mankiw, "The Pigou Club Manifesto"— http://gregmankiw.blogspot.com/2006/10/pigou-club-manifesto.html.

6 National Research Council, *Effectiveness and Impact of Corporate Average Fuel Economy (CAFE) Standards* (National Academies Press 2002) at Finding 7— http://www.nap.edu/catalog/10172.html. See also Jonathan Rauch, "A Higher Gas Tax is the Answer: Who'll Ask the Question," *Reason* (February 9, 2002)— http://www.reason.com/news/show/34594.html.

7 Hal Varain, "A Good Time to Raise Gasoline Taxes," *New York Times* (October 19, 2000). See also Gregory Mankiw, note 4 this chapter.

8 New York Times/CBS News Poll (February 22-26, 2006)— http://www.nytimes.com/packages/pdf/national/20060228_poll_results.pdf.

9 Philip Sharp, Testimony before Committee on Energy and Commerce, U.S, House of Representatives (May 3, 2006) at p. 3.

10 New York Times/CBS News Poll, note 8 this chapter.

11 See, for example, Mark Delucchi and James Murphy, "U.S. Military Expenditures to Protect the Use of Persian-Gulf Oil for Motor Vehicles" (University of California, Davis, revised Oct. 2006); National Highway Traffic Safety Administration, U.S. Department of Transportation, "Final Regulatory Impact Analysis, Corporate Average Fuel Economy and CAFE Reform MY 2008–2011 Light Trucks" (March 2006); Doug Koplow, "Subsidies to Energy Industries," *Encyclopedia of Energy* (2004); Milton Copulos, *America's Achilles Heel: The Hidden Costs of Imported Oil* (National Defense Council Foundation 2003); Doug Koplow and John Dernbach, "Federal Fossil Fuel Subsidies and Greenhouse Gas Emissions," *Annual Review of Energy and the Environment* (2001); General Accounting Office, "Tax Incentives for Petroleum and Ethanol Fuels" (Letter to Senator Tom Harkin, September 25, 2000); Energy Information Administration, *Federal Financial Interventions and Subsidies in Energy Markets* (May 2000); Doug Koplow and Aaron Martin, "Fueling Global Warming: Federal Subsidies to Oil in the United States" (Greenpeace 1998); International Center for Technology Assessment, *The Real Price of Gasoline* (1998).

12 See Energy Information Administration, "This Week in Petroleum: Gasoline"— http://tonto.eia.doe.gov/oog/info/twip/twip.asp.

13 *Ibid* (showing average gasoline demand of roughly 9.2 million barrels per day, equal to roughly 141 billion gallons per year). A tax would reduce demand, but very little in the short-term due to gasoline's low elasticity of demand. On elasticity of demand for oil products, see John C. B. Cooper, "Price Elasticity of Demand for Crude Oil: Estimates for 23 Countries," *OPEC Review* (March 2003); George Perry, "The War on Terrorism, the World Oil Market and the U.S. Economy" (Brookings Analysis Paper 2001) at p. 7; Patrick Anderson et al., "Price Elasticity of Demand" (Nov. 1997).

14 Bureau of Labor Statistics, U.S, Department of Labor, "Inflation Calculator"— http://www.bls.gov/cpi.

15 When Henry Kissinger was Secretary of State, he reportedly once quipped "The only options memos I get around here give me three choices—abject surrender, prudent diplomacy or thermonuclear war. I'm tired of being manipulated to choose the middle option!"

16 The average car or light truck in the United States is driven roughly 12,000 miles, Oak Ridge National Laboratory, *Transportation Energy Data Book* (2006) at Chapter 3, and gets roughly 21 miles per gallon. U.S. Environmental Protection Agency, "Light-Duty Automotive Technology and Fuel Economy Trends: 1975 through 2006—Executive

Summary" at Highlight #1. Calculating 12,000 miles at 21 miles per gallon = 571 gallons per year. Assuming no change in vehicle, fuel supply or driving habits, an extra 10 cents per gallon would cost $57 per year.

17 U.S. Census Bureau, *Income, Poverty and Health Insurance Coverage in the United States 2005* at p.6 (Table 1) and p. 31 (Table A-1) —http://www.census.gov/prod/2006pubs/p60-231.pdf.

Memorandum from the Secretary of Energy: Role for Coal

1 National Research Council, *Coal: Research and Development to Support National Energy Policy* (National Academies Press 2007) at p. 41. The National Research Council report raises questions about the data behind the widely repeated claim that U.S. coal supplies will last 230 years at current consumption rates.   See Energy Information Administration, "U.S. Coal Consumption" (1.1 billion short tons in 2005) and "Recoverable Coal Reserves" (267.5 billion short tons in 2005)—
http://www.eia.doe.gov/cneaf/coal/page/acr/table26.html and
http://www.eia.doe.gov/cneaf/coal/page/acr/table15.html.

2 See B.D. Hong and E.R. Slatick, "Carbon Dioxide Emission Factors for Coal," *Quarterly Coal Report* (Energy Information Administration January–April 1994). Some sources report carbon content as low as 25% for some kinds of coal, generally because the weight of water present in mined coal is included in making the calculation.

3 See American Coal Council, "Coal: An Abundant Resource" (2005)—
http://www.americancoalcouncil.org/pubs/abundant_energy_resource.pdf.

4 The cost of natural gas is highly variable. Even during periods of low prices natural gas has generally been twice as expensive as coal as a source of electricity. In recent years, natural gas has often been four times more expensive than coal. See Energy Information Administration, "Monthly Energy Review-Electricity," Table 9.10, "Cost of Fossil-Fuel Receipts at Electric Generating Plants"—
http://www.eia.doe.gov/mer/pdf/pages/sec9_15.pdf; Coalition for Affordable and Reliable Energy, "Fueling Growth" (2006)—
http://www.careenergy.com/fueling_growth/competitive.asp.

5 See generally, Energy Information Administration, "Annual Energy Outlook 2007 with Projections to 2030—Electricity"—http://www.eia.doe.gov/oiaf/aeo/electricity.html.

6 See, for example, David McAteer and Tom Bethel, "Coal: Planning Its Future and Its Legacy" (2004) at p. 2—http://www.energycommission.org/files/finalReport/IV.2.b-Coal-PlanningitsFut.pdf.

7 World Coal Institute, "Coal: Liquid Fuels" at p. 8—
http://www.worldcoal.org/assets_cm/files/PDF/wci_coal_liquid_fuels.pdf.

8 Liquid coal supplied more than 90% of the Nazi regime's fuel during World War II. In 1944, there were 25 coal liquefaction plants in Germany producing more than 124,000 barrels per day. National Mining Association, "Liquid Fuels from U.S. Coal"—
http://www.nma.org/pdf/liquid_coal_fuels_100505.pdf.

9 Production in 2005 was approximately 160,000 barrels per day. World Coal Institute, note 7 this chapter, at p. 5. This is equivalent to roughly 1.3% of U.S. transportation fuel consumption.

10 See Montana Official State Website, "Frequently Asked Questions about Synthetic Fuel"—http://governor.mt.gov/hottopics/faqsynthetic.asp.

11 National Academy of Sciences, National Academy of Engineering and Institute of Medicine *The Government Role in Civilian Technology: Building a New Alliance*, (National Academies Press 1992) at pp. 58–59.

12 See National Coal Council, Coal: *America's Energy Future* (March 2006)—
http://nationalcoalcouncil.org/report/NCCReportVol1.pdf. One ton of coal contains about as much energy as 3.8 barrels of oil. See Energy Information Administration, "Apples, Oranges and Btu" (June 2006), with Btu values for each fuel—
http://www.eia.doe.gov/neic/infosheets/apples.html.

13 See Sohbet Karbuz, "The U.S. military oil consumption," *Energy Bulletin* (February 25, 2006)—http://www.energybulletin.net/13199.html.

14 Energy Information Administration, "Petroleum Navigator-Crude Oil Production"—
http://tonto.eia.doe.gov/dnav/pet/pet_crd_crpdn_adc_mbbl_a.htm: Energy Information Administration, "Crude Oil Proved Reserves, Reserves Changes, and Production"—
http://tonto.eia.doe.gov/dnav/pet/pet_crd_pres_dcu_NUS_a.htm.

15 FuturePundit, "The Chinese are planning to start converting coal into liquid fuels" (December 31, 2005)—http://www.futurepundit.com/archives/003199.html.

16 John Sichinga, "Enabling a Coal to Liquids Industry in the U.S," (Sasol October 2, 2006) at slides 15, 17 and 22—
http://www.gasification.org/Docs/2006_Papers/06SICH.pdf.

17 See Future Pundit, "Rapid Switch from Oil to Coal Possible" (April 18, 2006)—
http://www.futurepundit.com/archives/003382.html; World Coal Institute, note 7 this chapter, p. 12.

18 Future Pundit, note 17 this chapter.

19 See "The Wedge from Capturing CO2 at Coal-to-Synfuels Plants"—
http://www.princeton.edu/~cmi/resources/Wedges/Capture%20CO$_2$%20at%20coal-to-sy
nfuels%20plant8.16.pdf; Montana Environment Information Center, "Coal to Liquid
Fuels-A Better Way"—http://www.meic.org/energy/coals-to-liquid-fuels/coal-to-liquid-
fuels-a-better-way.

20 See Robert Socolow, "Can We Bury Global Warming," *Scientific American* (July 2005);
David Hawkins, Testimony before Committee on Energy and Natural Resources, United
States Senate (April 24, 2006); Robert Williams and Eric Larson, "Comparison of Direct
and Indirect Liquefaction Technologies for Making Fluid Fuels from Coal," *Energy for
Sustainable Development December* (2003)—
http://www.princeton.edu/~energy/publications/pdf/2003/dclversussicl.pdf.

21 See Robert Socolow, note 20 this chapter, at p. 52; Robert Socolow, Testimony before
the Finance Committee, U.S. Senate (February 26, 2007) at p. 8.

22 See MIT Faculty Group, *The Future of Coal* (Massachusetts Institute of Technology
2007); Robert Socolow Senate testimony, note 21 this chapter, at p. 2.

23 See Montana Environment Information Center, "Coal to Liquid Fuels: Carbon"—
http://www.meic.org/energy/coals-to-liquid-fuels/coal-to-liquid-fuels-carbon.

24 Robert Socolow Senate testimony, note 21 this chapter.

25 Robert Williams and Eric Larson, note 20 this chapter (claiming CTL processes could
be designed so life-cycle GHG emissions are approximately 0.8 times that of petroleum,
with potential GHG benefits from coproducts displacing coal-fired electricity generation).
See also Eric Larson and Ren Tingjin, "Synthetic Fuel Production by Indirect Coal
Liquefaction," *Energy for Sustainable Development* (December 2003)—
http://www.princeton.edu/~energy/publications/pdf/2003/indirect.pdf.

26 See Robert Williams, "Climate-Compatible Synthetic Liquid Fuels," from "Coal and
Biomass with CO2 Capture and Storage" (Presentation to California Energy Commission,
December 19, 2005)—online at http://www.climatechange.ca.gov/documents/2005-12-
19_WILLIAMS.PDF.

27 MIT, *The Future of Coal*, note 22 this chapter.

28 MIT, *The Future of Coal*, note 22 this chapter, at p. 104 (recommending $440 million for
coal-related research and development).

"Jon Tester: Senator-Farmer"(*Profile: Jon Tester*)

1 Article written by David Sandalow for this book. Sources: Conversation between Senator Tester and Sandalow (2007); Jon Tester, "A New Energy Future," Buzzflash.com (April 27, 2006)—Montana Coal Council, "Montana Coal Production and Employment"—http://www.montanacoalcouncil.com/production_employment.html; and Duane Johnson, "Oil Seed Crops for Energy Production" (Montana State University)—

Memorandum from the Secretary of Energy: Hydrogen Fuels

1 See "Information Specific to Liquid Hydrogen," Harvard Division of Engineering and Applied Science website—http://www.safety.deas.harvard.edu/services/hydrogen.html.

2 See generally National Academy of Engineering, *The Hydrogen Economy: Opportunities, Costs, Barriers and R&D Needs* (National Academies Press 2004); Joseph Romm, *The Hype about Hydrogen: Fact and Fiction in the Race to Save the Climate* (Island Press 2004).

3 The chemical symbol for hydrogen is H. Water is H_2O (two parts hydrogen and one part oxygen). Natural gas is made up mainly of methane, which is CH_4 (one part carbon and four parts hydrogen). Oil and coal have more complex chemical formulas, in which hydrogen atoms abound.

4 See "Hydrogen," *Columbia Encyclopedia*, 6th edition (2001)—http://www.bartleby.com/65/hy/hydrogen.html.

5 Jules Verne, *The Mysterious Island* (Wesleyan University Press 2001) at pp. 327-328.

6 See Jeremy Rifkin, *The Hydrogen Economy* ,(Tarcher 2003) at p. 207.

7 See U.S. Department of Energy, "The President's Fuel Cell Initiative—http://www1.eere.energy.gov/hydrogenandfuelcells/presidents_initiative.html.

8 See Governor Arnold Schwarzenegger's California Hydrogen Highway Network Action Plan (2004)—http://www.hydrogenhighway.ca.gov/vision/vision.pdf.

9 Dolf Gielen and Giorgio Simbolotti, *Prospects for Hydrogen and Fuel Cells* (International Energy Agency 2005) at p. 15—http://www.iea.org/textbase/nppdf/free/2005/hydrogen2005.pdf.

10 See National Academy of Engineering, note 2 this chapter at p. 3.

11 Steam reformation of methane generates 50% of global hydrogen and 90% in the United States. See Joseph Romm, note 2 this chapter, at pp. 72-73.

12 A catalyst (such as nickel) is required. The process has two stages: first $CH_4 + H_2O \rightarrow 3H_2 + CO$ and then $CO + H_2O \rightarrow CO_2 + H_2$. See Joseph Romm, note 2 this chapter, at p. 73.

13 See American Physical Society, "The Hydrogen Initiative" (March 2004) at p. 6— http://positron3.aps.org/public_affairs/upload/Hydrogen-Initiative.pdf.

14 Energy Information Administration, "World Proved Reserves of Oil and Natural Gas" (January 9, 2007)—http://www.eia.doe.gov/emeu/international/reserves.html.

15 Joseph Romm, note 2 this chapter, at pp. 149–150 (citing M. Weiss et al., "Comparative Assessment of Fuel Cell Cars." Laboratory for Energy and the Environment Report (February 2003).

16 American Physical Society, note 13 this chapter, at p. 6.

17 Joseph Romm, note 2 this chapter, at p. 76.

18 See John Deutch and Ernie Moniz, *The Future of Nuclear Power*, (MIT 2003)— http://web.mit.edu/nuclearpower.

19 See Energy Information Agency, "A Primer on Gasoline Prices"— http://www.eia.doe.gov/bookshelf/brochures/gasolinepricesprimer/eia1_2005primerM.html.

20 Joseph Romm, note 2 this chapter, at p. 101; see Marianne Mintz, et al., "Hydrogen: On the Horizon or Just a Mirage?" (Society of Automotive Engineers 2002)— http://www.its.ucdavis.edu/education/classes/pathwaysclass/H2HorizonorMirage-Mintz.pdf.

21 Joseph Romm, note 2 this chapter, at p. 103.

22 Lou Ann Hammond, "Hydrogen Internal Combustion Engines" (Carlist.com, December 6, 2006)—http://www.carlist.com/autonews/2005/autonews_136.html.

23 Joan Ogden, "High Hopes for Hydrogen," *Scientific American* (September 2006) at p. 100.

24 Amy Raskin and Savrin Shah "The Emergence of Hybrid Vehicles" (AllianceBernstein, June 2006), p. 39. Available online at http://www.calcars.org/alliance-bernstein-hybrids-june06.pdf.

25 Dolf Gielen and Giorgio Simbolotti, note 9 this chapter, at p. 15

26 See Dan Baum, "GM's Billion-Dollar Bet," *Wired* (August 22, 2002); Karim Nice and Jonathan Strickland, "How Fuel Cells Work," How Stuff Works (site)—http://www.howstuffworks.com/fuel-cell.htm.

27 Joseph Romm, note 2 this chapter, p. 40.

28 Joseph Romm, note 2 this chapter, at pp. 121–122; for the $1 million per car figure: see Joe Wiesenfelder, "BMW Hydrogen 7 prototype," www.cars.com (million dollar cars); Jim Motavalli, "Fuel Cells in the Deep Freeze," *New York Times* (Dec. 11, 2004).

29 See Jeremy Rifkin, note 6 this chapter, at p. 207; Keith Damsell, "Ballard Power, Daimler-Benz cement fuel cell partnership," *Financial Post* (August 27, 1997); Associated Press, "Ford to Develop Fuel Cell Cars" (December 15, 1997).

30 See Gemma Crawley, "Fuel Cell Today Market Survey: Light Duty Vehicles," *Fuel Cell Today* (February 2007).

31 Joan Ogden, note 23 this chapter, at p. 97.

32 See Bluewater Network, Hydrogen-Fueled Hybrid Internal Combustion Engines—http://www.bluewaternetwork.org/reports/rep_ca_global_hydrogenengine.pdf.

33 See "BMW Hydrogen 7" (Sept. 20, 2006)—http://www.gatago.com/aus/cars/31469171.html.

34 Lou Ann Hammond, "Ford gives hydrogen to Las Vegas"-www.carlist.com/autonews

Memorandum from the Secretary of Transportation: Smart Growth

1 Oak Ridge National Laboratory, *Transportation Energy Data Book* (2006) at Chapter 3—http://cta.ornl.gov/data/tedb26/Edition26_Chapter03.pdf.

2 *Ibid.*; Robert Puentes, "A New Vision for Federal Transportation Policy" (Brookings July 2007); National Research Council, *Effectiveness and Impact of Corporate Average Fuel Economy (CAFE) Standards* (National Academies Press 2002) at p. 19—http://www.nap.edu/catalog/10172.html; Naomi Friedman, "It's About How and Where We Build: Connecting Energy and Smart Growth," (ACEEE 2006) at pp. 11–51—http://www.eesi.org/publications/aceee%20paper.pdf.

3 The fuel efficiency of new vehicles in the United States has been roughly constant for almost 20 years, so older vehicles ready for scrappage have roughly the same fuel efficiency as the fleet as a whole. New vehicles make up roughly 7% of the fleet (16.5 million new vehicles sold divided by 240 million total). If the fuel efficiency of new vehicles were improving 4% each year, fleetwide efficiency would increase by 0.28% (7%×4%) in Year 1, roughly 0.57% (7%×8.16%) in Year 2 and 0.875% (7%×12.5%) in Year 3. This ignores the fact that fewer cars are scrapped each year than manufactured (about 80% in recent years). See "Vehicles in Operation and Scrappage," *AutoExec Magazine* (May 2004). However, that fact does not materially change the results or basic conclusion—that significant fuel efficiency improvements in the new car and light truck fleet would be required to offset 2% annual increases in VMT.

4 ABC News/Time Magazine/Washington Post Poll: Traffic (January 2005)— http://abcnews.go.com/images/Politics/973a2Traffic.pdf. See, generally, Anthony Downs, *Still Stuck in Traffic* (Brookings Institution 2004) at pp. 128–129.

5 Washington Post Poll (2005)—http://www.washingtonpost.com/wp-srv/polls/2005027/index.html.

6 ABC News Poll, note 4 this chapter; Smart Growth America, "National Survey on Growth and Land Development," (September 2000)— http://www.smartgrowthamerica.org/poll.pdf; Bruce Katz and Robert Puentes, "Remaking Transportation Policy for the New Century" (Speech to Institute of Transportation Engineers January 23, 2006). See, generally, Anthony Downs, *Still Stuck in Traffic* (Brookings Institution 2004); David Shrank and Tim Lomax, "2005 Urban Mobility Report," (Texas Transportation Institute, Texas A&M, May 2005).

7 Andres Duany, Elizabeth Plater-Zyberk and Jeff Speck, *Suburban Nation: The Rise of Sprawl and the Decline of the American Dream* (North Point Press, 2001) at chapter 1.

8 Antonio Bento et al., "Impact of Urban Spatial Structure on Travel Demand in the United States," (World Bank Policy Research Working Paper, March 2003)— http://ssrn.com/abstract=636369.

9 Naomi Friedman, note 2 this chapter.

10 See Andres Duany et al., note 7 this chapter at pp. 91–92.

11 David Shrank and Tim Lomax, note 6 this chapter.

12 See generally, Smart Growth America (www.smartgrowthamerica.org) and the Smart Growth Network (www.smartgrowth.org). For a discussion of smart growth policy options

see, "Getting to Smart Growth II," Smart Growth Network—
www.smartgrowth.org/pdf/gettosg2.pdf.

13 See "Center for Transit Oriented Development," New Urbanism—
www.newurbanism.org/centerfortod.html.

14 For an interesting discussion of this point, see Russell Train, *Politics, Pollution and Pandas: An Environmental Memoir* (New Island Press, 2003) at p. 108–109.

15 Andres Duany et al., note 7 this chapter, at p. 225.

16 Robert Fishman, "The American Metropolis at Century's End: Past and Future Influences" (Fannie Mae Foundation Winter 1999)—
http://www.fanniemaefoundation.org/programs/hff/v114-metropolis.html.

17 Antonio Bento et al., note 8 this chapter, at p. 30. See also the same, highly regarded study at p. 6: "Attempts to reduce auto dependence by altering urban form and increasing supply of public transit are likely to have modest effects." The authors' focus appears to be on a package of measures at p. 30 and individual measures at p. 6.

18 Linda Bailey, "Public Transportation and Petroleum Savings in the U.S.," (American Public Transport Association, January 2007).

19 Anthony Downs, *Still Stuck in Traffic* (Brookings Institution 2004)
at p. 102.

20 Andres Duany et al., note 7 this chapter, at p. 89.

21 See Edward Beimborn and Robert Puentes, "Highways and Transit: Leveling the Playing Field in Federal Transportation Policy" (Brookings Transportation Reform Series, December 2003).

22 See the Telecommuting Coalition's website at http://www.telcoa.org/id33.htm.

23 See "Fuel Smart Economy: It's No Gas," Telework Exchange (September 21, 2005)—
http://www.teleworkexchange.com/FuelSmartStudy.pdf. According to this presentation, 233 million gallons/week would be saved from all white collar workers telecommuting 2 days/week. 233 million gallons/week × 48 weeks/year = 11.2 billion gallons/year = approximately 8% of U.S. annual consumption.

24 See Wendell Joice, "The Evolution of Telework in the Federal Government" (General Services Administration February 2000)—http://www.gsa.gov/graphics/ogp/EvolutionteleworkPDF.pdf.

25 Public Law 108-199, Division B, § 627.

26 "Status of Telework in the Federal Government" (Office of Personnel Management, June 2007)—http://www.telework.gov/surveys/2006_TW2oReport.pdf. See also Stephen Barr, "Working from Home a Work in Progress," *Washington Post*, June 19, 2007.

27 See Nicole Belson Goluboff, "Taxing Telecommuters," *The New York Times* (August 6, 2006); Telecommuter Tax Fairness Act of 2007 (S.785, HR 1360).

28 The Federal gas tax is 18.4 cents/gallon. This tax is allocated to the Highway account (15.44 cents/gallon) and to the Mass Transit account (2.86 cents/gallon). See U.S. Department of Transportation, "Infrastructure—When Did the Federal Government Begin Collecting the Gas Tax?"; American Public Transportation Association website—www.apta.com.

29 See Edward Beimborn and Robert Puentes, note 21 this chapter.

"A Visit to Biotown, USA" (*Profile: Reynolds, Indiana*)

1 Article written by David Sandalow for this book. Sources: Conversation in Reynolds among Charlie van Voorst, Brandon Seitz, Eric Burch and Sandalow (2007); Monica Davey, "One Farm Town's Drive for Energy Independence," *New York Times* (June 4, 2006); Ashley Heher, "U.S. Farm Town Tries for All-Renewable Energy," AP (July 10, 2006); Reynolds website at http://www.biotownusa.com.

Memorandum from the Secretary of Energy: Strategic Petroleum Reserve

1 U.S. Department of Energy, "Strategic Petroleum Reserve Inventory"—http://www.spr.doe.gov/reports/dir.htm.

2 For background on the SPR, see David Goldwyn and Michelle Billig, "Building Strategic Reserves," in David Goldwyn and Jan Kalicki, eds., *Energy and Security: Toward a New Foreign Policy Strategy* (Woodrow Wilson Press 2005); Robert Bamberger, "The Strategic Petroleum Reserve: History, Perspectives and Issues" (Congressional Research Service Report, April 2006); U.S. Department of Energy, "Strategic Petroleum Reserve-

Quick Facts and Frequently Asked Questions"—
http://fossil.energy.gov/programs/reserves/spr/spr-facts.html.

3 Energy Information Administration, "Industry and Government-Controlled Petroleum
Stocks in the OECD Countries," *International Petroleum Monthly* (April 2007)—
http://www.eia.doe.gov/emeu/ipsr/t16.xls; Timothy Considine and Kevin Dowd, "A
Superfluous Petroleum Reserve?" *Regulation,* (Summer 2005) at pp. 18-25 . See also Randy
Kirk, "The Impact of Additions to Strategic Petroleum Reserves on World Oil Demand,"
Energy Bulletin (December 2005).

4 Energy Information Administration, note 3 this chapter; Timothy Considine and Kevin
Dowd, note 3 this chapter at 18-25.

5 International Energy Agency, "IEA Response System for Oil Supply Emergencies,"—
http://www.iea.org/dbtw-wpd/Textbase/nppdf/free/2007/fs_response_system.pdf.

6 *Ibid.* at p. 12.

7 Building a multilateral coalition to challenge Iran's nuclear program, for example, has
been more difficult because of fear among some governments that Iran would withhold oil
from world markets. Securing cooperation from Saudi Arabia on important national
security matters (such as Khobar Towers) has been more difficult because of the priority
attached to maintaining Saudi cooperation in managing world oil markets.

8 See David G. Victor and Joshua C. House, "Politics Dog the Oil Reserve," *Los Angeles
Times* (August 22, 2004, making this proposal.

9 See David Goldwyn and Michelle Billig, note 1 this chapter, at p. 525, proposing Global
Strategic Petroleum Reserve.

Memorandum from the Secretary of State: Diplomatic Strategy

1 See *BP Statistical Review of World Energy 2007* (Historical Data Workbook)—
http://www.bp.com/productlanding.do?categoryId=6848&contentId=7033471; Paul
Leiby et al., "Oil Imports: An Assessment of Benefits and Costs" (Oak Ridge National
Laboratory, November 1997).

2 See *BP Statistical Review*, note 1 this chapter; International Monetary Fund World
Economic Outlook 2007.

3 Ben Bernanke, "Global Economic Integration: What's New and What's Not," Speech at the Federal Reserve Bank of Kansas City's Thirtieth Annual Economic Symposium (August 25, 2006).

4 See, generally, David Victor, *National Security Consequences of US Oil Dependency* (Council on Foreign Relations, 2006); James Woolsey, "The High Cost of Crude," Testimony before the Senate Foreign Relations Committee (November 16, 2005); Amy Myers Jaffe, "U.S. and the Middle East: Policies and Dilemmas" (National Commission on Energy Policy 2004).

5 More than 78% of Japan's oil and 17% of Europe's oil comes from the Mideast. Energy Information Administration, "Persian Gulf Oil and Gas Exports Fact Sheet" (September 2004) at p. 5— http://commercecan.ic.gc.ca/scdt/bizmap/interface2.nsf/vDownload/CABS_0059/$file/p gulf.pdf. Such direct physical flows might be less important in this scenario than the increase in world oil prices, but nevertheless provide a sense of the disruption.

6 International Trade Administration, U.S. Department of Commerce, "Employment Related to Manufactured Exports 2003"— http://ita.doc.gov/td/industry/otea/jobs/Reports/2003/jobs_by_state_totals.html; see also World Trade Organization, "Merchandise Trade of the United States by Region and Economy"—http://www.wto.org/english/res_e/statis_e/its2006_e/section3_e/iii16.xls.

7 See, e.g., Hearing on Oil Diplomacy, U.S. House of Representatives Committee on International Relations (June 20, 2002). See, generally, Daniel Yergin, "Ensuring Energy Security," *Foreign Affairs* (March/April 2006); David Victor at note 4 this chapter; Jan Kalicki and David Goldwyn, eds., *Energy and Security: Toward a New Foreign Policy Strategy* (Woodrow Wilson Press 2005; Daniel Yergin, "Energy Security and Markets" in Kalicki and Goldwyn.

8 See, generally, Worldwatch Institute, *Biofuels for Transportation* (2006); Center for American Progress, *Resources for Global Growth* (2005).

9 See Energy Information Admnistration, "To World Oil Producers and Consumer?— http://www.eia.doe.gov/emeu/cabs/topworldtables1_2.html.

10 Energy Information Administration, "Petroleum Navigator-U.S. Imports by Country of Origin"— http://tonto.eia.doe.gov/dnav/pet/pet_move_impcus_a2_nus_ep00_im0_mbblpd_a.htm.

11 See Energy Information Administration, "OPEC Revenues: Country Details"— http://www.eia.doe.gov/cabs/OPEC_Revenues/OPECDetails.html; see also Statistics

Canada, "Exports of Goods on a Balance-of-Payments Basis, by Product (2006)—http://www40.statcan.ca/l01/cst01/gblec04.htm.

12 See Rachel Bronson, *Thicker Than Oil*, (Oxford 2006).

13 See Bushan Barree, "Why OPEC Idles," *The Wall St Journal* (May 25, 2007). See also Alan Greenspan, Testimony before Committee on Foreign Relations, U.S. Senate (June 7, 2006), noting this as part of Saudi Aramco strategy.

14 See, generally, "Saudi non-oil exports build new economy" (CNN.com Feb 8, 2007)—http://www.ameinfo.com/110097.html.

PART III: DECISION

Note from the Secretary of Energy: Big Government and Oil

1 Daniel Yergin, *The Prize: The Epic Quest for Oil, Money and Power* (Free Press 1991) at p. 395.

2 *Ibid.* at pp. 394ff.

3 State of the Union Address (Jan. 24, 1980).

4 Speech to Joint Session of Congress (September 11, 1991).

Memorandum from the Director of Speechwriting

1 Nexis search performed 2007

Memorandum from the Vice President

1 See Pietro Nivola and Robert Crandall, *The Extra Mile: Rethinking Energy Policy for Automotive Transportation* (Brookings Institution 1995), at pp. 84–111.

Index

Acknowledgments

The list is long. It starts with Strobe Talbott—hero, mentor and friend. Under his leadership, Brookings thrives. It continues with many Brookings colleagues who offered comments, critiques and encouragement, including Bill Antholis, Ann Florini, Mark Muro, Pietro Nivola, Mike O'Hanlon, Carlos Pascual, George Perry, Ken Pollack, Rob Puentes, Susan Rice and Jeremy Shapiro. Dan Yergin, a Brookings trustee, taught me volumes many years before I met him and even more since.

Several research assistants helped with different stages of this project, including Hannah Volfson, Nalin Sahni and Ben Barry. I'm especially grateful to Anu Prasad, who showed extraordinary dedication and did an excellent job keeping the research for this project organized.

Many friends and colleagues reviewed this manuscript or earlier papers. Their comments, critiques and encouragement were essential. They include Rosina Bierbaum, Hank Chesbrough, Reid Detchon, Jon Elkind, TJ Glauthier, David Goldwyn, Eugene Linden, Larry Linden, Lisel Loy, Alan Madian, Ron Minsk, Peter Fox-Penner, Ken Novak, Les Silverman, PJ Simmons, Todd Stern and Kirk Talbott.

Bob Carter, Aimee Christensen, Robbie Diamond, Sherri Goodman and Mark Helmke provided introductions that helped make the profiles possible.

To all of you, thanks.

Special thanks to my editor Herb Schaffner, who pushed me to write a different book than I originally proposed. Many thanks as well to my agent David McCormick.

Of my many blessings, none surpass my wonderful family. My parents Terry and Ina, brother Marc and sister Judith laid the foundation with a lifetime of love and encouragement. Their comments on this manuscript helped a lot, too. My father-in-law Don Hammonds provided invaluable assistance on all aspects of this project.

My extraordinary children Ben, Maya and Holly are at the core of everything I do. An afternoon on the Tidal Basin with Maya and Holly played a central role in shaping my thinking about parts of this book. Ben provided excellent edits on parts of the manuscript.

Above all, thanks to my remarkable wife Holly Hammonds love of my life and partner for the journey.

About the Author

David B. Sandalow is Energy & Environment Scholar and a senior fellow at the Brookings Institution. He is chair of the Energy & Climate Working Group of the Clinton Global Initiative. Mr. Sandalow has served as Assistant Secretary of State for Oceans, Environment & Science; Senior Director for Environmental Affairs, National Security Council; and Associate Director for the Global Environment, White House Council on Environmental Quality. His opinion pieces and articles have appeared in the *New York Times, Washington Post, Washington Times, Financial Times, International Herald Tribune, Science* and many other periodicals. He is a graduate of the University of Michigan Law School and Yale College. He lives in Washington, D.C. with his wife and three children.